Somewhere I Have Never Travelled

Somewhere I Have Never Travelled

*The Second Self
and the Hero's Journey
in Ancient Epic*

THOMAS VAN NORTWICK

New York   Oxford
Oxford University Press
1992

Oxford University Press

Oxford   New York   Toronto
Delhi   Bombay   Calcutta   Madras   Karachi
Petaling Jaya   Singapore   Hong Kong   Tokyo
Nairobi   Dar es Salaam   Cape Town
Melbourne   Auckland

and associated companies in
Berlin   Ibadan

Published by Oxford University Press, Inc.
200 Madison Avenue, New York, NY 10016

Oxford is a registered trademark of Oxford University Press

Library of Congress Cataloging-in-Publication Data
Van Nortwick, Thomas, 1946–
Somewhere I have never travelled : the second self
and the hero's journey in ancient epic / Thomas Van Nortwick.
p. cm.   Includes bibliographical references and index.
ISBN 0-19-507149-2
1. Epic poetry, Classical—History and criticism.
2. Aeneas (Legendary character) in literature.
3. Achilles (Greek mythology) in literature.
4. Split self in literature.
5. Heroes in literature.
6. Travel in literature.
7. Virgil, Aeneis.
8. Homer. Iliad.
9. Gilgamesh.   I. Title.
PA3022.E6V36
1992   883'.01'09352—dc20
91-8315

2 4 6 8 9 7 5 3 1

Printed in the United States of America
on acid-free paper

For Mary

gladly beyond any

experience . . .

Preface

It comes over me that I had then a strange *alter ego* deep down
somewhere inside me, as the full-blown flower is in the small
tight bud, and I just took the course, I just transferred him to
the climate, that blighted him once and for ever.

Henry James, "The Jolly Corner"

Everyone, late or soon, turns his or her own "jolly corner," as James calls
it, coming face-to-face with an undiscovered blossom, a self as yet unrealized. The encounter may be pleasant, but more likely it will be bewildering
at best and possibly terrifying. Rather than confront such a specter, most
of us will find a way to "transfer it to the climate," make it go away, by
projecting it onto someone or something else. This act of *objectifying* parts
of ourselves, of putting a little distance between the person we know and a
new version, might not be such a bad thing, since it could afford a perspective not available within our subjectivity. The rub is that of course we
would have to acknowledge these other parts as our own in order to learn
anything about ourselves, and we project them so as *not* to have to acknowledge them. In imaginative literature (itself one of our most engaging
forms of projection, but that is for another book) we are happily allowed
to suspend these intractable realities for a time—if someone else is doing
the projecting, we may yet learn something about ourselves. So it is that in
ancient epic poetry, a literature centrally focused on the evolution of the
self, we sometimes find the tendency to embody parts of the hero in another
character, often the faithful companion. By so doing, the author creates the
opportunity to dramatize objectively what is in real life an inner, subjective
process, to explore, for him or herself and for us, the moral, psychological,
and spiritual dynamics of growing up.

Any model we may choose for understanding this mysterious inner journey will begin with the premise that self-knowledge is primary to the task

of reaching maturity. We must first recognize those parts of ourselves that we have somehow missed or denied. But this is only the first step, because of course knowing something intellectually is not the same as accepting it in that other, less rational, less accessible part of ourselves, call it the heart, the emotions, the soul, whatever. After self-knowledge must come self-acceptance, and the gap between these two is often the hardest chasm to bridge. Once we have crossed, once we have welcomed (or grudgingly accepted) those other selves, then the possibility of a different way of being in the world opens up before us — we may not choose it, we may not achieve it to the degree we would like, but at least we can entertain it.

Each of the works I will be discussing presents the heroic journey in such a way as to make it, among other things, a metaphor for the process of growing up. More particularly, the hero's second self is a vehicle for exploring the pain and the rewards of knowing and learning to live with our imperfect selves — the key, in this way of understanding how humans evolve, to reaching what I call a more *integrated* existence. Paradoxically, the rewards these works envision can only be realized as a result of a terrible loss: the second self must die before the hero can grow up; spiritual death must precede spiritual rebirth. This means that our study will prompt reflection on another puzzling truth, that full participation in life demands that death must finally be understood as not a negation but an integral part of living.

In what follows I will be looking at three works, the *Epic of Gilgamesh*, the *Iliad*, and the *Aeneid*, as the preeminent explorations in ancient western epic of the process I have been discussing. In each case, the search for self-realization or integration is pursued within the context of other central themes, the nature of which help to determine the makeup of the hero's second self. The two earlier works offer the hope of integrating other selves, of movement toward spiritual wholeness; the *Aeneid* draws on the same motifs to suggest the potential for such healing, but finally offers a much bleaker picture.

It will not escape my readers that this book is primarily about the experience of males — given the materials, it could hardly be otherwise. Though some of what I say about human nature may be applicable to all humans, and though I hope that I will not lose the chance to converse here with women as well as men, I do think that much of the dynamic of self-realization as it appears in these three works is peculiar to the male way of looking at the world. For this reason I make no pretense to gender-neutral language when talking about heroes — these are men, and their fictive lives are not, I believe, always germane in helping us understand how women make *their* way in the world. Neither will I enter the fray to settle the question of whether the gender-specificity of the stories reflects nature or culture, though it will be evident that I believe, based on what I know of my own and other lives, that there are certain universal dilemmas common to males as they try to grow up.

Even if I did not believe this, I would insist that what I am doing here is valid, even useful. There are, of course, myriad good reasons for reading any literature (leaving aside the bad ones). Scholars struggle to learn as much as possible about how a work of Classical literature might have been received by its original audience, so as to avoid importing anachronistic notions from another time. (And then perhaps citing the resulting interpretation of the ancient work to buttress the modern preoccupation, coming full circle.) But there is also a sense in which these poems are *here*, *now*, and if we cannot learn something about ourselves and our world as it now is by reading them, even if we "read in" anachronistic issues, then this is dead literature indeed. My approach looks to the latter sort of reading, but necessarily rests firmly on the foundations built by Classical scholars, and so hovers uneasily, in no sense *pure* in its perspective. Which brings me to one further *caveat*: I make no great pretense to objective detachment in this book. Though I hope that my prejudices and preoccupations do not distort the poems or make my analysis so private that it is of no use to anyone else, I was brought back to these particular stories, and learned to love them in a new way, because of my own struggles with death and change. More specifically, I could not have begun to understand what I say here without having turned my own "jolly corner," without having met, and in some cases learned to accept, versions of myself that I never knew were there.

I hope that what I write will be of interest to Classical scholars, but I am also eager to reach and converse with others who may be interested in literature or in the way imaginative constructs can help us to see things about ourselves not available firsthand. Because the poems I am looking at are complex and sometimes daunting for nonspecialists, I want to make my work as friendly to these particular readers as I can. With this in mind, I have given more space to retelling the original stories than might be necessary for experts, and I have tried to provide a discussion that stands by itself as much as possible without asides and elaboration in footnotes. The Further Reading section at the end of the book is also aimed at nonspecialists, in the hope of stimulating more reflection on the poems, rather than attempting to give a detailed scholarly provenance for my analysis.

For specialists, I also append a short bibliographical essay, saying how I see my work proceeding from previous scholarship on the poems. This latter group of readers will also know what a reading of the bibliography I list will show—that I am indebted for many of my ideas to the work of other scholars, and that my reading is by no means the only valid and fruitful approach to the material.

Again with a view to encouraging further exploring by those who may not read the original languages in which the poems were composed, I use well-known, easily available translations of extended passages from the *Iliad* and the *Aeneid* rather than my own. In the case of the *Epic of Gilgamesh*, I have no choice about using others' translations. Passages from the Standard Babylonian version of the *Epic of Gilgamesh* are from the translation of John Gardner and John Maier (Gardner and Maier 1984); for the Old Babylonian version I have used E. A. Speiser's translation in Pritchard 1969; for the *Iliad*, I have used Richmond Lattimore's version (Lattimore 1951), for the *Odyssey* and *Aeneid*, Robert Fitzgerald's (Fitzgerald 1963; Fitzgerald 1980). In the last two cases, the translator uses a shorter line than the original, and so has line numbers that do not correspond to the original text. My numbers refer to the numbering in the original texts, which Fitzgerald lists at the top or bottom of each page.

Readers will observe some discrepancies in the spelling of Greek names between my prose and Lattimore's translations of the *Iliad*: where Lattimore has Achilleus, I use Achilles, and so on. The choice reflects two preferences: for the familiar and accessible in general, and for honoring the presence of the Romans in particular as intermediaries between our civilization and the Greeks.

This book is a product of my association with Oberlin College in many ways. The bulk of the writing was supported by a research leave granted by the College during the academic year 1988–89; teaching there for sixteen years has brought into my life countless intelligent and forbearing students on whom I have tested out many of the ideas in this study; my colleagues, Nathan Greenberg and James Helm, have been an unfailing source of enlightenment, friendship, and support; Karen Barnes has helped me to prepare the manuscript and simply been there for me in many ways — everyone should be so lucky as to work with people like these.

Several people have helped to improve the final version of this book by reading and commenting on various earlier versions (I hope that I have not left anyone off the list, but if so, please, whoever you are, forgive me): Carol Beran, Andrew Bongiorno, Fred Feddersen, Barbara Horan, Brad Liebl, Joe Snider, Grover Zinn, the two anonymous readers for Oxford University Press, and my editor there, Rachel Toor, to whom special thanks are also due, for her acute editorial advice and enthusiastic support — working with her has been a pleasure indeed.

Three people occupy a special place in the history of this book. William H. Armstrong, who taught me ancient history, among many other things, at Kent School, was the first male who took me seriously and encouraged me to do the same. The older I get, the more grateful I feel for his attentions. Mark Edwards has been my teacher, my mentor, and my friend for almost twenty years. He has read virtually everything I have written and by his judicious advice has added valuable insights to the final versions and saved me from all kinds of errors. His contribution to this book, in conversation and in writing, has been enormous. And finally my wife, Mary K. Kirtz. My central thesis about the role of the second self in the poems came into bloom during a time spent tagging along with her in the summer of

1988 as she pursued her own research through the libraries of western Canada—somewhere I had never travelled. Rambling through the parks in that beautiful country, sharing my ideas and hearing her response to them, I felt a mix of serenity and excitement the richness of which I had never known and will never forget. The book is dedicated to her with love.

Oberlin, Ohio   T. V. N.
March 1991

Contents

Somewhere I Have Never Travelled

Metaphors

Those who write analyses of literature these days must begin by walking across the hot coals of the methodology test: what method are you using to get at the stories? Are you aware of your own prejudices? Is your way of seeing valid? The heat is especially intense for those who want to write about issues of personal behavior or motivation that may be said to cross over between literature and "life" (whatever that is). Recent theories have insisted that the whole idea of *self-expression* in literature must be seen as problematical: the texts produced are subversive, in that they may say things the author never knew they said, may autonomously send disquieting messages reflecting hidden presuppositions of the culture. This book will, in one sense, heartily endorse that sort of view, since it is about the potential for ignorance about oneself and the resistance to enlightenment. But as my earlier remarks indicate, I am reluctant to claim much dispassionate perspective on the issues I see raised in the poems, and I am stubborn about the *subjective* basis for much of what I say, so my methodology (or lack of it) may well give me a hot-foot. Nevertheless, I can at least try to be as open as I can about what *I* think I am doing, and hope for a sympathetic reading.

Everything in my approach follows from the assumption that the psychological or spiritual (more anon about these terms) dynamic the poets are dramatizing cannot be apprehended directly. The parts of ourselves we project originate in an inner darkness and are accessible to us only after they have entered the conscious mind, always in forms altered to fit the requirements of cognitive thought on the conscious level. So poets create metaphors to describe something which is by nature mysterious, unknowable. But this means that psychologists too must work with metaphors, and who is to say that theirs are any more accurate or illuminating than the poets'? The point here is that there is no reason that I can see to privilege the analyses of psychologists so as to make their metaphors the ultimate validation of any reading of the poems, or to turn the process on its head, using the poets for the purpose of awarding any prizes to a particular psychological school. This is not to say that I find all psychological models equally helpful *in addressing this particular set of issues* — the next paragraph would give that claim the lie — only that my primary aim here is not to validate a set of psychological theories but to describe a way literature reflects life. And, of course, I cannot claim primacy for my own metaphors (that is what my "analysis" comes to, after all) — given the extent to which psychological theories have become part of our common parlance in talking about human behavior, my observations from life may inevitably come out sounding like warmed-over Jung anyway. What I offer is a reading of the poems as metaphors, illuminated by other metaphors, none of which has a claim to ascendancy in apprehending the unknowable. If this sounds closer to a mad hatter's tea party than scholarship, I can only reply that Alice's journey is, after all, a metaphor quite like the ones I will be describing.

Having said all of that, I now confess to a certain preference for one particular school of psychology. My initial response to the poems and my own personal experience, both of which preceded any detailed knowledge of psychological theory, incline me to Jung's model of developmental psychology over Freud's. The reasons are various. First, my reading of, say, the end of the *Iliad* is essentially positive, in that I see Homer portraying in Achilles the potential for spiritual renewal, for a new wholeness born out of terrible loss. This kind of reading is commensurate with Jung's prospective method of addressing psychic problems, of building up out of the actual situation toward the possibility of growth in the future, as opposed to Freud's reductive method, which attempts always to resolve the present problem into a past incident or complex. Second, Jung was simply more interested than Freud in the relationship between life and art, in the myth-making capacity of humans as a therapeutic way of coping with the world than was Freud, so Jung gives you more to go on when studying literature. Finally, there is the quite subjective matter of temperament. I am inclined by nature to optimism (perhaps more than is helpful, but that is one of my "jolly corners"), to the feeling that things are generally going pretty well, and to the belief that if things are bad, I can make them better. So I am attracted to the insistence in Jung that self-realization is a moral decision, that the tenor of my life is something I to some extent choose. Freud's model, though hardly discounting conscious choice, sees life more as a kind of holding action, mopping up after the mess of our childhood and the grim realities of the world, trying for some kind of standoff between what one or another part of us wants and what we are likely to get.

While I am sure that all art has its roots in the psychic configuration of the artist, and while I also hold the view that art is at least in part the conscious shaping of unconscious material, I am not interested here in speculating on the psyche of any author. And luckily for me, the temptation is diminished since virtually nothing is known for sure about the creators of any of these works. Indeed, in the case of the *Iliad*, the questions of *who* composed what we have, and *how*, are veritable chestnuts, and ones which I do not propose to roast. For my purposes, the *Iliad* we now have will be considered to be the work of one mind, whatever antecedents there may have been, however the poem may have reached its present form.

A few words about terminology. Though I will draw on the work of psychologists, I prefer to call the overall process of growth we will explore here *spiritual*, rather than *psychological*. The latter term is rather too scientific for what I envision, and appears to elevate one set of metaphors over others. I do not mean to raise any doctrinal issues by my use of "spiritual" — this is not a book about religion and literature — but only to emphasize the centrality and primacy of the inner process the poets and psychologists are trying to get at. For this reason, "emotional" will not do, since the integration I am exploring, while it includes the accommodation of emotions, finally transcends feelings alone. In this sense, though discussion of any particular religion or doctrine will not be germane here, the metaphors of religious faith may sometimes help to illuminate the process. One person's god is another's archetype, and what I am after is not a final explanation of *what* the Other we all sense from time to time is, but rather *how* poets try to dramatize our inner struggles and what we can learn about ourselves by thinking about the poems.

Likewise, I prefer "second self" (borrowed from Keppler, see below) to "double" or "alter ego." Of the latter two, "double" sounds rather too exclusively literary, "alter ego" too clinical. My phrase, though perhaps slightly cumbersome, has the virtue of being sufficiently descriptive while avoiding constrictive overtones. And finally, the word "therapeutic" may be initially misleading when applied to the role of the second self, because it too carries echoes of the therapist, droning softly in our modern ear. I mean to use it because it is an economical way of expressing the function I have in mind, but let me request that for the duration of this study my reader listen not so much for the modern clinical buzzing but rather for the Greek root of our English word, *therapeuo*, meaning "to heal" in a wider sense.

The scholarship on the second self in literature is quite extensive. The great bulk of it is aimed at nineteenth- and twentieth-century realizations of the theme, and for that reason has a particular slant. The emphasis is on the second self as a dark, sinister figure, who often stalks the unsuspecting hero, driving him to what feels like murder, but is really a kind of suicide. The nineteenth century's fascination with undercurrents of feeling forbidden expression by the proprieties of the time make the sinister second self a familiar figure. After Freud's work on the unconscious became generally known, the second self of course entered the realm of science, but kept most of the dark qualities that writers like Poe and Stevenson had given it — Baudelaire's blossoms grew very well in Faulknerian soil. One striking aspect of the second self in the poems we will be looking at is the basically bright, positive qualities associated with it — try as we might, neither Enkidu nor Patroclus can be cast as a sinister figure. The effect of this is to open up the dynamic considerably: the hero may appear less exclusively bright, what has been hidden less dreadful; failure to incorporate the second self may reflect a much wider range of issues than simply fear of what seems unacceptable or evil. Indeed, the emphasis in all of the works we will study is not so much on the unacknowledged evil that lurks in all of us as it is on the potential for spiritual growth in every person, the possibility that even the most painful loss may open the door to a richer life.

There is in each of our works, as I have said, a close relationship between particular overarching themes and the makeup of the second self, so it seems best to consider each poem separately, rather than trying to develop a kind of typology of the second self in ancient epic from abstracted examples. But before looking at the poems it will be helpful to lay out some common characteristics of the second self in literature. I am not suggesting that all of these tendencies fit our poems, and in fact we will sometimes be noting contrasts between our works and this set of generalizations, but they will provide a kind of baseline for discussion. By far the most helpful survey for this purpose is Carl Keppler's *The Literature of the Second Self* (Keppler 1972) a comprehensive, sane overview, grinding no particular axes. Here is list of characteristics that Keppler sees as common in the dynamic of the second self:

> The first and second selves are not identical, but complementary; each possesses what the other lacks.
>
> The intrusion of the second self cannot be entirely accounted for by "the facts."
>
> The second self always appears when the first self is most vulnerable to its influence.
>
> There is an instant, strange, and inexplicable affinity between the two selves.
>
> Whatever the feelings between the two, they are always *intense*, often more intense than "the facts" can explain.
>
> The feelings and reactions of the first self are always in the foreground, those of the second in the background.
>
> The encounter with the second self is always potentially therapeutic.

If we do find that our poems sometimes fit these characteristics, the exercise will not be entirely circular, as Keppler has included the *Epic of Gilgamesh* in his survey, but not, as far as I can see, the *Iliad* or the *Aeneid*. Keppler's analysis of the Gilgamesh epic, though brief, is very good, though I see the dynamic of the second self as fitting into the overall structure of the poem differently than he does.

The Wild Man:
The Epic of Gilgamesh

Since it has been said that you are my twin and true
companion, examine yourself so that you may understand who
you are . . . I am the knowledge of the truth. So while you
accompany me, although you do not understand (it), you
already have come to know, and you will be called "the one
who knows himself." For whoever has not known himself has
known nothing, but whoever has known himself has
simultaneously achieved knowledge about the depth of all
things.

Book of Thomas the Contender 138

Robert Bly makes a useful distinction between the *savage* man and the *wild* man:

> We could distinguish between the wild man and the savage man by looking at several details: the wild man's possession of spontaneity, the presence of the female side in him, and his embodiment of positive male sexuality. None of this implies violence toward or domination of others. . . . (in old European initiation rituals) The older males would teach the younger males how to deal with the shadow material in such a way that it doesn't overwhelm the ego or the personality. They taught the encounter more as a kind of play than as a fight. (Bly 1988.53)

Enkidu, dropped to earth as the gods' pinch of clay, is such a man as Bly describes: wild but not savage, spontaneous, at one with the rhythm of nature, exuding raw sexuality that seems to draw, especially in his opposition to Gilgamesh, on a reservoir of femininity. The *Epic of Gilgamesh* is driven by two interconnected polarities, nature/culture and mortal/immortal, and the pivot for the entire structure is the relationship between Gilgamesh and Enkidu. The wild man crosses, hand-in-hand with a harlot, the boundary from nature into culture, then crosses again, this time alone as we all must, beyond the pale of life itself. In each journey he travels as and for both himself and his friend Gilgamesh; at each crossing he draws illumination, like a lightning rod, to the opposing territories. As Gilgamesh follows, he must learn not to walk in the same footprints but to absorb his second self and make his own way, to make one man, new and yet familiar, from two. Looking on lets us think about some knotty and abiding problems: how can we live at peace with what is, letting go of what we wish would be; how can we learn to accept death as a part of life; how exactly do we know when we are "grown-up"? This is the first realization we have of the second self in western literature, and it is an impressive debut.

Preliminaries

Two problems of a different sort need attention before we go further: first, the difficulty of my not knowing either Sumerian or Akkadian; second, the question of which epic of Gilgamesh we ought to be thinking about. As to the former, I am well aware of my limitations, being one who has struggled to learn other ancient languages. My devilishly clever interpretation of a particular passage may depend on a word that my translator says means "soul" but some other expert reads as "lentil." To which I can only reply that, aware of the dangers, I have tried to inform myself of the intricacies of the text as best I can, and that I have relied on as many experts as I can to maintain quality control. It is also the case that most of what I have to say will be about broad themes and structures, not individual elements of the language (but, then, the themes are carried by individual lexical units, so . . .).

About the second issue I am less nervous, since it is more a matter of assessing needs and making a choice. There are three major extant groupings of stories about Gilgamesh: an early set of individual tales composed in Sumerian around 2100 B.C.; an expanded narrative or narratives, composed around 1600 B.C. in Akkadian, having thematic connections with the Sumerian stories but no verbal parallels (Old Babylonian version, OB); a final, more homogenized, more structurally integrated version in Akkadian, showing many verbal and thematic parallels to OB, composed sometime between 1600 and 1100 B.C. by a priest named Sîn-leqi-unninni, and reaching us through a copy dated to about 600 B.C. (Standard Babylonian version, SB). The most complete version is SB, and this, for the most part, is what I mean by the epic of Gilgamesh. What we have of SB is divided into a twelve-tablet format, with six columns to a tablet, and I will refer to the text by noting tablet (Roman capitals), column (Roman lowercase), and line (Arabic numerals). There are gaps in SB, and in these cases I follow the usual method of scholars in the field, making conjectures based on OB or the earlier fragments, if there are enough parallels to make this feasible.

There seems to a general esthetic preference for OB among those who read the original languages, as the author of SB (call him Sîn, for short) wrote in a more repetitive style, with longer lines and less variety of wording. The differences are evident even in translation, and I find myself in agreement with the experts. Unfortunately, since we need to be as confident

as we can about the integrity of the entire story in order to discuss the
second-self motif in the larger context of the epic, and since the fragments
of OB are too scarce to tell for sure even whether it represents the remains
of an integrated, continuous epic or another set of individual stories, esthetic pleasure must in this case yield to other values.

   One other aspect of the textual tradition is of interest here. As we follow
the development of the story from the earliest to the latest versions, we
see that the second-self motif becomes ever more prominent, adding new
complexities to the story. In the Sumerian stories we have, Enkidu appears
to be somewhat inferior in status to Gilgamesh, a squire rather than a peer.
In OB the relationship changes to one between equals, and with this change
come new elements related to it, an account of Enkidu's origins, the outsized response of Gilgamesh to Enkidu's death, and an increased attention
to Gilgamesh's obsession with and quest for immortality. All of this in turn
is related to the introduction, for the first time, of the motif of the second
self.

   SB has the same basic plot, but a more self-consciously artistic structure.
It begins with a new and somewhat unusual prologue, which stresses neither
the heroic adventures of the first half of the poem nor the subsequent
search for immortality, but focuses instead on the outcome of the quest,
increased knowledge and maturity. One emblem of this growth appears to
be acceptance of the fact of human mortality, and a consequent appreciation of the works of human culture. Sîn underscores the point by introducing language in the prologue that matches almost verbatim something Gilgamesh says at the end of tablet XI, creating a frame around the main
body of the story:

> Ascend the walls of Uruk, walk around the top,
> inspect the base, view the brickwork.
> Is not the very core made of oven-fired brick?
> As for its foundation, was it not laid down by the seven sages?
> One part is city, one part orchard, and one part claypits.
> Three parts including the claypits make up Uruk.
>
> SB I.i.16–21

> Gilgamesh said to him, to Urshanabi, the Boatman,
> "Go up, Urshanabi, onto the walls of Uruk.
> Inspect the base, view the brickwork.
> Is not the very core made of oven-fired brick?
> Did not the seven sages lay down its foundation?
>
> In [Uruk], house of Ishtar, one part is city, one part orchards, and one part
>   claypits.
> Three parts including the claypits make up Uruk."
>
> SB XI.vi.303–307

Since Gilgamesh's final insights reflect his experience of looking for the secret of immortality, a quest spurred by the death of Enkidu, we see that Sîn is building on the motif of the second self, first introduced in OB, to underscore a major theme in his version of the story.

Two other new features of SB are less germane to my project: the account of the flood, told Gilgamesh by Utnapishtim to explain the latter's immortality (XI.i–iv.197), and the story told in tablet XII of Enkidu's trip to the Underworld to retrieve a drum that Gilgamesh had dropped. The flood narrative is of great interest to those who want to study the relationship of the Old Testament to other Near Eastern texts, since it parallels the story of Noah fairly closely, but it is basically a large-scale digression having nothing directly to do with the second self. The story in tablet XII is more anomalous, giving an account of Enkidu's death that is not consistent with what comes before. The episode is, in fact, a faithful reproduction of part of a Sumerian episode, "Gilgamesh, Enkidu, and the Nether World," and the reasons why Sîn included it are obscure. In any event, for my purposes here, the epic ends with tablet XI.

Gilgamesh as Hero

The presence of the second self would seem to indicate, as I have said, a potential problem, something that might be explored. More specifically, there is something the hero has lost track of or does not yet know and therefore cannot accept about himself—his spiritual development as a man is incomplete in some significant way. The Gilgamesh story has barely begun when problems arise. It seems that Gilgamesh is endowed with extraordinary energy, and his exercise of it is causing distress to his fellow citizens:

> He runs wild with the young lords of Uruk through the holy places.
>
> Gilgamesh does not allow the son to go with his father;
> day and night he oppresses the weak—
> Gilgamesh, who is shepherd of Uruk of the Sheepfold.
> Is this our shepherd, strong, shining, full of thought?
> Gilgamesh does not let the young woman go to her mother,
> the girl to the warrior, the bride to the young groom.
>
> SB I.ii.11–17

The exact nature of Gilgamesh's misbehavior here is slightly obscure, though it seems to be at least partly sexual in nature. As king, he might be demanding the "privilege of the first night" with all the brides; he might also be performing his part in a sacred marriage rite, playing the role of the king who insures the fertility of the crops by sleeping with a surrogate for the goddess Ishtar; then again, it may be that he is simply winning all the potential brides by defeating his male rivals in wrestling matches. For our purposes, it suffices to say that he is overpowering the city in some way that is harmful.

The root cause of this appears in the opening lines of the narrative:

> Two-thirds of him is divine, one-third human.
> The image of his body the Great Goddess designed.

>   SB I.ii.1–2

Gilgamesh is the first in a long line of western heroes who straddle the boundary between human and divine. Such creatures are by nature problematical, to themselves and those around them. They might exhibit all the strengths and weaknesses of deities, exerting their enormous power for good or evil, depending on where their appetites drive them; they sometimes transcend the reach of human morality, because they are simply too powerful. All of this sounds very appealing for the hero, if not for his fellows, but a mixed lineage is also a mixed blessing. Being akin to the gods clearly raises large expectations; being human may impair their fulfillment. Too powerful to have real peers among mortals, not strong enough to mix with the gods, the hero may be an isolated, lonely man. Most pressing of all is the problem of mortality: will the hero escape death? The answer, in all but a very few cases, has been no, and learning to accept that verdict is certainly one of Gilgamesh's greatest challenges.

Viewed from the author's perspective, the hero of mixed lineage affords the opportunity to explore one of life's most significant turning points. All of us, if we live long enough, come to a moment when we accept the fact that our life is finite, that we will die. In the aftermath, nothing is quite the same. Life had looked like a collection of possible futures, some realized, some only waiting for our attention. Suddenly those roads not taken appear to be definitely *behind* us; instead of standing at the beginning of an open vista, we are in *the middle* of something finite, with a past stretching in one direction, and a future that looks somehow narrower. At the end of the journey now stands a boundary we had not seen before, and it changes the way we see everything on this side of it.

Such a realization need not be entirely depressing. If death will take away the world, its prospect also clarifies what it is that we most treasure, removes false issues, adds perspective. If life's finitude seems to restrict our possibilities, it also relieves us of the burden of unlimited potential — we are what we are, we do what we can, and we can more easily learn to love ourselves and others as flawed but game mortals than as unfulfilled deities. All of this means that the acceptance of one's own mortality, painful though it may be, is one prerequisite for emotional maturity, because without it we cannot really know ourselves for what we are.

It should not surprise us to find the second self as part of the exploration of life's finitude. If the fact of mortality can bring us to be easier on ourselves, then one aspect of this would be the acceptance of parts of ourselves that our former godlike perspective would not accommodate. In the Gilgamesh epic, the two elements are firmly linked: Enkidu is created as a solution to the problems brought on by Gilgamesh's extraordinary nature. Let us note immediately two things: the overtly therapeutic function of Enkidu within the framework of the story—he is sent on a mission from the gods, who want things to get better in Uruk—and the lack of mystery about Enkidu's origins. We are a fair distance from the dark, haunting stranger who appears as from nowhere in nineteenth-century fiction to torment the unsuspecting hero. The gods' expectation within the story is that this new creature will bring relief to the citizens of Uruk; looking from without as readers familiar with the motif of the second self, we are curious about how the wild man fits into the dynamic of spiritual growth in the hero.

Exploring this distinction will help us keep our bearings. Though the gods' explicit intervention and intent may appear to make the therapeutic role of the second self that we are discussing *a part of the fabric of the story*, as it is not in, say, *Doctor Jekyll and Mr. Hyde*, this is not so. The drive toward spiritual growth in the logic of our story is a dynamic imposed from *outside* the frame of the narrative by its author, not from within by fictional transcendent powers. Though the gods of ancient epic, Mesopotamian, Greek, or Roman, may intervene in the life of mortals to good effect, they do so to please themselves, not to forward the progress of mortals toward spiritual wholeness as a worthy goal in itself. If they save a city, it is because they feel a personal sense of ownership, and they might just as well destroy a city for equally private reasons. Just so, they may have favorite mortals or ones they hate—the *Odyssey* is driven by the counterbalancing love of Athena and hatred of Poseidon for its hero. In this sense, the fact that Enkidu is sent by the gods is coincidental to his role as a second self. Likewise, though Gilgamesh has his divine protectors, principally his mother, as a group the gods are indifferent to his spiritual state, except as it forwards or impedes their personal aims. They will give Gilgamesh a companion if being less lonely will divert him from wearing out the citizens, not because they feel sorry for him in his isolation, and they certainly have no interest in what is our present preoccupation as readers outside the story, his need to integrate the second self.

The Advent of Enkidu

The citizens cry out, and the gods respond:

> When [Anu the sky god] heard their lamentation
> he called to Aruru the Mother, Great Lady: "You, Aruru, who created
> humanity,

create now a second image of Gilgamesh: may the image be equal to the time
  of his heart.
Let them square off one against the other, that Uruk may have peace."

When Aruru heard this, she formed an image of Anu in her heart.
Aruru washed her hands, pinched off clay and threw it into the wilderness:
In the wilderness she made Enkidu the fighter; she gave birth in darkness and
  silence to one like the war god Ninurta.
His whole body was covered thickly with hair, his head covered with hair like
  a woman's;
the locks of his hair grew abundantly, like those of the grain god Nisaba.
He knew neither people nor homeland; he was clothed in the clothing of
  Sumuqan the cattle god.
He fed with the gazelles on grass;
with the wild animals he drank at waterholes;
with the hurrying animals his heart grew light in the waters.

SB I.ii.29–41

There is much to be learned from these few lines. First, and most important
for us, is the explicit naming of Enkidu as "second image" of Gilgamesh —
from the beginning, Enkidu is named as a second self to Gilgamesh. The
new creature is further defined in some detail: a leader, created out of the
image of Anu, the head god of the pantheon, in Aruru's heart; a fighter,
like the war god Ninurta; a wild man, at home in the wilderness, covered
with hair, ignorant of humans, at ease with animals; and, finally, a man
with hair like a woman's.

Enkidu is to provide relief for the citizens by fighting with Gilgamesh,
not, apparently, in order to kill the king, but rather to occupy that overwhelming energy — fighting in this case will bring peace. We begin to see
that Sîn presents the motif of the second self rather explicitly: arranging for
Gilgamesh to confront his "second image" will bring peace to the citizens;
ostensibly, in the gods' view from within the story, this will be so because
the king will be diverted, will wrestle with someone else for awhile; from
our vantage point, and presumably Sîn's, it is no great leap to see this new
"peace" as something to be achieved by Gilgamesh inside himself. The
rudiments of self-realization are laid out neatly.

But just confronting the second self brings no guarantee of growth. Next
must come acceptance and integration (if the qualities of the second self
have never been active in the hero) or reintegration (if the qualities have
been present before and then somehow "lost"). What this will mean in
Gilgamesh's case remains to be worked out, and much will depend on the
peculiar nature of Enkidu. We may begin with the notion of *complementarity*, which Keppler and others see as a common part of the relationship
between the first and second selves: the second self embodies qualities not
identical with but complementary to those of the hero, so that the two may

be seen as adding up to a third, richer entity. Because Sîn has taken such pains to describe Enkidu's qualities for us early on (again suggesting that the dynamic of the second self is primary), we can isolate rather easily the parts of him that complement Gilgamesh: he is wild, in tune with the natural world, while Gilgamesh is a man of the city; his ties are to animals, Gilgamesh's to humans; he dresses in animal skins, Gilgamesh (we suppose) in the finery of a king. Taken all together, the list seems to show a clear polarity between nature and culture. The entrance of Enkidu into the life of the city will confirm this.

Enkidu is not entirely unlike Gilgamesh. He must be a good fighter, in order to give the king some competition, and like Gilgamesh, his power is disruptive to the regular order of things. Enter "the Stalker," a man given only as much definition as suits his role, to be bothered: he finds Enkidu's presence among the animals upsetting, as the wild man is sabotaging his traps and pits, and says as much to his father. The advice given is to go to the city and tell Gilgamesh, which he does, getting this time more detailed instructions: take a temple courtesan to the watering place and lie in wait for the wild man; have the woman strip and "show him her strong beauty;" once the wild man makes contact with her, the animals will turn from him. The Stalker and the courtesan (another minimalist character) wait by the watering hole for three days; Enkidu arrives, and the woman presents herself to him with the predicted effect: seven days of uninterrupted lovemaking.

The aftermath is rich and instructive. As predicted, the animals shun Enkidu, and his former fleetness is gone. The encounter has severed the wild man's seamless connection to the rhythms of the animal world — having arrived at the watering hole as "man-as-he-was-in-the-beginning" (SB I.iv.6), he has now entered the alluring but complex world of human culture. Although it might well be seen as something animalistic, a way for humans to participate in the natural world, sex in this instance is clearly an emblem of culture. The priestess has lured Enkidu across the boundary into civilization, ironically enough, by tapping his animal energies; from now on, he will have to find ways to compensate for the loss of direct access to the world of nature:

> "You have become wise, like a god, Enkidu.
> Why did you range the wilderness with animals?
> Come, let me lead you to the heart of Uruk of the Sheepfold,
> to the stainless house, holy place of Anu and Ishtar,
> where Gilgamesh lives, completely powerful,
> and like a wild bull stands supreme, mounted above his people."
>
>   SB I.iv.34–39

As for Adam, so for Enkidu knowledge is an ambivalent thing: to gain access to its rewards, he must give up another kind of power; once in possession of it, he must go where it can be used, the city.

Before setting out for civilization with the courtesan, Enkidu reveals to her a new longing for a "deeply loving friend" (SB I.iv.42) — deprived of the company of animals, he craves a companion. Curiously enough, this desire is immediately balanced by what appears to be a more antagonistic mood: he will go to the temple to challenge Gilgamesh; he, Enkidu alone, is powerful; he, born in the wild, "changes fates" (SB I.v.2).

Enkidu's assertiveness signals his new condition. In place of the unreflective interaction with nature that he forfeited by sleeping with the priestess, we find the vaunting typical of epic heroes; now that he has begun to become civilized, he must adopt new modes of behavior that will give him a status commensurate with his self-esteem. At the same time, we might say that self-esteem and status only become issues *because* Enkidu has entered civilization, where one's place in the order of things is not so often assured by a "natural" order but by the rubbing and jostling between humans.

In the course of introducing Enkidu, Sîn offers a concise analysis of the polarity nature/culture. To live at one with nature requires unthinking adherence to a larger system, and offers in return a life of innocent exertion and unreflective interaction with the world and its inhabitants. To enter culture is to lose innocence, along with an assured place in the scheme of things. In return comes knowledge, which is needed because now it is necessary to *manipulate* nature in order to get what came without effort before, and with knowledge comes *self-consciousness* — who we are and where we stand become problematical in the world of culture as they are not in nature. Enkidu's boasting is, in this sense, a recognition of new opportunities but also new uncertainties.

All of this prompts some reflection on humility, a quality very much at issue in this poem. Heroes are outsized, extreme exemplars of ordinary human attributes, both positive and negative; they confirm the contours of human experience by testing its parameters. They are not usually credited with much humility, and this is hardly surprising, since as egregious carriers of humanness they tend to embody an extreme self-consciousness, and this militates against the sense of fitting into a larger scheme that is the essence of humility. One of the strengths of the Gilgamesh epic is to broaden finally the scope of its hero's vision, so as to make the achievement of humility one emblem of maturity. The price for this growth will be the loss of Enkidu.

First Contact

Gilgamesh's first contact with his second self is in a dream:

> Gilgamesh rises, speaks to Ninsun his mother to untie his dream.
> "Last night, Mother, I saw a dream.
> There was a star in the heavens.

Like a shooting star of Anu it fell on me.
I tried to lift it; too much for me.
I tried to move it; I could not move it.
Uruk, the land, towered over it;
the people swarmed around it;
the people pressed themselves over it;
the men of the city massed above it;
companions kissed its feet.
I myself hugged him like a wife,
and I threw him down at your feet
so that you compared him with me."

The mother of Gilgamesh, skilled, wise, who knows everything, speaks to her
    lord;
the goddess Ninsun, skilled, wise, who knows everything, speaks to
    Gilgamesh:

"The star of heaven is your companion,
like a shooting star of Anu he falls on you;
you tried to lift it; too much for you;
you tried to move it; you were not able to move it;
you lay him down at my feet
so that I compared him with you;
like a wife you hugged him."

SB I.v.25–47

Dreams in the Gilgamesh epic are prophetic, meant to reveal the future more than the inner state of the dreamer. Certainly this vision has much to tell us. Something is coming, which looks like a rival to Gilgamesh for the attentions of the citizens, but oddly enough, the king's response is to "hug him like a wife." Ninsun's interpretation helps to explain the latter: the star will be Gilgamesh's companion, someone to end the isolation of his existence. Still, there remains the curious mix, which first appeared in Enkidu's yearning for a friend and subsequent boasting, of love and competition.

Given the norms of male bonding, perhaps this is not so anomalous — men have always used competition as one basis for establishing relationships with other males. But we can go a bit further by considering the issue in light of the second self. The first response to undiscovered parts of oneself may well be antagonistic, fueled by wariness, even fear, which produces in turn denial — "I could never be(do) that!" At the same time, the intense affection that Gilgamesh envisions betrays the fact that finally, this creature knows the hero as no one else can, is by definition already *intimate* with him.

We need to be careful not to misunderstand this intimacy. My students often assume that Gilgamesh and Enkidu or Achilles and Patroclus are homosexual lovers, that the lack of any mention of sexual contact only reflects the author's tact. Likewise, it would be easy enough to see the wrestling-match-to-come between the hero and his second self as a metaphor for sexual contact. This is understandable, explaining something by the apparently obvious model closest to hand, but it can be reductive. Friendship in general is a difficult relationship to fix, seen in our modern cultures as existing on the boundaries of other bonds, familial or sexual, which provide the categories through which friendship itself is defined. The poems we will read here offer another model for friendship, one accommodating a greater degree of intimacy than is often accorded to nonsexual friendship these days. The first and second selves are intimate because they compose, together, a single entity, though the realization of that unity may be delayed or even destroyed—at this level of intensity, sexual love is sometimes inadequate as a model because it may not be intimate enough. As Keppler says: "There are no tepid relationships between hemispheres of the soul" (12).

At this point we may recall that Sîn has taken care in the initial description of Enkidu's creation to mention "his head covered with hair like a woman's" (SB I.ii.36). If there is no gain in seeing Gilgamesh and Enkidu as lovers, why this little detail? I want to be careful not to load too much significance onto one phrase, especially if it is not developed further, but the relevance of this to Bly's description of the wild man is tantalizing. Is it too much to see the "feminine" part of Enkidu as integral to his unique status at the poem's beginning, forming a complementary relationship with Gilgamesh's overbearing masculinity? Perhaps, especially given the habit in Near Eastern and Mediterranean cultures of associating women with the rhythms of nature, and men with the imposition of rational order on those rhythms as a way of channeling their power within human culture. If so, we ought to consider whether there is something about this particular trait in Enkidu that, once accepted by Gilgamesh, would contribute to his maturity. More of this later.

Ninsun goes on to say that the star in the dream "is a powerful companion, able to save a friend" (SB I.vi.1). Perhaps encouraged, Gilgamesh relates a second dream much like the first, but with Enkidu in the form of an axe. Ninsun "unties" the message in much the same way, adding one detail: "I treated him as your equal" (SB I.v.19). The stage is set for a meeting.

But Enkidu's progress is deliberate, as the priestess breaks him in to civilization gradually. The second tablet of SB is broken, and especially column one, so we depend on OB to conjecture here. Apparently, before reaching the city, they stop with some shepherds, traditionally boundary figures between nature and culture, and Enkidu undergoes further initiation: he is given clothes, he eats bread and drinks wine, thus tasting the two most universal examples of prepared food.

The beginning of the next column is broken, the middle missing entirely, but the end is intact, telling how the encounter between Gilgamesh and Enkidu begins. In the preceding lines, fragmentary but comprehensible, we learn that Gilgamesh is again on the verge of either pulling rank to sleep with a bride, or performing his function as king to reenact a sacred marriage. In any event, Enkidu finds him on the threshold of the bridal chamber:

> Enkidu, at the gate of the bridal house, planted his feet.
> He prevents Gilgamesh from entering.
> They seized one another in the bride-house gate;
> they fight in the street, through the city quarter;
> [they broke down part of] the wall.

> SB II.ii.46-50

The first forty or so lines of the next column are lost, but probably told the story of the fight. What remains from the very end seems to have Ninsun advising her son in the aftermath. The next column too is very fragmented, but we have enough to see that Gilgamesh makes a speech, perhaps praising Enkidu, who is moved to tears. Lines 12 to 13 are intact:

> They seized one another, embracing,
> took one another's hands like [brothers].

The first meeting of Gilgamesh with his second image is complete, and we might pause to consider what it tells us about the relationship. There are some continuities with Keppler's list: the complementary nature of the two men, the sudden intensity of their relationship, the sudden and mysterious appearance, from Gilgamesh's perspective, of Enkidu in his life. The departures are equally instructive: the vivid characterization of Enkidu, his essentially positive nature, and the prominence of his feelings in the story. We have seen that this poet makes the motif of the second self extraordinarily explicit; we should also note that the nature of the second self is exceptionally well defined, as if to focus as strongly as possible the impact he will have on Gilgamesh, and exceptionally positive, as if to underscore the king's less positive qualities. Finally, we note the strong, fundamental connections established immediately between Enkidu's emergence and the polarity nature/culture.

Adventure in the Cedar Forest

Once formed, the partnership is soon taken into the field. Gilgamesh has decided that the two should go to the Cedar Forest to challenge the monster who guards it, Humbaba. Exactly why Gilgamesh suggests this must remain a mystery, since none of the extant versions of the story preserve the explanation, but we can guess from what follows. Enkidu, knowing something of Humbaba, is not at all enthusiastic about the plan, and Gilgamesh's reassurance (here from OB — SB is broken in this spot) is instructive. Apparently, the goal of the quest, apart from adventure, is to gain glory:

> Gilgamesh opened his mouth,
> saying to [Enkidu]:
> "Who, my friend, can scale he[aven]?
> Only the gods [live] forever under the sun.
> As for mankind, numbered are their days;
> Whatever they achieve is but a wind.
> Even here thou art afraid of death.
> What of thy heroic might?
> Let me go then before thee,
> Let thy mouth call to me, 'Advance, fear not!'
> Should I fail, I shall have made me a name:
> 'Gilgamesh' — they will say — 'against fierce Huwawa
> has fallen!' (Long) after
> My offspring has been born in my house . . . "

> "[Thus calling] to me, thou hast grieved my heart.
> [My hand] I will poise
> and [will fe]ll the cedars.
> A name that endures I will make for me!"

>   OB III.iv.3–17; 22–25

If, as is likely, SB also has something like this, the theme of mortality enters the story here, in a form compatible with a typically heroic perspective: death will come when it comes, and meanwhile, we must gain as much glory — the one hedge against oblivion available to us insubstantial mortals — as we can. The other half of the polarity, immortality, will be brought into play initially by the goddess Ishtar, then grow yet more prominent after Enkidu's death, when Gilgamesh's bravado gives way to a different perspective.

Let us note an immediate effect of Enkidu's entrance into Gilgamesh's life. From the gods' perspective, things are going well. Not only has Gilgamesh been diverted from wearing out the citizens, he is leaving the city altogether. We, meanwhile, think about how the second self changes the hero's trajectory: from immersion in the life of the town, the arena of human culture, he now heads straight into the wilderness in the company of his new friend, the onetime wild man, thus reversing the journey of Enkidu from nature to culture. To say that this is evidence of Gilgamesh somehow absorbing Enkidu's wildness seems too pat — after all, Enkidu does not want to go. Indeed, Enkidu's fear would reflect his former integration with nature—why go out of one's way to kill another creature who is not threatening you directly and may kill you instead—while Gilgamesh's heroic aggression is fueled by the quest for glory so important within the pale of culture.

We may note here that though Enkidu has gone through an initiation into the world of culture and has lost his ability to live as he used to in the wilderness, he still seems to carry, or embody to some extent, the perspective on the world that his former existence provided. He continues to be a foil for Gilgamesh the city-dweller, and this function becomes if anything more prominent as the poem progresses. In this sense, Enkidu's symbolic function as we see it from our removed perspective takes precedence over his naturalistic characterization within the poem, or, to put it another way, his function as an objectified part of Gilgamesh takes precedence over his existence as a fully independent character.

Though Gilgamesh does not adopt the ways of the wild, the adventure does clearly reflect new influences in his life. His foray is driven by values from within the life of the city, but it has the effect of removing him from the arena of greatest potential responsibility as a ruler. From this perspective, the journey to the Cedar Forest might well be seen as postponing adult responsibility in favor of an adolescent brand of male bonding. The issue, in other words, is maturity. Though the arrival of the second self leads initially to something approaching immaturity, the adventure that follows the death of the second self, a more profound and perilous one, will eventually bring the king back to his people with a deeper understanding of his role.

The next two tablets, three and four, are very fragmented. They contain, as far as we can tell, the preparations for the journey to the Cedar Forest (III) and the journey itself (IV). A few important details survive: Gilgamesh's request of his mother, Ninsun, for intervention to secure the support of Shamash, the god of justice (III.i–ii), which seems to supply some further motivation for the adventure; the adoption of Enkidu by Ninsun (III.iv), further strengthening the ties between Gilgamesh and his friend; and Gilgamesh again encouraging Enkidu as the two enter the forest (IV.vi), a restatement of the heroic defiance of death. Speaking to Ninsun, Gilgamesh implies that Shamash will support the mission, because Humbaba is considered evil, something "Shamash hates" (II.i.30). Within the context of the story, then, a less self-serving motive for the adventure is suggested. The identification of Humbaba as evil, along with his position in the wild, indicates in fact that we have here an example of a very common motif in the Near Eastern hero story: the fight between the hero as agent of order and a monster representing chaos, disorder. Gilgamesh and Enkidu are elevated in this mythical pattern from playmates to enforcers of the cosmic order, and though a certain mixture of motives for aggression in real life should, alas, be no surprise to anyone familiar with the history of warfare, this use of the pattern in a work of imaginative literature might throw doubt on my earlier characterization of the adventure as somehow immature.

Once again, we need to keep the distinction between internal and external motivation clearly in mind. Within the frame of the story, Gilgamesh and his friend are exemplars of heroic exertion, but the author of our story has established another perspective outside the narrative, which identifies Gilgamesh's heroic self-assertion as a problem from the beginning. In this sense, a "mission from god" is hardly incompatible with the more solipsistic self-assertion which is the focus of our exploration of the second self in the episode.

Tablet V of SB offers little more comprehensible text than the previous two, but parallels from OB help us to fill out the story. The main subject of the tablet was probably three dreams that Gilgamesh has, with Enkidu's interpretations, followed by a description of the two heroes killing Humbaba. The dreams all seem ominous to Gilgamesh, but Enkidu, who now is comfortable with the mission, offers more positive interpretations, emphasizing the protection that Shamash will provide to them. In all the surviving versions of this episode, a debate about whether Humbaba, whom the heroes have apparently reduced to helpless pleading, should be killed precedes the deed. Gilgamesh inclines to mercy, but Enkidu is adamant that the monster must die. The disagreement reflects a telling difference between the two friends: Gilgamesh, seeing the conquest of the monster as part of a larger vehicle for getting status in the culture, not as a struggle for survival, can contemplate the possibility that reducing Humbaba to helplessness would be proof enough of his superiority; Enkidu, still more closely in tune with the elemental realities of nature, wants to finish the monster. The wild man prevails and they cut off Humbaba's head.

Ishtar and the Bull of Heaven

The chaos monster defeated, the heroes now relax in their glory. Tablet VI, which is much more complete than the previous three, opens with the two men back in Uruk. Gilgamesh bathes and changes from his grimy clothes back into the finery of a king, complete with crown. His beauty attracts the notice of Ishtar, the goddess of fertility, who makes overtures:

> "Come, Gilgamesh, be my lover!
> Give me the taste of your body.
> Would that you were my husband, and I your wife!
> I'd order harnessed for you a chariot of lapis lazuli and gold,
> its wheels of gold and its horns of precious amber.
> You will drive storm demons – powerful mules!

Enter our house, into the sweet scent of cedarwood.
As you enter our house
the purification priests will kiss your feet the way they do in Aratta.
Kings, rulers, princes will bend down before you.
Mountains and lands will bring their yield to you.
Your goats will drop triplets, your ewes twins.
Even loaded down, your donkey will overtake the mule.
Your horses will win fame for their running.
Your ox under its yoke will have no rival."

SB VI.i.7–21

Gilgamesh rejects the offer firmly. He begins with the reasonable observation that he, even though a king, cannot offer much to a goddess. Warming to the assignment, he begins to insult the goddess, calling her "a cooking fire that goes out in the cold,/ a back door that keeps out neither wind nor storm" and so forth. Then comes the most compelling charge, that none of her previous lovers has fared well:

"Which of your lovers have you loved forever?
Which of your little shepherds has continued to please you?
Come, let me name your lovers for you."

SB VI.i.42–44

The catalog takes up nearly all of the next column, a damning indictment. She loved the shepherd bird, then broke his wing; she loved a shepherd, then turned him into a wolf that his own dogs tore to pieces; the gardener ended up as a frog. Ishtar, understandably angry, goes to her father Anu to complain.

This is a striking episode, almost intrusive, with more than one function in the story. When the two friends return from the wilderness, their crossing back into civilization is marked by Gilgamesh's toilet, a sign that he has taken up again the role of king. Ishtar responds to Gilgamesh not only as a potent male, beautiful and pumped up with the success that the adventure brings, but also as a king, because the union she wants would be an enactment of the sacred marriage rite, this time with the real deity rather than a mortal surrogate. Gilgamesh, returned triumphant, is in this sense offered the chance to bring fertility not only to himself personally, but to his city as well. His adamant refusal has then at least two potential dimensions, and will repay careful attention.

The issue of the *personal* consequences for the king of accepting Ishtar's offer occupies the foreground of both speeches. She holds out a godlike existence for her lover: splendid equipage, groveling underlings, potent fertility in the crops and the king. Gilgamesh sees it differently. According to his reckoning, about the best he could hope for is to end his days as a frog, and the story pattern of the mortal mating with a goddess in ancient literature has more than one example of death as the man's reward.

The civic dimension of both Ishtar's offer and Gilgamesh's refusal is much more muted, never alluded to directly in the poem. This may suggest that we not lean too heavily on it as a guide to understanding the story—maybe this level of meaning is not a live one in the poem. But I am reluctant to let this dimension go too quickly—the story pattern of the sacred marriage is common enough in Near Eastern culture to suggest that it may well be something the poet could expect his audience to recognize without heavy prodding, and the importance in other ways of Gilgamesh's civic, even religious, function in Uruk is clear. If we allow Ishtar's offer to carry the promise of both personal and civic fertility, the portrait of Gilgamesh deepens: on the personal level, Gilgamesh's answer suggests some arrogance, even hubris, which we read in the context as a result of the heroic adventure—bravura denunciation is of a piece with the earlier defiance of death; at the same time, turning Ishtar down might also suggest that Gilgamesh is continuing to slight his responsibilities as a king in favor of the exciting new life that the encounter with Enkidu has opened up. Our poet keeps the issue of maturity in the foreground.

Though Ishtar does not explicitly hold out the promise of immortality to Gilgamesh, she seems to raise the issue by offering something akin to the life of the gods. His response, a seamless extension of his heroic self-assertion, rejects by implication the possibility of immortality: she seems to extend a hand across the boundary between humans and gods, but this looks to him like an invitation to go in the other direction, from man to animal. Gilgamesh's current way of seeing precludes even considering the prospect of immortality, not because humility dictates he let go of that hope, but because his arrogance blinds him to the reality of death.

By traveling to the Cedar Forest Gilgamesh reversed Enkidu's entrance into Uruk; by rejecting Ishtar, he mirrors (in the literal sense, reversed images) the encounter with the priestess. Enkidu's animal energy drew him across the boundary from nature into culture, into a status that the priestess compares to a god's; Gilgamesh's heroic self-assertion holds him back from access to what Ishtar claims is the world of the gods, but what he himself sees as the world Enkidu left. All of this is tantalizing, but pressing the analogies too hard is reductive. We are better off simply observing that Enkidu continues to foreshadow, in a puzzlingly reversed way, the journey of Gilgamesh toward maturity, and that this second instance begins to draw together the poem's two dominant polarities.

One adventure creates a second. Though Anu tries to calm Ishtar down, she eventually prevails on him to create the fearsome Bull of Heaven to punish Gilgamesh for his insults. Anu reminds his daughter that the creation of the bull will somehow take up all the wheat in Uruk for seven years, which suggests that the bull embodies the destructive power of famine, and that we have here a variant on the common story of the angry fertility deity who withholds food from the earth. Though she claims to have provided enough food for the citizens to live out the famine, when the bull actually arrives his very snorting opens up holes in the earth into which hundreds of men disappear—once again, Gilgamesh's heroism costs the citizens dearly.

The two heroes are undaunted, and after consulting double-team the monster (VI.iv.). The tablet is very fragmentary where the actual fight occurs, but becomes legible at the end of the struggle, when the two tear out the bull's heart in triumph (VI.v.153). Gilgamesh and Enkidu are now at the height of their powers, glorious heroes bringing back the carcass to be admired by the citizens. Ishtar confronts them with a curse for killing the bull, and Enkidu, true to his direct manner, insults the goddess and defiantly throws a thigh from the carcass into her face. This is followed by a corresponding show of arrogance in Gilgamesh:

> Gilgamesh speaks these words to the people assembled,
> to the women he says:

> "Who is the best-formed of heroes?
> Who is the most powerful among men?
> Gilgamesh is the best formed of heroes.
> [Enkidu is] the most powerful among men."
>
> SB VI.v.180–181; vi.182–185

This speech marks the farthest point in the trajectory that began with the advent of Enkidu. Gilgamesh, persuading his new friend to defy death and pursue glory as a guarantee of earthly fame, has reached the top of the mountain he has chosen to climb. Along the way, he and his friend experience all of the joys of this view of life, illustrating at the same time its less joyous consequences for others. Now a reckoning comes for the heroes as well.

The Death of Enkidu

The last line of tablet VI has Enkidu telling his friend about a disturbing dream, of the gods in council. The first column of tablet VII is broken, but seems to contain something of the dream, including the ominous phrase, "Now I have set down for you the day of fate" (VII.i.41?). A fragmentary Hittite text of the poem from the period 1600–1100 B.C. (Middle Babylonian Period) has a fuller version, with the dream reporting a demand for Enkidu's death by the gods Anu and Enlil, despite objections from Shamash that the two heroes were following his orders. Not Gilgamesh, but his second image will have to pay for the act of killing the bull.

The next two columns are fragmented and rather obscure in spots, but seem to contain Gilgamesh's attempts to console his friend, Enkidu's cursing of the Stalker and the priestess who first brought him to Uruk, and

finally Shamash's speech of consolation, which convinces Enkidu to let go
of his anger and bless the priestess at the beginning of column iv. This part
of the poem is important because Enkidu's response to impending death
previews in many ways the struggle of Gilgamesh in the remainder of the
story: first come fear and anger, then acceptance.

Enkidu's last days take us to the end of tablet VII. He continues to lead
the way for his friend, this time bringing Gilgamesh into contact with that
part of the cosmos that his heroic exuberance has kept hidden from him,
the land of the dead. Enkidu dreams:

> "He seized me and led me down to the house of darkness, house of Irkalla,
> the house where one who goes in never comes out again,
> the road that, if one takes it, one never comes back,
> the house that, if one lives there, one never sees light,
> the place where they live on dust, their food is mud;
> their clothes are like birds' clothes, a garment of wings,
> and they see no light, living in blackness:
> on the door and door-bolt, deeply settled dust.
>
> In the house of ashes, where I entered,
> I saw [the mighty], their crowns fallen to the dirt.
> I heard about crowned kings who ruled the lands from days of old,
> worldly images of Anu and Enlil, waiting table with roast meats,
> serving baked goods, filling glasses with water from cool steins.
>
> In the houses of ashes, where I entered,
> there lives the funereal priest who brings together gods and men, and the
>   funereal wailing priest;
> there lives the purification priest and the ecstatic shaman;
> there live the *pashishu*, priests of the great gods;
> there sat Etana, the human taken to the sky by an eagle; and there sat
>   Sumuqan the cattle god.
> There sits the queen of below-earth, Ereshkigal:
> Belit-tseri, tablet-scribe of the underworld, kneels before her.
> [She holds a tablet] and reads aloud to her.
> Lifting her head, [Ereshkigal] looked directly at me — *me*:
> '[Who] has brought this one here . . . ?'"

SB VII.iv.33–54

The last column of tablet VII, what remains of it, apparently chronicles
Enkidu's wasting death. Tablet VIII opens with Gilgamesh's lament for his
dead friend.

The Gilgamesh epic is the first treatment in western literature of the
universal human experience of grief. Though grief is a primary emotion —
there are no real analogies — the process raises issues central to the evolution
of Gilgamesh toward maturity. I have said that self-acceptance is prerequi-

site to growing up, and of all the things about ourselves we must learn to live with, mortality is one of the most fundamental and most difficult. This struggle is played out in our story through the vehicle of the second self: Gilgamesh must accept the loss of his friend and carry on in the world of the living; by doing so, he accepts the fact of his own mortality and the role it plays in his life in the present.

In the first rush of grief, Gilgamesh recalls what seems most important about Enkidu, his origins in the wild and their adventures there together. He then slips further into that world, becoming in his mind, and then the poet's, an animal:

"Like an eagle I circled over him."

Like a lioness whose whelps are lost
he paces back and forth.

SB VIII.ii.18–21

Next, a gesture characteristic of grieving but especially significant in this context: "He tears off and throws down his fine clothes like things unclean" (SB VIII.ii.22). Sîn has established regal finery as a symbol of Gilgamesh's role in the culture. His behavior here, taken together with his earlier reminiscing, shows him moving within himself back into the wild as a way of identifying with Enkidu. This is on one level a vain attempt to keep his friend with him in any way he can—we will see Achilles making a similar gesture by clinging to the body of Patroclus—but since Enkidu is Gilgamesh's second self, the need to be reunited has a special resonance.

What we have here is a heightened version of something common to many who grieve, the feeling that when someone you love dies, something of yourself dies, too. This kind of spiritual death has its analog in the feeling of being cut off from the world—life goes on, but we do not want to go with it, clinging instead to a lost world where death is not real. This is the dark side of grieving, but dying unto oneself, being taken however vicariously back into the undifferentiated, unhierachical limbo within ourselves, represented in this case by the world of the dead, can also be the first step to rebirth.

Whatever funeral arrangements Gilgamesh makes for Enkidu are lost to us. When we next see the king, he is acting out the roaming that began in his imagination. He goes again into the wilderness, looking for relief from his pain:

Gilgamesh for his friend Enkidu
bitterly cried. He roamed the hills.
"Me! Will I too not die like Enkidu?
Sorrow has come into my belly.
I fear death; I roam over the hills.
I will seize the road; quickly I will go

to the house of Utnapishtim, offspring of Ubaratutu.
I approach the entrance of the mountain at night.
Lions I see, and I am terrified.
I lift my head to the moon god Sîn;
For . . . a dream I go to the gods in prayer:
' . . . preserve me!'"

SB IX.i.1–12

This is the first direct statement of Gilgamesh's new attitude toward mortality. Gone is the easy heroic defiance of death. It has become real for him;
he fears it. At this point, aimless wandering gives way to a more purposeful
journey, as he sets out to find a way to ease his fear: he will go to see
Utnapishtim, the only mortal ever to escape death.

Journey to the Land of Dilmun

So begins a version of the definitive heroic adventure, the trip to the underworld. To look death in the face and return to the living is the ultimate
proof of a hero's extraordinary stature. On another level, the journey often
represents a going into the dark places of oneself, to find certain truths
hidden from us in our conscious life. Certainly Gilgamesh's trek beyond
the twin mountains and over the waters of death has this dimension, an
acting out of the "dying unto self" I have described above. In a way that
typifies the Gilgamesh epic's explicit representation of profound spiritual
issues, the king's overt reason for making the journey corresponds exactly
with its deepest level of significance: he goes to the underworld not as do
Odysseus and Aeneas, to find the way home, but to discover how to escape
being what he is, to escape death.

The journey takes Gilgamesh past various boundary figures, who test his
resolve and ultimately help him on his way. First are the Scorpion man and
his woman, guarding the gate to the twin mountains, called Mashu, beyond
which Shamash (the sun) passes each day. Gilgamesh is already pressing
against the normal bounds of human existence. Asked why he wants to go
through the gate, the king is brief and direct:

"I have come on account of Utnapishtim, my elder,
    who stands in the assembly [of the gods, and has found life].
Death and life [I wish to know]."

SB IX.iii.3–5

Gilgamesh eventually talks the Scorpion man, who is initially alarmed—no
man has ever made this journey before—into letting him through, and the
great journey begins. The first part, lasting eleven "double-hours," is all in

thick darkness. At the end of the eleventh "double-hour," it begins to brighten a little, and by the beginning of the twelfth, it is light. He finds himself in a grove made of stone, with carnelian fruit and lapis lazuli leaves, a garden of the gods. The last column of tablet IX, perhaps detailing his stay in the garden, is illegible.

Tablet X opens with Gilgamesh approaching the house of the next boundary figure, Siduri the female tavernkeeper, who lives on the edge of the waters of death. The king must cross these waters to reach Utnapishtim, and he needs guidance. Siduri has often been compared to Circe in the *Odyssey*, who gives Odysseus advice on how to reach the underworld and talk to the sage, Teiresias. The comparison is apt, and would be more so if SB had a parallel to the following advice from Siduri found in OB:

> Gilgamesh, whither rovest thou?
> The life thou pursuest thou shalt not find.
> When the gods created mankind,
> Death for mankind they set aside,
> Life in their own hands retaining.
> Thou, Gilgamesh, let full be thy belly,
> Make thou merry by day and by night.
> Of each day make thou a feast of rejoicing,
> Day and night dance thou and play!
> Let thy garments be sparkling fresh,
> Thy head be washed; bathe thou in water.
> Pay heed to the little one that holds on to thy hand,
> Let thy spouse delight in thy bosom!
> For this is the task of [mankind]!

OB X.iii.1–14

In this version, the advice to Gilgamesh to give up his quest for immortality is linked with the notion of enjoying life while one can, since death is inevitable. And since the barkeep is extolling the virtues of the civilized life, the polarities of mortal/immortal and nature/culture are neatly linked. Alas, SB does not have such a passage, and shows no lacuna where it might likely have been found, so we will have to go with what Sîn gives us. Even so, the linkage of polarities might be hinted at by putting Siduri, who as a barkeep is associated with the civilized pleasures of beer, at this point in the story.

Gilgamesh has by now assumed a frighteningly wasted aspect, causing Siduri to bolt her door. The king convinces her to open up, but she is still wary of someone whose strength is wasted, face sunken, a face "like that of a man who has gone on a long journey" (SB X.i.32–35). Gilgamesh explains himself:

"Barmaid, it is not that my strength is wasted, my face sunken,
not that evil fortune has entered my heart, done in my looks.
It is not the sorrow in my belly,
not that I look like a man who has gone on a long journey,
nor that the cold and heat have weathered my features —
not for that do I roam the wilderness in quest of a wind-puff, but because of
my friend, companion, who chased the wild ass, the panther of the steppe —
Enkidu, friend, loved-one, who chased the wild ass, panther of the steppe.
We overcame everything: climbed the mountain,
captured the Bull of Heaven and killed him,
brought Humbaba to grief, who lives in the cedar forest;
circling the mountain gates we slew lions.

My friend whom I love dearly underwent with me all hardships.
Enkidu whom I love dearly underwent with me all hardships.
The fate of mankind overtook him.
Six days and seven nights I wept over him
until a worm fell out of his nose.
Then I was afraid.
In fear of death I roam the wilderness. The case of my friend lies heavy in me.
On a remote path I roam the wilderness. The case of my friend Enkidu lies
    heavy in me.
On a long journey I wander the steppe.
How can I keep still? How can I be silent?
The friend I loved has turned to clay. Enkidu, the friend I love, has turned to
    clay.
Me, shall I not lie down like him,
never again to move?"

SB X.i.40–51; ii.1–14

This lengthy summation is helpful, though it also exemplifies Sîn's repetitious style. Indeed, nearly the same speech will be delivered before Urshanabi, the boatman who takes Gilgamesh across the waters, and yet again before the sage Utnapishtim. All the addressees initially give the same advice: give up the quest for immortality; the fate of mortals is to die.

Siduri tells Gilgamesh that no mortal has crossed the waters of death, but that he may try by getting Urshanabi the boatman to ferry him across. The ensuing encounter (X.iii–iv) is one of the more opaque portions of the story, as Gilgamesh apparently breaks some icons crucial to the crossing, perhaps does violence to the boatman, who may have wings, and so forth. In any event, he tells his story and makes it to the other side of the waters of death, finally reaching Utnapishtim, who he hopes will tell him how to escape the death sentence awaiting him.

The first part of column v is broken, and mercifully so the reader may say, as when the text becomes legible again, Gilgamesh is rounding the far turn on that speech again. But there is an important coda this time:

> "I said, 'I will go to Utnapishtim, the remote one about whom they tell tales.'
> I turned, wandering, over all the lands.
> I crossed uncrossable mountains.
> I travelled all the seas.
> No real sleep has calmed my face.
> I have worn myself out in sleeplessness; my flesh is filled with grief.
> I had not yet arrived at the house of the Barmaid when my clothing was used up.
> I killed bear, hyena, lion, panther, tiger, stag and [ibex] — wild beasts and creeping things of the wilderness.
> I ate their flesh, covered myself with their skins.
> She barred her gate against me. I slept in dirt and bitumen."
> [I lay down with animals, I touched . . .]
>
> SB X.v.24–34

Killing animals, wearing their skins, sleeping with them, Gilgamesh has come as close to the former life of Enkidu in the wild, gone as far from his former life in the city, as he ever will. We understand the gesture as denial, of Enkidu's death, as the king clings to his friend, and of Gilgamesh's own mortality, as he presses against the boundaries of humanity in his attempt to transcend them.

Utnapishtim, after reviewing the facts of Gilgamesh's mixed lineage, and after a lacuna in the text that we cannot fill, asks some troubling questions:

> "Do we build a house forever? Do we seal a contract for all time?
> Do brothers divide shares forever?
> Does hostility last forever between enemies?
> Does the river forever rise higher, bringing on floods?
> Does the dragonfly [leave] its husk . . .
> the face that looks at the face of Shamash?"
>
> SB X.vi.26–31

The conclusion to be drawn is an unhappy one for Gilgamesh, and is followed by a yet more explicit dashing of his hopes:

> From the beginning there is no permanence.
> The sleeping and the dead, how like brothers they are!
> Do they both not make a picture of death?
> The man-as-he-was-in-the-beginning and the hero: [are they not the same] when they arrive at their fate?
> The Anunnaki, in the Assembly of the Great Gods —

Mammetum with them, mother of Destiny — sets the ends of things.
They settle death and life.
As for death, its time is hidden. The time of life is shown plain.

SB X.vi.32–39

Here is the simple truth, put so directly it almost takes us by surprise; the rest of the story tells us how Gilgamesh comes to accept it. This means more denial, but no more success at evading the reality. Tablet XI is taken up with Utnapishtim's explanation of how it is that *he* of all mortals escaped the inescapable (the flood story), Gilgamesh's vain attempt to beat death's twin, sleep, his loss of the plant that would have conferred agelessness, and his final return to Uruk, clothed again in his kingly robes. The last lines of the tablet and of the story take us back to the very beginning:

"Go up, Urshanabi, onto the walls of Uruk.
Inspect the base, view the brickwork.
Is not the very core made of oven-fired brick?
Did not the seven sages lay down its foundation?

In [Uruk], house of Ishtar, one part is city, one part orchards, and one part claypits.
Three parts including the claypits make up Uruk."

SB XI.vi.304–307

The story's quiet close belies the significance of Gilgamesh's return. He is back where he started but a changed man, his description of Uruk here suggesting in the context a new acceptance of the meaning of the city in his life, an embracing rather than defiance of the limits it represents. The friendship with and loss of Enkidu, the journeys into the wild and into the dark, all suggest that the king has evolved from the hubristic, dominating male of the poem's opening, full of pride and eager to distinguish himself from lesser beings, into a wiser man, accepting the limitations that his mortal side imposes, and especially the fact itself of mortality, which in turn has let him begin to see not those things that separate him from other humans, but rather the emblems of his essential kinship with all creatures who must die.

The Return of Enkidu

Utnapishtim's sobering questions begin a profound thematic synthesis that integrates various strands of the story. At the center stands the figure of the second self, "man-as-he-was-at-the-beginning." Though he comes from the wild into the city, Enkidu's effect on Gilgamesh has been to separate him from the rest of the citizens. Before the wild man's appearance, the king's energy is a problem, but he is at least fully immersed in the life of the city. Meeting his "second image" stirs up in him the desire for adventure, in particular that kind of glory-seeking which has the goal of distinguishing the two heroes from the rest of the citizens, raising them to some higher plane by virtue of their extraordinary skill and strength. The apogee of this movement comes in Gilgamesh's speech to the citizens after the killing of the Bull of Heaven.

The death of Enkidu provides a check to heroic self-assertion, but not to the separation of Gilgamesh from his fellows. Now driven by fear of death rather than defiance of it, the king travels yet further beyond the pale of human culture, to the poem's version of the dark Underworld. There has been some gain realized already, in that Enkidu's destruction has made death real for Gilgamesh, in a way that his former heroic perspective prevented. But as I have said, knowing something and accepting it are not the same — denial must have its day, and this latter form proves no less strong than the heroic brand.

Gilgamesh's journey into darkness, an outward representation of an inward process, brings him to a new source of truth, deeper and more profound than anything he has yet experienced. Utnapishtim, who corresponds on some level to the nonrational, inner part of Gilgamesh's self, delivers the bad news that Gilgamesh cannot escape the mortal part of his nature. The particular way he puts the point, noting the identical fate awaiting both Gilgamesh and Enkidu, effects an abrupt and significant shift in the role Enkidu plays in the evolution of Gilgamesh toward maturity. Suddenly, Gilgamesh's intense identification with his second self becomes not a force isolating him from the rest of humanity, but rather the ultimate example of his essential kinship with all other mortals. To put it another way, Enkidu becomes a goad to humility, not hubris.

The motif of the second self has been closely integrated throughout the story with the polarities nature/culture and mortal/immortal. Enkidu's transition from the wilderness to Uruk provided Sîn with a vehicle for exploring the former, his death, the latter. As a result, the two antitheses have been woven together in ways that illuminate both. The heroic perspective dominating the earlier adventures was a reflection of the cultural preoccupation with renown as a hedge against oblivion, and led to an easy defiance of the reality of death. So it is, we have observed, that Gilgamesh can contemplate a reprieve for Humbaba, since the monster's begging would provide sufficient proof of the two heroes' prowess — the reality of death is less important than glory. In the world of nature, survival is a genuine issue, death a real possibility, and so Enkidu, still in touch with these necessities, insists on killing the monster.

Once death intrudes into the artificial world of culture, it destroys the illusion of invulnerability that man's creativity can provide. At the same time, it reminds us that we, as mortal creatures, participate in the world of nature, of death and renewal — culture cannot insulate us from the destiny that we share with wild animals. In this sense, Enkidu's journey into Uruk at first suggests a misleading dichotomy between humans and animals, between creatures of the wild and those of the city. His death and Gilgamesh's reactions to it then offer a corrective to the original view, displacing our attention from the boundary between nature and culture, or animals and humans, which turns out to be less absolute than we thought, toward the definitive boundary between mortals and immortals.

This new focus reinforces, as I have said, the need for Gilgamesh to let go of the perspective that emphasized the ways in which the extraordinary part of his nature set him apart from other humans, and to embrace instead those parts of himself that he shares with all other creatures who must die. At the same time, manipulating the polarities allows Sîn to explore the original "problem" of Gilgamesh, his domination and the hubris that it at least implied, from a wider perspective, as the "problem" inherent in the human illusion of culture as a way of denying the reality of death. In this sense, Gilgamesh plays the typical role of the hero in any culture, representing an outsized version of every human, testing the limits of human life as a way of refining our understanding of them.

I have said that grieving raises critical issues for the spiritual evolution of Gilgamesh. Though Enkidu is not explicitly mentioned when Gilgamesh makes his final return to Uruk, one has the sense that Gilgamesh's period of grieving for his dead friend is at an end. The suffering that Enkidu's passing brought for Gilgamesh is tied closely in the story to the king's quest for a way to escape his own death. Both were a form of denial, specifically culture's denial of the reality of the wilderness, and in accepting the inevitability of his own mortality, Gilgamesh by implication accepts the wild man as a part of himself: he reintegrates the second self. In this sense, when Utnapishtim orders that Gilgamesh wash off the dirt of the journey, put aside the animal skins, and dress again in the clothes of the city, he signals an end to the period of grieving. But the shedding of clothing from the wilderness need not anymore signal a break with the reality of the wild, because Gilgamesh has now accepted, on a deeper level, the presence of the wilderness inside himself. The loss of Enkidu has, then, made a difference in the way Gilgamesh sees the world: death, once something to be defied, then to be denied, has become a part of life; Enkidu, lost forever, is at the same time found again.

Conclusion: Life from Death

This synthesis, satisfying though it may be, leaves the troublesome question with which we began. Why does the wild man have to die in order that Gilgamesh be able to accept him as alive *within himself*? Why must one kind of gain be preceded by another kind of loss? The answer, such as it is, lies in the nature and function of the second self as metaphor within the story.

Enkidu's creation ties him to the wilderness as opposed to the culture of Uruk, and marks him as *complementary* in some sense to Gilgamesh. We might suppose then that the embrace that brings their initial confrontation to an end might also mean that Gilgamesh has accepted the complementary qualities that the wild man embodies. But the story does not go this way. Rather, the appearance of Enkidu seems to drive Gilgamesh further into the heroic perspective to which the wild man stands in opposition. This might seem puzzling, but not if we consider how a confrontation like the one before the bridal chamber in the poem often works in "real life." Faced with parts of ourselves that we do not recognize, would like perhaps not to recognize, we deny the kinship, and often lean away from the new and into the old, accentuating the familiar qualities that complement the strange new ones. So it is when Gilgamesh faces a specter of the unacknowledged "wilderness" inside himself, a complex of attitudes and feelings opposed to the heroic view of life and death that is on display in the first half of the story. Instead of becoming more "wild," he launches an adventure that is driven by a more intense version of the same way of seeing the world that seems to have informed his behavior when he was overwhelming the city: everything he does presupposes the importance of marking the *difference*, in strength, determination, birthright, between the king and his subjects. The events that follow, the killing of Humbaba and the bull, the proposition of Ishtar, seem to lead him further along the same trajectory toward the extreme position reflected in his boasting speech after the death of the bull.

The death of Enkidu is seen within the story as retribution for killing the bull. It also suggests by its placement some kind of punishment for the hubristic excess of the two heroes. From where we stand, on the other hand, the death looks like the final act of denial, of pushing away from the strange qualities of the wild man—Gilgamesh "kills" Enkidu by running away from what he represents.

We note here that the flow of interior events that we see as students of the second self seems to run counter to the surface logic of the story: Sîn tells us that Gilgamesh is thrilled to have a friend, someone to end his isolation, to share the adventures that now suddenly open up. To see his behavior as a *denial* of what his new friend represents seems perverse, somehow flying in the face of what the story says. But again, is it so unusual to discover that what felt good at the time turns out to have been harmful, or "good" in some way we could not foresee, that what seemed a token of our superiority was actually a sign of vulnerability, *if only we could have seen it for what it really was*? The motif of the second self has the effect, then, of opening up for our consideration the gap between what we see in the sometimes narrow vision of conscious life and the different vista afforded by including truths from the darkness inside us.

With this in mind, consider again the implications of Enkidu's death. From inside the story, Enkidu's passing looks entirely negative: Gilgamesh has lost his friend, and worse yet, he himself must be held partly responsible, since he seems to have initiated the adventures. We too hold Gilgamesh "responsible," but see the affair in a different context, one that supplies a level of motivation not evident on the surface of the story and makes the king's complicity less ironic. But *still*, why death as a prelude to self-realization?

The insistent question drives us back to metaphor. I have said that in response to Enkidu's death Gilgamesh appears to return, first within himself and then without in the search for Utnapishtim, to a state that is represented by two symbols within the poem: the wilderness and the underworld. Both imply the presence of elemental forces outside the reach of culture, and a corresponding diminishment of human control. The analogous state in the metaphor of psychology is of course the unconscious, and the notion that the journey to the underworld is a symbol of the confrontation of the unconscious is not a new idea.

So Enkidu's death drives Gilgamesh into a dark place where his heroic mastery avails him nothing. He emerges from that state a changed man, different in ways that suggest the influence of just those qualities that characterized the wild man: a respect for the limits of human control over nature, a sense of kinship with his fellow creatures enforced by the universality of death. The second self returns, not as a separate being, but as part of the hero, and we may say that from our perspective this is appropriate: the second self appears when there is a "problem" in the hero, particularly something he has not realized about himself that is leading him to act badly; by objectifying what is unacknowledged, the second self allows the hero to react to his deficiency, by denying it, pushing away from it, finally killing it; the act of killing the second self pushes the hero out of the world he has created to serve his denial, and into the darkness, variously characterized; this darkness forces the hero to face and accept the reality he has been trying to escape, and he can then welcome the stranger back. The second self as a separate being is no longer necessary, because his mission is complete, and he can return to where he always was, inside the hero.

As it happens, Jung's metaphors are particularly apt to this configuration. In this perspective, Enkidu represents the Shadow, the unacknowledged parts of the self present in the personal unconscious. For the conscious mind to come to terms with these parts of the self is the first step, in this model, toward psychic wholeness. But often the Shadow is initially frightening, repugnant, to the conscious mind, not fitting the persona—an

arbitrary conflation by each person of elements from the collective unconscious with his or her own characteristics—we want to show to the world.
Denial follows fear, but the repressed always returns, because the self, the
totality formed by the conscious mind (ego), the personal unconscious and
the collective unconscious, regulates the flow of energy within the psyche.
If the conscious mind (Gilgamesh) refuses to admit the Shadow (Enkidu),
then the qualities the Shadow embodies become more active in the unconscious, eventually causing trouble again on the conscious level.

How does Gilgamesh's story reflect as art what we call life? What can we
learn about ourselves by reading the poem? Large questions, but suitable
for a work of art as deep and comprehensive as this. There is certainly much
to be learned here about the interrelations between maturity, humility, and
acceptance—lessons, indeed, that seem to contradict some of the common
connotations of the word "heroic." The word conjures up other words:
young, powerful, defiant (Odysseus is something of an exception here).
Certainly Gilgamesh is all of these, and yet the poem, taken as a whole,
offers an implicit critique of the association of these qualities with the fully
realized male. To grow up in the fullest sense, what I have called spiritually,
the poem suggests that Gilgamesh must learn to see himself not as preeminent among men, but as part of a larger whole, ruled by forces often
beyond his ability to control. Rather than challenge his limitations, he must
learn to accept them and live within them: maturity requires humility,
which requires acceptance—not defiance, not denial.

Ideas like this are not very often associated with young men. Rather, the
kind of realignment of perspective Gilgamesh seems to achieve is usually
part of what we now call the "mid-life crisis," when the first rush of self-
assertion has played itself out for most men, often leaving them puzzled
and lost, less in control of their lives and the world than they once thought.
This is also the time when parents begin to die, then perhaps a friend or
two as well, and the realization that Ereshkigal or her surrogate looks at
"me, *me*" begins to come over us, with the attendant feeling of options
closed off, roads not taken receding out of reach.

Gilgamesh, then, traverses while still obviously a young man the territory
now covered by most men in the years from twenty to forty (picking round
numbers). While perhaps straining the bounds of naturalism, this is appropriate in another sense, in that heroes in western literature often function,
as I have said, as boundary testers, traveling conspicuously through some
stretch of life and lighting it up for the rest of us. It may surprise us that
his journey leaves us with a "middle-aged" view of the world, but we will
see that this perspective is in fact common to all the poems we explore
here.

As a second self, Enkidu leads the king around a "jolly corner," to face
the truths he has been denying. In this sense, the wild man is for Gilgamesh
what Gilgamesh is for us, one who leads into undiscovered country, testing

and redefining the meaning of life. The story of the second self may then be a kind of hero story within a hero story, with one part of the self showing the way for another until a final reintegration is possible. This last thought suggests another: that the world as we see it, particularly in the challenges and obstacles it throws up before us, is more about us and our ways of seeing and less about the others we share it with than we may think; the key to growing up may be in taking ownership of what was always ours:

> . . . and when the light surrounded me
> I was born again: I was the owner of my own darkness.
>> Pablo Neruda, *100 Love Sonnets*

Into Prison:
The Iliad *(1)*

But if you will not know yourselves, then you dwell in poverty,
and it is you who *are* that poverty.

Gospel of Thomas 32

Achilles sends his friend Patroclus into battle with a prayer:

"Father Zeus, Athene and Apollo, if only
not one of all the Trojans could escape destruction, not one
of the Argives, but you and I could emerge from the slaughter
so that we two alone could break Troy's hallowed coronal."

Iliad 16.97–100

This is a fitting envoi, capturing in brief the qualities in Achilles that will soon cost him his companion: cosmic grandiosity, intense love, and above all, a stunning solipsism. Patroclus is going to fight in his friend's place, and will die in his place, sacrificed to Achilles' sense of honor. No figure in ancient literature embodies so purely as Achilles the destructive aspects of the heroic code, the terrible imperatives that drive men to wall themselves off from their fellows in pursuit of glory. Shut away in a self-imposed prison, he keeps Patroclus beside him as a fragile link to the world. But Patroclus dies, the tie is severed, and Achilles surges yet further away, roaming the edges of human life in a vengeful rampage. He can only return by contacting Patroclus again, by welcoming into himself the spirit of his second self. The *Iliad* explores the paradoxical nature of heroism, its alluring absolutism, its lethal isolation. In such a setting, we are not surprised to find competition, hostility, and self-absorption all around, but the greatness of Homer's poem lies in its final transcendence of that milieu. Of the many lessons to be learned from the *Iliad*, none is more profound than what it teaches us about self-knowledge and the ability to love.

Looking at Achilles and Patroclus will immediately remind us of Gilgamesh and Enkidu — appropriately enough, as there are many genuine parallels. This is almost certainly not evidence of any conscious reminiscence, but rather of how deeply embedded the story pattern is in the mythical substratum of the Mediterranean and the Near East. The similarities will be helpful to us, as a basis for comparison, but can only take us partway toward understanding the Greek poem. Where the Mesopotamian work is relatively simple and direct, with the surface of the story often presenting the deepest issues in the work, the Greek is elaborate and sophisticated, working on many different levels at once; Gilgamesh and Enkidu command Sîn's attention almost exclusively, while Achilles and Patroclus are woven into a complex tapestry, full of incident, expansive in its focus; Gilgamesh's journeys are usually actual, those of Achilles symbolic, figurative. Finally, the direct, complementary relationship between Gilgamesh and his second self gives way in the Greek poem to a more elusive, triangulated dynamic played out among Achilles, Patroclus, and Hector.

The Anger of Achilles

Homer's first words look toward the "problem" of Achilles which the motif of the second self may be said to address:

> Sing, goddess, the anger of Peleus' son Achilleus
> and its devastation, which put pains thousandfold upon the Achaians,
> hurled in their multitudes to the house of Hades strong souls
> of heroes, but gave their bodies to the delicate feasting
> of dogs, of all birds, and the will of Zeus was accomplished
> since that time when first there stood in division of conflict
> Atreus' son the lord of men and brilliant Achilleus.
>
> *Iliad* 1. 1–7

The Greek word for Achilles' anger, *menis*, is in fact the very first word in the poem — it is Homer's major theme. In the course of the story, the object of this wrath will shift, from Agamemnon, to Hector, to Achilles himself, but it remains the driving force behind the narrative. Exploring the motif of the second self in the *Iliad* will mean first of all working out the nature of Achilles' wrath, its motivation, what it tells about Achilles, and how it affects those around him.

To begin with, it is not an ordinary, human emotion — apart from Achilles, only gods are visited by *menis*; there are other words for the anger of mortals. This is not surprising because Achilles' mother is divine, and as for Gilgamesh, so for Achilles, a mixed parentage is a mixed blessing. The outsized appetites of deities find reflection in the grandiose attitudes of Thetis' son, in particular his absolutist, rigid perspective, which drives him away from other mortals: the price for being different is loneliness, isolation. At the same time, the urge in Achilles to separate from those he cannot bring to see the world as he does has a devastating effect on the larger society of the poem, essentially the Greek army and, less directly, the civilization of Troy. In this sense, the issues of community raised by Gilgamesh's behavior toward the citizens of Uruk are very much to the fore here, and the heroic perspective will be presented to us again as problematic. Likewise, the isolation of Achilles will cause him to bind Patroclus to him so as to make that relationship initially harmful to the common good, keeping the Greek hero from facing what drives him into loneliness.

There is no analog in the *Iliad* for the elaborate entry of Enkidu into Gilgamesh's life. The story begins in the tenth year of the war at Troy, and the relationship of Achilles and Patroclus is already firmly established. Nor is Patroclus ever as fully characterized as his Mesopotamian counterpart — he remains quietly in the background for the first half of the poem, rarely speaking except when addressed, has a few crucial exchanges with Nestor and Achilles, then goes into battle and dies. All of this means that the complementarity of Achilles and his second self is not presented to us as clearly and forcefully, right from the beginning, as it is in the Gilgamesh epic. This, in turn, makes the dynamic of the second self unfold more slowly here, so that though the "problem" of Achilles is evident early on, the relationship of this problem to any *lack* or blind spot in the hero that might be made up by the second self is also less evident. But Patroclus' *actions*, though few, are in fact crucial, his entrance into battle as Achilles' surrogate and his resulting death being the motivation for much of what happens in the last third of the poem.

The Quarrel

The first flaring of Achilles' anger comes early, in the dispute with Agamemnon, leader of the Greek expedition. The latter has angered Apollo by keeping the daughter of his priest as a part of the spoils of battle, and the god responds in typically brutal fashion, visiting plague on the Greek camp. Achilles calls an assembly and asks the seer Calchas to advise the Greeks. Agamemnon is blamed, and he does not take it well, bullying the seer — why always *bad* news, never good? — defending his preference for the priest's daughter over his own wife Clytemnestra with a repellently specific set of comparisons. Still, he will give the girl back, if that will keep the army safe. But — here the trouble begins — if he must lose his "prize of honor," then let the Achaians give him someone else's.

The issue of personal honor is prominent here, and we see that it is tied to material possessions — the woman in question is nothing more than a "prize," in the same category as, say, a handsome tripod. What a man *has* counts for more in the estimation of his worth in Homer's world than we perhaps expect, conditioned as we are by distinctions that became more prominent later in western cultures between inner worth and outer appearance. In the warrior culture of the *Iliad*, which puts rather more emphasis on results than intentions, what you see of another person is taken to be a good measure of his worth — if Agamemnon loses this woman, another of equal value in his and in others' eyes will restore his lost honor.

Agamemnon's preoccupation with his own honor is fierce, but he does struggle to balance it against the needs of the community. The same concern colors Achilles' answer to Agamemnon: the Greeks would gladly give him a new prize, but all the available booty has been distributed; as soon as more is gotten from raids on neighboring cities, he will have three or four times as much as he has lost. So far, a fairly restrained debate.

Things heat up quickly in Agamemnon's response:

> "Not that way, good fighter though you be, godlike Achilleus,
>   strive to cheat, for you will not deceive, you will not persuade me.
>   What do you want? To keep your own prize and have me sit here
>   lacking one? Are you ordering me to give this girl back?
>   Either the great-hearted Achaians shall give me a new prize
>   chosen according to my desire to atone for the girl lost,
>   or else if they will not give me one I shall myself take her,
>   your own prize, or that of Aias, or that of Odysseus,
>   going myself in person; and he whom I visit will be bitter."
>
> *Iliad* 1. 131–139

The last threat shows where things are headed: Agamemnon is finding his thoughts focused increasingly on Achilles. But once again he veers away from the sore spot, turning back at the end of his speech toward responsibility to the community by commissioning an embassy to return the priest's child.

But Achilles can hear only the attack on him, and his anger is ignited. Civic concern is now swept away in a tidal wave of emotion:

> "O wrapped in shamelessness, with your mind forever on profit,
>   how shall any one of the Achaians readily obey you
>   either to go on a journey or to fight men strongly in battle?
>   I for my part did not come here for the sake of the Trojan
>   spearmen to fight against them, since to me they have done nothing.
>   Never yet have they driven away my cattle or my horses,
>   never in Phthia where the soil is rich and men grow great did they
>   spoil my harvest, since indeed there is much that lies between us,
>   the shadowy mountains and the echoing sea; but for your sake,
>   o great shamelessness, we followed, to do you a favour,
>   you with the dog's eyes, to win your honour and Menelaos'

from the Trojans. You forget all this or else you care nothing.
And now my prize you threaten in person to strip from me,
for whom I laboured much, the gift of the sons of the Achaians.
Never, when the Achaians sack some well-founded citadel
of the Trojans, do I have a prize that is equal to your prize.
Always the greater part of the painful fighting is the work of
my hands; but when the time comes to distribute the booty
yours is far the greater reward, and I with some small thing
yet dear to me go back to my ships when I am weary with fighting.
Now I am returning to Phthia, since it is much better
to go home again with my curved ships, and I am minded no longer
to sit here dishonoured and pile up your wealth and your luxury."

Iliad 1. 149–171

This is the Achilles we will see from now on until the very end of the poem: uncompromising and fiercely protective of his prerogatives, proud of his skill and what it has done for the Greeks, unconcerned with the cost to his friends of his intransigence. Typical too is the threat of leaving. Achilles, like no other warrior in the poem, is characterized by being *apart*, from his friends and from the community informed by the values they espouse: if they do not see the world as he wants them to, he leaves.

Agamemnon's reply is scornful, fueled by escalating anger. Let Achilles go home by all means, *he* will not beg him to stay; as king, Agamemnon may count on Zeus for support. And if Achilles is strong, it is only some other god's gift. He ends with a specific threat: the compensation for Agamemnon's loss will come from Achilles; Briseis, his prize of honor, will take the place of the priest's daughter in Agamemnon's tent. Achilles, meanwhile, is on the verge of passing beyond words to action, considering whether to kill Agamemnon and be done with it. Athena appears and restrains Achilles, promising him yet more gifts to compensate for the loss of Briseis, convincing him to confine himself to verbal abuse. This he does, unleashing another blistering attack that ends with his own threat:

And this shall be a great oath before you:
some day longing for Achilleus will come to the sons of the Achaians,
all of them. Then stricken at heart though you be, you will be able
to do nothing, when in their numbers before man-slaughtering Hektor
they drop and die. And then you will eat out the heart within you
in sorrow, that you did no honour to the best of the Achaians.

Iliad 1. 239–244

This prediction will come true, and once again we see the astonishing solipsism that can contemplate the destruction of men Achilles has fought beside for ten years, in order to serve his sense of honor.

Nestor, seeing the destructive course that the exchange has taken, tries to strike a compromise. After a characteristically lengthy recounting of his own youthful valor, he encapsulates the dispute neatly, drawing a critical distinction: Achilles, though a better fighter, must give way to the king, who has Zeus' sanction; Agamemnon meanwhile owes allegiance to the man who stands as "a great bulwark of battle over all the Achaians" (*Iliad* 1.284). Agamemnon, the political leader, is "greater," because he rules over more men; Achilles is "stronger" by nature, because his mother is divine. Nestor is walking a tricky line here, and his overtures fail in any event, but he brings to light a major question that has been embedded in the furious debate: how is honor to be awarded? Since honor is for the moment taken to be the supreme measure of worth in this society of warriors, the quandary could not be more fundamental.

The "Problem" of Achilles

It will be helpful at this point to invoke again the distinction between the perspective from within the story and our own, colored by an interest in the motif of the second self. Seen from the former, Achilles' imminent desertion of the Greek camp is motivated by the immediate circumstances, his anger over the quarrel and Agamemnon's threats. We look on from a different angle, one that lines up the present separation of Achilles with other manifestations of his basic *apartness*: his enormous physical gifts, his tendency to go to extremes, his emotional contact with the world beyond the battlefield, his detachment from the heroic value system that governs the warrior's life. And finally the most potent symbol, his semi-divine nature, explosive like an unstable chemical compound: shake it up and it blows. All of this, from our perspective, is of a piece, and it takes us to the heart of Achilles' "problem:" the famous anger is a response to the frustrations created by being who he is, by the brute fact that what makes him great is also what isolates him.

Pressing the distinction further, we observe that from inside the story, the immediate problem is how to either find a fitting substitute for the best of the Achaians or get Achilles back into the camp and into the fighting, by offering gifts and other compensations. The first alternative is tried in books 2 through 8 of the poem, with Diomedes filling the role for a time, and when this fails, the second, in the embassy to Achilles in book 9. But from our position, the attempts to appease Achilles are somehow beside the point. It is not a matter of finding the right set of arguments to convince Achilles to bend—he is what he is, and this will prevent him from giving in until, like Gilgamesh, he pushes the parts of himself represented by the second self far enough away to "kill" them. This, in turn, will prompt a journey into the dark, painful and frightening, but holding out finally the prospect of healing.

The opening scenes of the poem have established with extraordinary economy the major characters and themes of the story. Out of the potentially enormous range of possible topics offered by the basic set of events, Homer has focused our attention on the problematic heroic value system, and in particular on its dangerous ambivalence in Achilles, its most egregious embodiment. Myriad other issues are raised in the course of this the richest of all ancient poems, the relation of body to soul, material to immaterial, the bittersweet quality of love, death as end and then beginning, the gulf between human and divine, but they are part of, or follow from, the central focus. And integral to that focus is the motif of the second self.

The Debut of the Second Self

Nestor's gambit fails, the two men fling yet more abuse, and Achilles storms from the camp after a final gauntlet: Briseis he will not fight over, but this is the end of concessions; the next challenge will bring blood. Making good on his own threat, Agamemnon sends two heralds to collect Briseis, vowing to go himself if there is any trouble. The men are not keen and who could blame them, but after an initial show of displeasure, Achilles makes a generous gesture:

> "Welcome, heralds, messengers of Zeus and of mortals.
> Draw near. You are not to blame in my sight, but Agamemnon
> who sent the two of you here for the sake of the girl Briseis.
> Go then, illustrious Patroklos, and bring the girl forth
> and give her to these to be taken away. Yet let them be witnesses
> in the sight of the blessed gods, in the sight of mortal
> men, and of this cruel king, if ever hereafter
> there shall be need of me to beat back the shameful destruction
> from the rest. For surely in ruinous heart he makes sacrifice
> and has not wit enough to look behind and before him
> that the Achaians fighting beside their ships shall not perish."
>
> *Iliad* 1. 334–344

This is our first glimpse of Patroclus, not a memorable debut. Unlike Enkidu, who holds our attention with his striking entry into the poem, Patroclus appears here as one servant among many, silent, obedient. We note that the relationship sketched here—and barely at that—is more akin to Keppler's model than anything in the *Epic of Gilgamesh*: the dominant primary self, the shadowy second self, defined for the moment solely by his relationship to his friend.

But one aspect of Patroclus' importance to Achilles is already hinted at: he shares with his friend a kind of *intimacy* not found elsewhere in the poem. Even Hector and Andromache, moving and rich as their exchanges in book 6 are, have a public function as a couple, commensurate with Hector's role as defender of the city. Not so Achilles and Patroclus, whose scenes together are all *away* from the main camp, away from the public world of the warrior culture. In this sense we are tempted to see Achilles and Patroclus, even more than Gilgamesh and Enkidu, through the lens of romantic love. Lovers define themselves *as lovers* within a *private world*, created by themselves alone, accessible to themselves alone, and certainly this is how Achilles seems to view his friend. But again we must resist making that move unless the author insists, as Homer does not, because it imports into the relationship elements that only distract us from the real function of Patroclus as the second self—the second self *can* also be a paramour, as we will see later, but this is rare. To quote Keppler (12), the first and second selves "are preoccupied with each other, affect each other, exist for each other, whether for good or ill."

The Hero and His Mother

The other intimate bond in Achilles' life is to his mother, and having dispatched the heralds with Briseis, he turns to her, pouring out all of his pain. Fated to have a short life, he deserves honor at least; Agamemnon has instead dishonored him, taking Briseis. After a further lengthy recapitulation of Agamemnon's offenses, Thetis replies, echoing and expanding on the issue of mortality in her son's appeal:

> "Ah me,
> my child. Your birth was bitterness. Why did I raise you?
> If only you could sit by your ships untroubled, not weeping,
> since indeed your lifetime is to be short, of no length.
> Now it has befallen that your life must be brief and bitter
> beyond all men's. To a bad destiny I bore you in my chambers."
>
> *Iliad* 1. 413–418

It is not surprising to find such sentiments in Thetis: when the subject of Achilles' mortality appears, she is inevitably near. The tenacity of the association is significant and ironic, making her at once Achilles' link with the divine world and the harbinger of his ultimately mortal nature. At the same time, going to his mother for help puts Achilles in the mainstream of the heroic tradition. It is often part of the hero's journey to move from the sphere of his mother, source of unquestioning support and nurture, into the world of his father, source of wisdom, however painful. We recall that Gilgamesh began the journey to the Cedar Forest by going to Ninsun to ask her to intervene on his behalf with a powerful male god, and attained wisdom from Utnapishtim, whom he calls "my father" (SB IX.3.3). So too

Achilles will reach a new level of understanding by making contact with his
father, Peleus.

All of this suggests a telling complex of associations embedded in the
relationship of Achilles and Thetis, and implies from our perspective a
corresponding set of intertwined imperatives: to reach maturity, Achilles
must leave the sphere of his mother and come to an accommodation with
his father; in doing so, he will also separate from the part of his nature that
is divine and come to accept his own mortality. It is one measure of the
richness of the *Iliad* that Homer's ironic linking of Thetis with the imminence of Achilles' death can also represent the tension men often feel between their mother's urging of them toward maturity and the counter-tug
that keeps them close.

Next comes the trip to return the daughter of Apollo's priest, a distinctly
communal exercise, juxtaposed pointedly to Achilles' solitary exile:

> Afterwards they scattered to their own ships and their shelters.
>   But that other still sat in anger beside his swift ships,
> Peleus' son divinely born, Achilleus of the swift feet.
> Never now would he go to assemblies where men win glory,
> never more into battle, but continued to waste his heart out
> sitting there, though he longed always for the clamour and the fighting.
>
> *Iliad* 1. 487–492

Isolation and divinity go together in Achilles, nor is it surprising to find
Thetis in the next episode, which takes place on Olympus. Making good
her promise, she appeals to Zeus, calling in an old debt. He agrees to help
Achilles by punishing the Greeks — again that destructive solipsism — though
doing so will bring him grief from Hera. But no matter: because nothing
can change what they are, the gods' existence within their own sphere is
inevitably without consequence, and the quarrel on Olympus is entirely
comic. The essentially frivolous nature of the conjugal disagreement, which
ends with the gods laughing in typically cruel fashion at the cripple Hephaestus, only points up by contrast the dire consequences of the preceding
quarrel among mortals: the divine couple end up sleeping together compan-
ionably; the Greeks are doomed by the pride of their own leaders.

The Embassy to Achilles

We see no more of Achilles for seven books of the poem, some 4,300 lines,
while the Greeks try, with the help of various surrogates, to live (in a literal
sense) without him. As Homer expands the focus, reviewing the history of
the war, establishing the civilization at Troy, examples of heroic excellence
pass before us: Diomedes, Ajax, and of course, Hector. All in their own
way display admirable characteristics that Achilles for the moment decid-

edly lacks: civic responsibility, devotion to one's fellows, a sense of proper limits. But splendid as all these men are, none is Achilles, who hovers at the edges of our attention, brooding in his quarters.

Making good on his promise, Zeus ends the brief resurgence of the Greeks and helps the Trojans drive them back against the sea, pinning them in their camp and forcing Agamemnon to send the conciliatory embassy to Achilles at the beginning of book 9. This famous episode has generated great controversy and veritable forests have fallen to fuel all that has been written about it. Does Achilles put himself in the wrong by refusing the overtures, the offer of gifts? Is he still living by the "heroic code" — whatever exactly that is? Does he speak a different language than the other Greeks, pressing at the boundaries of expression established by Homer's traditional poetic style? All of these issues are important in one way or another to Homer's larger purposes in the poem, but remain peripheral to our perspective. Likewise there is great tension within the story: will the embassy be successful; will Achilles relent, considering Agamemnon's gestures sufficient to reestablish his honor in the eyes of the Greeks; will Ajax shame Achilles into ending the destruction of his fellow Greeks, whom he claims to love? Again, important issues in some contexts, but to us, looking through the lens of the second-self motif, Achilles is still far away from the crisis that can bring significant change.

Achilles' speeches here are among his most powerful, in particular his reply to Odysseus, where content, sentence structure, and pacing contribute to the picture of a man barely in control, struggling to keep from being overwhelmed by his emotions. But looking at the entire set of speeches, we find a curious dissonance between form and content. As it happens, Achilles does soften his position, is apparently affected by the arguments. To Odysseus, he vows to sail home the next morning; after Phoenix speaks, he will wait until the next morning to decide whether to leave; Ajax reminds him of the friends who love him and depend on him, and he swears to stay and not reenter the fighting until Hector brings fire to his ships. And yet these changes are obscured by the consistent tone in Achilles of high emotion, anger, and defiance: *what* he says shows some softening; *how* he says it undercuts that message. Though circumstances change, Achilles' anger remains constant, suggesting that it is somehow fueled from outside the context of the issues raised in book 9.

Patroclus appears again in this episode, much as he was in book 1, the silent and obedient helpmate, companion for Achilles in his solitude:

> Now they came beside the shelters and ships of the Myrmidons
> and they found Achilleus delighting his heart in a lyre, clear-sounding,
> splendid and carefully wrought, with a silver bridge upon it,
> which he won out of the spoils when he ruined Eetion's city.

> With this he was pleasuring his heart, and singing of men's fame,
> as Patroklos was sitting over against him, alone, in silence,
> watching Aiakides and the time he would leave off singing.
> Now these two came forward, as brilliant Odysseus led them,
> and stood in his presence. Achilleus rose to his feet in amazement
> holding the lyre as it was, leaving the place where he was sitting.
> In the same way Patroklos, when he saw the men come, stood up.
>
> *Iliad* 9. 185–195

Patroclus has not yet spoken a word in the poem, but has begun nonetheless to have a certain presence. First of all, he is *close* to Achilles: there are others who serve Achilles, but none who sit apart with him. He also exhibits some characteristics that fit Keppler's idea of *complementarity*: where Achilles is assertive, vivid, forceful, he is passive, opaque, retiring; Achilles is voluble, he is silent; Achilles is entirely concerned with himself, he seems to exist only to serve others, principally Achilles for the moment, though this will soon change. And finally, the silent passivity of Patroclus is consistent with his function as representative of parts of Achilles which are for the moment dormant, unrealized. This will not last much longer.

The Emergence of Patroclus as a Second Self

Patroclus' inactivity comes to an end with what looks initially like a trivial errand. Book 11 opens with the arming of Agamemnon for the second day of battle, an elaborate, almost baroque expansion of one of Homer's standard scenes. The stylized, elevated tone continues through the initial battle encounters in a profusion of similes, usually a sign of significant movement in the story. Though invincible at first, Agamemnon is eventually dealt a small but debilitating wound and must leave the field. His exit brings Hector into the battle, and things look less promising for the Greeks. Then Odysseus, Diomedes, and Eurypolos, who have come forward to fill the gap left by Agamemnon, are all driven from the battle by injury, and there appears to be a crisis: once again, the absence of Achilles is costing the Greeks heavily. Ajax becomes the last bulwark of the Greeks, beginning a long, stubborn holding action that will last the rest of the day.

Paris has been busy in this part of the battle, shooting several Greeks from a distance – true to his unheroic nature – and his least illustrious victim is one Machaon. In other circumstances, we might not hear more of a minor character like this, but Homer has plans for Machaon: Nestor is told to take him from the field, and Achilles, reconnoitering from his ship, catches a glimpse. His curiosity is piqued, and he makes a fatal request of Patroclus:

> At once he spoke to his own companion in arms, Patroklos,
> calling from the ship, and he heard it from inside the shelter, and came out
> like the war god, and this was the beginning of his evil.
> The strong son of Menoitios spoke first, and addressed him:
> "What do you wish with me, Achilleus? Why do you call me?"
> Then in answer again spoke Achilleus of the swift feet:
> "Son of Menoitios, you who delight my heart, o great one,
> now I think the Achaians will come to my knees and stay there
> in supplication, for a need past endurance has come to them.
> But go now, Patroklos beloved of Zeus, to Nestor
> and ask him who is this wounded man he brings in from the fighting.
> Indeed, seeing him from behind I thought he was like Machaon,
> Asklepios' son, in all ways, but I got no sight of the man's face
> since the horses were tearing forward and swept on by me."
>
> *Iliad* 11. 601–614

This is Achilles' first appearance since dismissing the embassy in book 9, and it is a delicate piece of characterization. Great curiosity about such a minor player seems to show him missing the action, eager to get any kind of news, but to show this too openly would hurt his position, so he begins with a piece of bravado to cover up. As in the embassy scene, so here there is some distance between what Achilles says and the overall import of his appearance.

Patroclus arrives as Nestor and his henchmen are taking refreshment in the hut. No rest for him, however, feeling the threat of Achilles' anger if he dawdles:

> "No chair, aged sir beloved of Zeus. You will not persuade me.
> Honoured, and quick to blame, is the man who sent me to find out
> who was this wounded man you were bringing. Now I myself
> know, and I see it is Machaon, the shepherd of the people.
> Now I go back as messenger to Achilleus, to tell him.
> You know yourself, aged sir beloved of Zeus, how *he* is;
> a dangerous man; he might even be angry with one who is guiltless."
>
> *Iliad* 11. 647–653

Nestor's answer is again characteristic of him. After sarcastic notice of Achilles' newfound solicitude for the Greeks—he does not even know yet about Odysseus, Diomedes, Agamemnon, or Eurypolos—the old man launches on a long reminiscence of his own past glories as a fighter. Finally, after some 90 lines or so, he circles back briefly to Achilles—he will enjoy his valor in loneliness—then reminds Patroclus of the obligation put on him by Achilles' father as the Greek expeditionary force was being formed: as the older of the two, Patroclus must temper Achilles' great strength with good counsel. This last piece of history is to prime Patroclus for the crucial

message to follow: Patroclus must try to honor Peleus' request by persuading Achilles to rejoin the battle; if not, maybe he will let Patroclus become
another stand-in, wearing his armor and going in his place, masquerading
to scare the Trojans and buy time. The fatal chain of events leading to
the deaths of Patroclus, Hector, and finally, beyond the scope of the *Iliad*
but in the cycle of Trojan stories, to the death of Achilles himself, begins
here.

Stepping back for a moment to look at larger structures in the poem, we
see that the surge of energy generated by the quarrels in book 1 is rechan-
nelled to some extent by the end of the embassy scene in book 9. We might
have expected some resolution there of the impasse created by Achilles'
withdrawal from battle—the Greeks have paid dearly for not acquiescing
to Achilles, and he has had a chance to reconsider—but Homer delays,
putting Achilles in an even more anomalous position and generating new
tension by leaving the Greeks in a perilous pinch. After a lull in the night
raid of book 10—clearly an interlude and probably the least successful part
of the poem—a fresh impetus is signaled in the almost operatic style of the
opening of the next day's battle.

Patroclus' emergence as a major player coincides with this second wave
of energy in the story, and appropriately so: the first nine books are somewhat self-contained, and could be (may have been?) a shorter version of
the story of Achilles' prideful wrath, the withdrawal ending, amity restored
between Agamemnon and Achilles, perhaps some version of the death of
Hector appended; after the embassy, the issues generated by the quarrels in
book 1 are considerably blurred—when Agamemnon tries to make recompense again in book 19, Achilles brushes him off, not caring in the least
about the insults that completely paralyzed him earlier. The "problem" of
Achilles, now becoming more defined as we come to know Patroclus better,
comes to the fore in place of the original dispute, and with it the motif of
the second self, which, though present, is relatively dormant in the first ten
books.

Nestor tells us more about Patroclus than we have learned in the previous
7,000 lines of poetry. The story of his arrival in Phthia and entry into
Achilles' life there establish the friendship as one of long standing, and
make Patroclus a surrogate for Peleus, an older, wiser source of advice
and restraint for his more powerful but less reflective companion. This
particular role for Patroclus is somewhat puzzling, since what we have seen
of the relationship so far clearly shows Achilles to be dominant—readers
of the *Iliad* are invariably surprised to find that Patroclus is *older* than
Achilles—and the trend will continue when the two reappear in book 16,
with Achilles using a simile that casts him in the role of parent to Patroclus.
But this only reflects the dominance of Achilles' *perspective* in the poem,
something that will not change until the very end of the story. Nestor,
removed by his age and experience from Achilles' way of seeing, distorted

as it is by his "problem," has a different angle on the relationship, and one that will finally prevail, but only after Achilles pays the price for enlightenment by losing Patroclus.

What we learn from Nestor is complemented by what Patroclus himself says and does while on his errand. This is the first time we hear him conversing or indeed having anything significant to do with anyone other than Achilles, and though little enough, it is expressive. In the phrase, "You know yourself, aged sir beloved of Zeus, how *he* is" (*Iliad* 11. 652 — the emphasis is in the Greek as well) we hear Patroclus distancing himself from his friend's dangerous monocular vision, reaching out for sympathy from the other Greeks — he is Achilles' friend, but also has his own perspective. Some disapproval, however benign, is suggested as well, a prelude to the much stronger challenge he will offer to Achilles' view later in the poem. The more positive aspect of this change is the sympathy he shows for his fellow warriors: in moving slightly away from Achilles, Patroclus is also moving *toward* the other Greeks. As the episode closes, Homer leaves us focused on this latter aspect of Patroclus. Hurrying back to Achilles, he meets Eurypylos, limping along. The sight evokes pity for the Greeks, dying as they are, and a question: will they be able to hold Hector? Eurypylos is pessimistic, and asks Patroclus for first aid, the other healers, including Machaon, being unavailable. Patroclus does not disappoint him:

> Then in turn the strong son of Menoitios spoke to him:
> "But how shall this be, my lord Eurypylos, how shall we do it?
> I am on my way carrying a message to wise Achilleus
> given me by Gerenian Nestor, the Achaians' watcher.
> But even so I will not leave you in your affliction."
>   He spoke, and holding the shepherd of the host under the arms led him
> to his shelter, and a henchman seeing them spread out some oxhides,
> and Patroklos laid him there and with a knife cut the sharp tearing
> arrow out of his thigh, and washed the black blood running from it
> with warm water, and, pounding it up in his hands, laid on
> a bitter root to make the pain disappear, one which stayed
> all kinds of pain. And the wound dried, and the flow of blood stopped.
>
> *Iliad* 11. 836–847

Patroclus will not appear again until book 16, but Homer prepares for the return pointedly, calling our attention to his strong sympathy for the other Greeks and his power to heal.

The Development of the Second-Self Motif

In this short stretch of the poem, Patroclus has gone from a silent adjunct to Achilles to a significant force in the story. The second-self motif, only potential until now, has suddenly become more prominent in the presentation of Achilles. We might profitably pause here to consider how the development of the motif so far differs from what we found in the Gilgamesh epic.

We have noted that while Enkidu's complementarity to Gilgamesh is established immediately and forcefully, Patroclus only emerges as a separate personality in book 11. The result is a refocusing of the "problem" of Achilles. Certainly it has been obvious from the first lines of the poem that Achilles has a dangerously high level of pride, and that this, combined with his absolutist vision and violent anger, is a potentially debilitating package of traits. But the intensity of the quarrel in book 1 tends to draw us into the thicket of issues surrounding the proper allocation of honor. Likewise, the obvious shortcomings of Agamemnon complicate our judgment of Achilles—in the Mesopotamian epic, by contrast, the victims of Gilgamesh's pride are entirely innocent as far as we can see, so that his shortcomings are evident and relatively uncomplicated.

After the embassy, where Achilles brushes aside three different but compelling arguments for why the holdout ought to be ended, the original dispute seems to become less important, pushed offstage from there on by Achilles' excesses. At this point, Patroclus emerges as a more independent presence, isolating his friend yet further, making the latter's stance yet more problematical. Now the lack in Achilles stands out more clearly for us. He is missing what Patroclus has in ready abundance, the ability to see himself as part of a larger picture and so, at least at times, to put the interests of others before his own honor.

As we have seen from Agamemnon's behavior in book 1, this blind spot is not confined to Achilles; the heroic emphasis on competitive virtues pervades the *Iliad*. But in a creature already disposed by nature to grandiosity and solipsism—he is a hero, by definition carrying the traits of ordinary mortals beyond normal limits—the societal tendency becomes debilitating. Achilles' problem, though presented in somewhat different terms, is much like Gilgamesh's: his abundant gifts are, for him and others, unsettling; he is semi-divine, and in many ways his essential impact is best understood as like a god's—he can do great things, and he can do great damage; his moods are fickle, his attention focused primarily on himself; he lacks what the gods are missing by nature, humility, a trait proper (and necessary) only to mortals. Perhaps most representative of Achilles' peculiar liminal status and the pain it brings is the fact that while he knows and can choose between two different fated outcomes for his life, as no other mortal can, in either case he must finally die. Learning to accept the limitations of ordinary men is as hard for Achilles as it is for Gilgamesh, and like his Mesopotamian predecessor, the Greek hero must travel much further away from other mortals and from his own essential humanity before he can return to find a more fruitful balance between mortal and divine.

While these comparisons are helpful, at the same time we ought not to miss the exceptional richness of Homer's characterization. Achilles, unlike Gilgamesh, has a *history* outside of the immediate story, sketched in brief for us throughout the poem. He was once a little boy, dandled on the knee of Phoenix (*Iliad* 9. 485–489); tutored by the wise centaur Cheiron, he could be a healer like Patroclus as well as a killer (*Iliad* 11. 831–832); he is a man capable of long-term, intense friendships (*Iliad* 11. 769–778); other men *love* him and miss him when he is away (*Iliad* 9. 630–642); he has a father, sitting far away and pining for his only son (*Iliad* 11. 785–788); he *is* a father, and worries about his son (*Iliad* 19. 326–333); he has not always been so fiercely preoccupied with himself, has shown mercy to those he captured (*Iliad* 6. 425–427); he has always been a gracious host, no small thing in the world of the Homeric poems, and still is, even in the midst of his anger (*Iliad* 11. 776–779; 1. 334–344; 9. 193–204). In short, a complex, contradictory man, his essential nobility inextricably entwined with his destructive excesses. To watch him is to see the beginning of what we call the tragic vision in western literature.

Growing Opposition of the Second Self to the Hero

Book 15 ends with the fulfilling of Achilles' last condition: fire has reached the Greek ships. Book 16 opens:

> So they fought on both sides for the sake of the strong-benched vessel.
> Meanwhile Patroklos came to the shepherd of the people, Achilleus,
> and stood by him and wept warm tears, like a spring dark-running
> that down the face of a rock impassable drips its dim water;
> and swift-footed brilliant Achilleus looked on him in pity,
> and spoke to him aloud and addressed him in winged words: "Why then
> are you crying like some poor little girl, Patroklos,
> who runs after his mother and begs to be picked up and carried,
> and clings to her dress, and holds her back when she tries to hurry,
> and gazes tearfully into her face, until she is picked up?
> You are like such a one, Patroklos, dropping these soft tears.
> Could you have some news to tell, for me or the Myrmidons?
> Have you, and nobody else, received some message from Phthia?
> Yet they tell me Aktor's son Menoitios lives still
> and Aiakos' son Peleus lives still among the Myrmidons.
> If either of these died we should take it hard. Or is it
> the Argives you are mourning over, and how they are dying
> against the hollow ships by reason of their own arrogance?
> Tell me, do not hide it in your mind, so that we shall both know."
>
> *Iliad* 16. 1–19

Homer has left Patroclus frozen, on his way back to Achilles' quarters, for 2,500 lines while filling out the picture again. Now he restarts the film and, at least within the second-self motif, we take up right where we left off in book 11: Patroclus' sympathy for the suffering Greeks has pushed him away from Achilles, and now, angry himself, he provokes a confrontation:

> "Son of Peleus, far greatest of the Achaians, Achilleus,
> do not be angry; such grief has fallen on the Achaians.
> For all those who were before the bravest in battle
> are lying up among the ships with arrow or spear wounds.
> The son of Tydeus, strong Diomedes, was hit by an arrow,
> and Odysseus has a pike wound, and Agamemnon the spear-famed,
> and Eurypylos has been wounded in the thigh with an arrow.
> And over these leaders skilled in medicine are working
> to cure their wounds. But you, Achilleus; who can do anything
> with you? May no such anger take me as that you cherish!
> Cursed courage. What other man born hereafter shall be advantaged
> unless you beat aside from the Argives this shameful destruction?
> Pitiless: the rider Peleus was never your father
> nor Thetis was your mother, but it was the grey sea that bore you
> and the towering rocks, so sheer the heart in you is turned from us.
> But if you are drawing back from some prophecy known in your own heart
> and by Zeus' will your honoured mother has told you of something,
> then send me out at least, let the rest of the Myrmidon people
> follow me, and I may be a light given to the Danaans.
> Give me your armour to wear on my shoulders into the fighting;
> so perhaps the Trojans might think I am you, and give way
> from their attack, and the fighting sons of the Achaians get wind
> again after hard work. There is little breathing space in the fighting.
> We unwearied might with mere cry pile men wearied
> back upon their city, and away from the ships and the shelters."
>
> *Iliad* 16. 19–45

A remarkable set of speeches, worth lingering over. While Homer indicates real solicitude in Achilles, his mocking tone and vivid simile show him trying to keep the upper hand in the relationship, as parent to Patroclus' child. But there is something strained in the attempt at a light touch, and we may feel a hint of unease, even defensiveness, in this opening gambit, perhaps a recognition in Achilles of how extreme his position has become. The casting of Patroclus as a girl is of course belittling in the context of this poem, but from our perspective it inevitably raises the same issues as Enkidu's long hair: is it some kind of hint about an aspect of Patroclus' complementarity? The trouble with this is that Achilles is an unreliable narrator here, driven by attitudes already problematical in the story, and in any event, he casts *himself* in the role of mother, so that the contrast of gender is missing. Nor is it the first time Achilles portrays himself in the role of nurturing mother in the poem. Responding to Odysseus in book 9 (323–327), he became in his own vision a mother bird, tirelessly bringing morsels for her chicks, putting her own needs aside.

Gender issues, then, are blurred here. We do find the by now familiar attempt to cover genuine concern with a cavalier tone, a sign of stubbornness or perhaps denial in Achilles that does not bode well for Patroclus' mission. Even the order of topics, first the two fathers, then, almost by the way, the dying Greeks, suggests a certain studied indifference. And any worry about his friends is hedged, undercut by the final jab: if they suffer, they brought it on themselves; *they* are the arrogant ones, not Achilles.

Patroclus begins his answer calmly enough, but his feelings get the upper hand, and we see him angry for the first time in the poem. The resulting denunciation of Achilles pushes him further away from his friend. The "But" in line 36 does mark a break with the angry tone—having vented his feelings, Patroclus now gets back to business with his suggestion of himself as a substitute for Achilles—yet from our perspective the emotional distancing and the coming physical separation, first on the battlefield, then in death, are all of a piece, marking the growing spiritual crisis for Achilles.

By having Patroclus call Achilles a child of the rocks and sea, Homer shows him turning the model of parent and child around, putting his friend in the infantile role, looking for emotional leverage. At the same time, a remarkable chain of imagery is established, beginning with the darkrunning fountain just previous, including a haunting simile comparing Achilles' horses weeping over the death of Patroclus to stone funeral monuments (*Iliad* 17. 426–440), ending with the picture of Niobe in book 24, changed from a mother, weeping over her dead children, killed by Apollo and Artemis to pay for her own arrogance, to a rockface with water running down perpetually. Analysis of such a delicate and charged complex of images runs the risk of being reductive, but we may say at least that the imagery suggests a series of dualities: soft, yielding water and hard rock, deep love and arrogance, nature's continuity and death's finality. All of these are ordinarily understood as polarities, but each pair in its own way might also evoke elements in the *Iliad*, either in Achilles or the larger canvas of the poem, which coexist in a fragile but telling solution.

In reply to Patroclus, Achilles makes one last stand. Having reviewed his grievances, he seems ready to let them go, then pulls back again, clinging to denial just a bit longer, on what looks very much like a technicality:

> Still, we will let all this be a thing of the past; and it was not
> in my heart to be angry forever; and yet I have said
> I would not give over my anger until that time came
> when the fighting with all its clamour came up to my own ships.
>
> *Iliad* 16. 60–63

Fire has come up to the Greek ships, but not *his* ships, so he takes Patroclus' second alternative, sending his friend to die in his place. The mission is to be carefully circumscribed: Patroclus, disguised as Achilles, will drive the Trojans back to preserve the Greeks' chance of sailing home; he is *not* to fight so long or so well as to deprive Achilles of *his* glory, and the speech ends in the remarkable fantasy with which we began, Achilles and Patroclus storming Troy alone, all the others, Trojans *and Greeks*, dead so as not to diminish their glory. (Diomedes imagines a similar kind of heroic isolation for himself and his friend, Sthenalus, but in his version the other Greeks have gone *home*, not to Hades—characteristically, Achilles goes beyond the pale of "ordinary" heroism—cf. *Iliad* 9. 48–49.)

This moment corresponds in a rough way to the pinnacle of hubris reached by Gilgamesh after the killing of the Bull of Heaven. Like Gilgamesh, Achilles has reached the end of one trajectory, arrived at some kind of outer limit of arrogance, and a reckoning is coming for him and for Patroclus. Yet notice the difference in the dynamic: Enkidu's complementarity is evident from the beginning of the story, but he remains more or less identified with Gilgamesh's hubristic behavior right up to the time of his death; Patroclus' differences from Achilles are sketched in much more slowly, and he has already begun to distance himself from Achilles' excesses by the time retribution comes—the fantasy of the two heroes alone shows *Achilles* at the edge, but we suspect that Patroclus would not travel that far anymore.

This gradual distancing of Patroclus contributes to the complex characterization of Achilles. Homer not only dramatizes the isolation of his hero, but shows him becoming aware of it over time, as Gilgamesh never is until after Enkidu's death. The result is a much richer picture of the operation of *denial* in the Greek hero, in the curious dissonance between the tone and subject matter of his speeches in books 9 and 11, in the uneasy bantering of book 16. Achilles has a depth, a level of sophisticated self-consciousness, not found in Gilgamesh, whose spiritual evolution, though profound in its implications, is portrayed mostly through objectivized symbols rather than subjective, interior states.

The *exclusive* intimacy of the two friends, so damaging to the larger community of Greeks, also reaches its most extreme form in Achilles' fantasy—the fact that Patroclus does not apparently share this vision only emphasizes its isolating unreality. Achilles will detach still more from the world of mortals before the story ends, and he will be driven by what *he* experiences at the time as love for Patroclus. But his final return to the part of himself that must die will be possible only after he establishes a new kind of intimacy with his friend, one that urges him toward acceptance of his essential fellowship with all mortals.

The Death of Patroclus

Hector finally sets fire to a Greek ship, and Achilles urges Patroclus into the field. The arming scene that follows is based on the same set of formulaic phrases as the more elaborate preparations of Agamemnon in book 11, with one crucial exception:

> He took up two powerful spears that fitted his hand's grip,
> only he did not take the spear of blameless Aiakides,
> huge, heavy, thick, which no one else of all the Achaians
> could handle, but Achilleus alone knew how to wield it;
> the Pelian ash spear which Cheiron had brought to his father
> from high on Pelion to be death for fighters . . .
>
> *Iliad* 16. 139–144

Patroclus is not interchangeable with Achilles; disguise will not help. Homer's insistence on the point sounds a note of unease, echoing faintly the first such warning, when Achilles called Patroclus to see about Machaon:

> At once he spoke to his own companion in arms, Patroklos,
> calling from the ship, and he heard it from inside the shelter, and came out
> like the war god, and this was the beginning of his evil.
>
> *Iliad* 11. 601–603

Putting Patroclus so concretely in the place of Achilles suggests a merging of the hero and his second self that is, from our perspective, premature. Patroclus both is and is not Achilles, and in pressing the identification here Homer launches an appraisal of the terms of this curious ambivalence. Nestor's strategy works for a time, but it kills Patroclus in the end, foundering on a fatal mistaking of exterior show for interior substance. This confusion reverberates through the rest of the poem, echoed in the battle for the corpses of men already dead, pointing to the fundamental duality of body and spirit that Achilles must sort out before coming to understand his own true nature.

The death of Patroclus, like the death of Enkidu, prompts a major shift in the evolution of the hero. Typically for Homer, the change is prepared carefully, and book 16 of the *Iliad* is in many ways an overture to the last third of the poem. In particular, Patroclus' killing of the Trojan ally Sarpedon marks the beginning of a chain of deaths, of Patroclus, of Hector, and finally, beyond the scope of the poem but definitely in prospect, of Achilles himself. All are part of the evolution of Achilles toward maturity, and many of the themes central to that movement are highlighted in the first link of the chain.

After further preliminaries, Achilles sends Patroclus into battle. The ruse of the armor succeeds at first, the Trojans are fooled. Patroclus and the other Greeks make the most of this, and the first rush drives the Trojans back away from the ships. Patroclus himself has killed thirteen men before coming to Sarpedon. The latter was fathered, as it happens, by Zeus, who is disturbed at the prospect of his son's death:

> And watching them the son of devious-devising Kronos
> was pitiful, and spoke to Hera, his wife and sister:
> "Ah me, that it is destined that the dearest of men, Sarpedon,
> must go down under the hands of Menoitios' son Patroklos.
> The heart in my breast is balanced between two ways as I ponder,
> whether I should snatch him out of the sorrowful battle
> and set him down still alive in the rich country of Lykia,
> or beat him under at the hands of the son of Menoitios."
>
> *Iliad* 16. 431–438

In Homer's poetic world, each man has a specific and usually unalterable fate, set for him by a powerful and mysterious force, represented as three sisters spinning: when your "portion" has been spun out, the yarn is cut. Divine will, like fate, never goes unfulfilled, but it is not the same thing as fate, which originates outside of the gods. Though in a general sense the gods are guarantors of cosmic order, the relationship between divine will and fate is never fully worked out in Homeric poetry—it was apparently enough to know that the two forces always finally coincided and that in any case each presented unalterable necessity to mortals. So when Zeus contemplates *changing* Sarpedon's fate, we are given a glimpse into previously uncharted country: Zeus, it seems, *may* do it, but *should* not. Hera points out that if Zeus saves *his* son, other divinities will want to do the same, and this will cause resentment. Typically for the *Iliad*, the cosmic stakes are not spelled out, but we may understand dissension among the gods as at least potentially upsetting to the cosmic order.

Zeus relents, letting Sarpedon die, and the regular order of things is preserved. But the vignette is a telling one, a prelude to the playing out of several crucial themes in the last third of the poem, the relationship of fathers and sons, the dichotomy of body and spirit, the imperatives of death, even, as it turns out, for gods. All of these will be central to the second-self motif.

A fierce struggle follows, forming what will be a familiar tableau: on one side Greeks, on the other Trojans, in the middle, a corpse. The treatment of corpses is always in the forefront of Homer's imagination, as we may remember from the *Iliad*'s opening lines, with their description of the coming price of Achilles' anger, those bodies given to be "the delicate feasting/of dogs, of all the birds" (4–5). At the same time the armor of a dead man is a prime trophy for Homer's warriors, so taking it provides the enemy with a double benefit: honor for himself, dishonor for the dead man. And if the man's friends are kept from burying the naked corpse, so much the better, since the dead man's soul will then be consigned to eternal wandering in limbo, neither living nor resident in the underworld with the rest of the dead.

Sarpedon will suffer the first indignity, but not the second. The battle over his corpse is decided by Zeus, who routs Hector and the Trojans, having let them strip off the armor, but saves the body, to be carried to quiet burial in Lycia by the brothers Sleep and Death. Zeus' thoughts, as it happens, are already moving beyond Sarpedon:

> So they swarmed over the dead man, nor did Zeus ever
> turn the glaring of his eyes from the strong encounter,
> but kept gazing forever upon them, in spirit reflective,
> and pondered hard over many ways for the death of Patroklos;
>
> *Iliad* 16. 644–647

The fatal progression has begun. As Sarpedon dies, Patroclus' death comes into view; in Patroclus' last moments, Hector is already marked:

> Phoibos
> Apollo now struck away from his head the helmet
> four-horned and hollow-eyed, and under the feet of the horses
> it rolled clattering, and the plumes above it were defiled
> by blood and dust. Before this time it had not been permitted
> to defile in the dust this great helmet crested in horse-hair;
> rather it guarded the head and the gracious brow of a godlike
> man, Achilleus; but now Zeus gave it over to Hektor
> to wear on his head, Hektor whose own death was close to him.
>
> *Iliad* 16. 792–800

Hector is next; Achilles will kill him, as Patroclus predicts in his last words. By training our attention on the helmet as the Trojan's impending death comes before us, Homer creates a powerful symbol, a kind of harbinger, which is passed from one dying man to the next. As an emblem of fighting, the helmet connects the heroic view of the world with this chain of deaths; as a lovely object, once pristine, now fouled in the dust, it stands by metonomy for all the beautiful bodies of dead men killed in the war, and previews in particular the gruesome fate of Hector's corpse; as an extension of Achilles, it presents again the persistent dichotomy of exterior show and interior substance that pervades the end of the poem. And as a tangible link between Patroclus, Hector, and Achilles, it suggests other ties, especially those dramatized in the second-self motif.

Conclusion and Prospect

Hector's assumption of the armor of Achilles, and the fatal linkage it signals, mark a clear and unique departure from the dynamic of the second self as it appears in the Gilgamesh epic. Up to this point, Homer's treatment, though elaborated differently, follows the same basic structure as that of the Mesopotamian poem. But now Hector seems to have taken on something of what Patroclus carried, something of Achilles. The effect is to create another second self, whom Achilles will kill in his turn, and to complicate by elaboration the progress of the Greek hero toward integration. Assuming that Hector does in some sense "inherit" something of Achilles from Patroclus raises difficult questions: if Patroclus represents unrealized parts of Achilles, what is *Hector*'s function; why does Homer create another second self at all—leave out the link of the armor, and the story could proceed identically, with Patroclus still "found" again at poem's end, with the same implications for Achilles' maturation as Enkidu's "return" has for Gilgamesh—what, in other words, is gained by the elaboration?

Not Alone:
The Iliad (2)

When you make the two one, and when you make the inside
like the outside and the outside like the inside . . . then you will
enter [the Kingdom].

Gospel of Thomas 37

Patroclus is dead, killed, Homer tells us, by Euphorbos, Hector, and
Apollo. But we may say that in one important sense Achilles was the killer.
Faced, even more explicitly than Gilgamesh, by parts of himself as
yet unacknowledged, he pushed them away until he "killed" them. And
as it did Gilgamesh, so loss will at first drive Achilles into the dark and
further still from integration with other mortals in general and with his
second self in particular. The corresponding alienation from self represented by this journey takes on several forms: descent into savage behavior,
simultaneous ascent toward divinity, numbed withdrawal into grief. All are
parallel realizations of the basic *apartness* that has characterized Achilles
from the beginning of the poem, and in this sense preserve a certain continuity in the character. But the stakes become higher, escalated from a
personal to a nearly cosmic level, so that the resolution achieved in book 24
in the interchange between Achilles and Priam is part of a larger thematic
synthesis with implications beyond the personal evolution of the Greek
hero.

What exactly did Achilles "kill"? What qualities must he somehow find
again to reach a fuller existence? The social aspect of Gilgamesh's behavior
is certainly present here: by isolating himself from the society of his fellows,
Achilles causes pain and death to others. And his motive for withdrawing
is also familiar. Like Gilgamesh, Achilles sees the world through the heroic
prism, valuing individual honor above the common good, justifying it as
consistent with the intensely competitive ethic that is so prominent in the
poem: the highest good is to be the best at something the warrior culture

values, and the struggle for excellence, even within one or the other of the armies, takes precedence over group values.

The nature/culture polarity, instrumental in the characterization of Gilgamesh, is present in the *Iliad*, but not so vital to the portrayal of Achilles. The earlier poem presents the duality as one raising issues about the extent of human ability to control and rechannel the intrinsic order of the natural world; the *Iliad* tends rather to oppose two human worlds, the civilization of Troy, which along with the vignettes contained in similes stands for life beyond the battlefield, and the warrior culture. Priam's family, and in particular Hector and Andromache, represent an alternative to the explosive competitive relationships between warriors. Patroclus' behavior toward his fellow Greeks shows the same qualities, reversing the hierarchy of individual over group, self over others, and Achilles must learn to accept this part of himself in order to "return" from the frightening outer edges of human experience which he reaches by the beginning of book 24.

The second crucial polarity in the Gilgamesh epic, mortal/immortal, is a critical theme in the entire *Iliad*, and especially prominent in the portrayal of Achilles in the last third of the poem. After Patroclus dies, Achilles' own imminent death hangs persistently over his head, brought to his attention by—as always—his mother (*Iliad* 18. 94–98), but also even by his immortal horses (*Iliad* 19. 404–410), present in his own thoughts as he attends to the killing of Lykaon (*Iliad* 21. 106–113), and then Hector (*Iliad* 22. 365–366), poignantly with him as he makes a last gesture to Patroclus:

> And now the brilliant swift-footed Achilleus remembered one more thing.
> He stood apart from the pyre and cut off a lock of fair hair
> which he had grown long to give to the river Spercheios, and gazing
> in deep distress out over the wine-blue water, he spoke forth:
> "Spercheios, it was in vain that Peleus my father vowed to you
> that there, when I had won home to the beloved land of my fathers,
> I would cut my hair for you and make you a grand and holy
> sacrifice of fifty rams consecrate to the waters
> of your springs, where is your holy ground and your smoking altar.
> So the old man vowed, but you did not accomplish his purpose.
> Now, since I do not return to the beloved land of my fathers,
> I would give my hair to the keeping of the hero Patroklos."
>
> *Iliad* 23. 140–151

When Enkidu dies, Gilgamesh looks his own death in the face and is afraid. But he does not *accept* the fact of his mortality, and tries to escape his fundamental nature by traveling to see Utnapishtim. When acceptance finally comes, it brings with it a humility, an understanding of his place in a larger scheme. Patroclus' demise brings death close to Achilles as well, but the denial we saw in Gilgamesh is hardly evident here: Achilles seems not only to recognize the nearness of death, but to *accept* it. What, then, stands between him and spiritual fulfillment?

Once again, we need to recognize the greater level of internalization in the Greek character. The reactions and motives of Gilgamesh, though profound in their implications, are never complex. Enkidu's death makes him sad and afraid, and his denial takes a straightforward, externalized form; when Patroclus dies, Achilles too is sad, but also both enraged and guilty—his famous anger is now directed outward and inward simultaneously; he says that he is ready to die, and yet his actions tell a different story, of a man who is far from accepting the death of Patroclus, let alone his own, of one whose recognition of his place in any larger scheme of things is still far in the distance. Here, as earlier in the poem, Achilles' words are not in themselves always accurate reflections of his true state—denial is present, but dramatized subtly, tangled in a web of sometimes conflicting emotions. And certainly, this is not a man at peace with himself or anyone else.

Grieving, for Patroclus, for Hector, dominates the last third of the *Iliad*. Achilles, like his Mesopotamian forerunner, must live through his grief, must come to accept the fact of his friend's death, before he can accept his own mortality and make contact with his buried self. To grieve entails withdrawing from the world into oneself, and so Achilles' apartness has, as I have said, yet another analog after Patroclus dies. At the same time, the linking of the deaths of Patroclus, Hector, and Achilles, one bringing on the next in the larger plan of Homeric destiny, means that any grieving that Achilles does for Patroclus must at some level, however unconsciously at first, be directed at his own impending demise as well. And *denial* of one death is, on that level, denial of the others; holding onto one body is clinging to all. In this perspective we may begin to explore the question that ended the last chapter: why does Homer, after Patroclus dies, invest *Hector* with something of Achilles?

Hector as Second Self

Given its preparation, the linking of Hector to Achilles through the armor invites us to see Hector as some kind of extension of the second self. Is Patroclus then displaced in the pattern? Yes and no. One common interpretation—basically Freudian—of Hector's function in the story distinguishes his role clearly from Patroclus': Hector represents Achilles to himself, and in particular the part of himself responsible for the death of Patroclus. Thus, guilt over Patroclus' death is discharged indirectly in the killing of Hector, which becomes a kind of suicide.

This model, though helpful in recognizing the importance of guilt in the portrayal of Achilles, does not accommodate any notion of spiritual regeneration—Patroclus' presence in the poem diminishes after his burial. My own version, while incorporating the displacement of guilt, allows for some conflation of the functions of Hector and Patroclus, all in the service of the second-self motif. The key, in my view, to Hector's function lies in the complexity of Achilles' response to Patroclus' death. We return to Achilles' anger.

The wrath of Achilles, Homer's leitmotif, has been consistently present in the poem. I have said that the disparity between what Achilles says and the tone of his speech gives the anger a life of its own. It has often been noted in this connection that after Patroclus dies, the object of Achilles' anger shifts—Agamemnon is forgotten; Hector, before a dangerous foe but not someone at whom Achilles was angry, becomes the principal focus of the wrath. Now there is nothing impossible from a naturalistic point of view about this turn of events—Hector, after all, did kill Achilles' best friend. But if we look at Achilles' behavior from the peculiar perspective of the second-self dynamic, as reflecting an underlying "problem" whose solution has been only loosely connected to the surface of the story, then the persistence of anger tells us something different: its focus may change, but the emotion will continue until its deeper causes are addressed. More than this, Achilles' wrath *carries* his problem in the text: from this perspective the anger *is* Achilles.

Artistic function has here, as it often does, its analog in life. Anger is often what we call a "secondary emotion," generated in response to some other unexpressed feeling. We may recognize the displacement, but more often we do not. In any case, we are unable to acknowledge it, unable to face the presence of the real emotions in ourselves—anger is more acceptable than, say, fear or shame, which make us feel vulnerable. And often anger is a tool for self-motivation, propelling us past the barriers to action, a little piece of self-deception with a payoff in self-esteem. How many do we know who seem to use anger in these ways with such frequency that we call them "angry" people, who make anger part of what defines them?

Achilles, in his struggle with unacknowledged parts of himself, may be understood in this way. And if so, then the puzzle of Homer's doubling of the second self begins to yield: Hector becomes the new focus of Achilles' anger, motivating him to act in spite of his residual pride; but by also investing him with something of Achilles, Homer creates a vehicle for the playing out of the less acceptable emotions, guilt and self-reproach. The wrath, which seems to define Achilles in the poem, can now be directed, as I have said, outward and inward simultaneously, while the process driving Achilles toward reintegration with Patroclus proceeds apace. Hector is part of the second-self motif, but plays a different role than Patroclus. The latter represents what Achilles must recover or discover in himself; the former is a vehicle for the journey toward that integration.

Turning again for a moment to psychological metaphors, we note that while Hector's role as target for Achilles' displaced emotions fits a basically Freudian model rather well, it complicates the Jungian paradigm I outlined in response to the Gilgamesh epic. If Patroclus already occupies the same role as Enkidu, is the "shadow" of Achilles, then where does Hector come in? My answer, which may or may not convince a Jungian analyst, goes like this: Patroclus dies, driving Achilles further into denial, but also into a dark place within himself—so far, similar to Gilgamesh; but Homer now does something remarkable, splitting Achilles' inner self again, so that Hector, in his civic responsibility and relatively uncomplicated heroism, carries at least a version of what Achilles is, however unconsciously, working toward—a difference here from the Freudian model, in which Hector's particular character matters less than the fact that he killed Patroclus.

We have at this point, then, two representations of the second self, one dead, one still alive. In order to reach the inner darkness where, in the paradoxical mode of the second self, enlightenment can occur, Achilles must in effect kill his second self twice. Patroclus' death, though it pushes him toward the goal of his spiritual journey, only begins the trip; training his sights on Hector propels Achilles yet further away from the world of mortals, and, as we will see, from Patroclus himself in particular. By elaborating on the basic pattern we have seen in the Gilgamesh epic, Homer preserves the central facet of Achilles' characterization, his anger, while at the same time suggesting a complexity of motivation missing from Gilgamesh: anger at Hector is also anger at himself, driven by guilt.

Pressing further, we note how rich the portrait of *denial* in Achilles has become: he chases with murderous intent a version of the self that has been lost to him; angered by the result of his own selfishness, he duplicates the original error while trying somehow to correct it; thinking to express his love for Patroclus by his hatred of Hector, he is, in fact, pushing Patroclus further away; anger, the overt manifestation of a fundamental alienation, alienates him further. And finally, Hector's investment with Achilles' lost self allows the portrayal of a common human weakness: how often we despise just those parts of another person that we hate or fear in ourselves.

Circling back to Jung again, we note that the complexity of Homer's story does not end with splitting the shadow, complicating but also enriching the dynamic of self-realization as Jung described it. If there is anyone in the story who displays a character we would call "dark," it is neither Hector nor Patroclus, but Achilles. And this coloration intensifies after the death of Patroclus, as if his death releases Achilles' dark side. True to the internalized drama of Achilles' spiritual journey, the movement into darkness is symbolized not by an outward trip to the underworld, as in Gilgamesh, but rather by a kind of invocation, the conjuring up of a darkness *that is Achilles himself*, so that the metaphorical identification of the Land of Dilmun and Gilgamesh's innermost self becomes here something much more direct: the Hades that Achilles visits is himself.

Grieving for the Second Self

The journey begins in book 18. Movement in the story has been slowed in book 17 by the tense but inconclusive battle over Patroclus' corpse. Homer cuts away in the beginning of 18 to show us Achilles' reaction to the news of his friend's death. Antilochos has found him, alone as usual, and delivered the news, that Patroclus has fallen, Hector has stripped off the armor, the battle for the corpse continues:

> . . . and the black cloud of sorrow closed on Achilleus.
> In both hands he caught up the grimy dust, and poured it
> over his head and face, and fouled his handsome countenance,
> and the black ashes were scattered over his immortal tunic.
> And he himself, mightily in his might, in the dust lay
> at length, and took and tore at this hair with his hands, and defiled it.
>
> *Iliad* 18. 22–27

The gestures are typical of grieving figures in antiquity, representing sorrow, of course, but also a certain sense of *mortification*, which may be understood as a way of identifying with the deceased, delaying separation. In Achilles, whose own death is so overtly linked to both Patroclus' and Hector's, such acts have a special relevance: he mourns for his friend, he mourns for himself; he will kill Hector, he will kill himself. Thetis arrives immediately—her son's mortality is at issue—and solidifies the connection with a gesture, cradling her son's head in her arms. To hold Achilles this way is to treat him like a corpse—Thetis too sees where this grief is leading.

Achilles is impatient to go after Hector, but has no armor. Thetis will remedy that by having Hephaestus make replacements, the description of which takes up the rest of book 18. Book 19 opens with the presentation, splendid and suggestive:

> The goddess spoke so, and set down the armour on the ground
> before Achilleus, and all its elaboration clashed loudly.
> Trembling took hold of all the Myrmidons. None had the courage
> to look straight at it. They were afraid of it. Only Achilleus
> looked, and as he looked the anger came harder upon him
> and his eyes glittered terribly under his lids, like sunflare.
> He was glad, holding in his hands the shining gifts of Hephaestus.
>
> *Iliad* 19. 12–18

The inert metal carries something of the divine: glittering and beautiful, but also vaguely menacing. Its reflection in Achilles' eyes seems to stir up an elemental fiery substance in him, pointing forward to his coming rampage. Achilles was born with some godhead inside him, and now its fullest potential is to be tapped. The results are true to their origin, releasing a terrible power the moral import of which is not easy to fix.

Meanwhile, Patroclus' corpse lies unburied. It has been washed and mended, but Achilles fears corruption will set in. Once more, Thetis intervenes, embalming the corpse with nectar and ambrosia. According to her nature — as mother of the hero — Thetis gives her son unquestioning support, even though we begin to see that this may not be in the interest of his spiritual evolution. And it is significant that her support takes this particular form, holding back the regular rhythm of nature to please her son. In order to evolve into a fully mature man, as the second-self motif seems to define it, Achilles will have to move out of the sheltering embrace of his mother and come to terms with a hard but profound wisdom, in tune with the inexorable flow of life and death, which will come to him from his father.

Why does Achilles not bury his friend, and so let his soul come to rest in the land of the dead? The stated reason is retribution:

> "But seeing that it is I, Patroklos, who follow you underground,
> I will not bury you till I bring to this place the armour
> and the head of Hektor, since he was your great-hearted murderer.
> Before your burning pyre I shall behead twelve glorious
> children of the Trojans, for my anger over your slaying.
> Until then, you shall lie where you are in front of my curved ships
> and beside you women of Troy and deep-girdled Dardanian women
> shall sorrow for you day and night and shed tears for you, those whom
> you and I worked hard to capture by force and the long spear
> in days when we were storming the rich cities of mortals."
>
> *Iliad* 18. 333–342

Notice that the intense and exclusive bond with Patroclus still has destructive consequences for others, but that the victims are now to be Trojans instead of Greeks. We may say that, in the context of the war, this shift is positive — better to kill the enemy than one's friends. But the issues generated by Achilles' spiritual journey will eventually reach beyond the parameters set by battle, will draw our attention to other, more fundamental boundaries. In this wider view the revenge envisioned by Achilles here is no different from the earlier punishment meted out to the Greeks.

From our perspective, through the prism of the second-self motif, there is another level of significance in postponing the burial: by clinging to the body of Patroclus, Achilles seems to delay the final separation that death imposes — in this sense he is typical of those who grieve, in Homer's culture or our own; but because of the chain of deaths in the last third of the poem, the gesture has special force, as denial not only of Patroclus' death, but also, as we have seen, of his own mortality. Once again Achilles' words are an incomplete guide to his true state of mind.

The attention to armor and corpses as somehow invested with the essence of a man is typical of the culture of the *Iliad* as a whole, and not necessarily pernicious. But for Achilles, whose spiritual fulfillment is in the balance, the risks in mistaking the body for the soul are especially high, since Patroclus represents a part of himself that must be recovered. In order to achieve spiritual integration Achilles will have to effect a revolution in his perspective, letting go of the flesh and welcoming back the spirit of his friend.

The End of the Quarrel

The body preserved, Achilles has one other little detail to attend to before heading into battle. Turning to Agamemnon, he abruptly announces the end of his anger over losing Briseis; he is eager to put the quarrel aside and get on with the business of avenging Patroclus' death. This news ought to be momentous: Achilles renounces all of the prideful emotions that seemed to fill up his entire world in the first sixteen books of the poem, that drove him to sentence his friends to death in the service of his honor. It is all dismissed, and yet it already seems very distant, somehow beside the point. Such is the force of Achilles' presence in the poem that once he has turned away from these issues to another focus, we turn away with him.

Agamemnon has not sensed the change, and responds with a long-winded and self-serving speech, ready to stop quarreling but unwilling to take responsibility for his acts — Zeus sent savage delusion over him, he says. Achilles, who once might have taken exception to this waffling, brushes it off with the equivalent of "whatever," and presses again for action. The contrast between the two men is telling: Achilles is somehow *beyond* all of this, while Agamemnon seems petty; just where Achilles is now remains to be demonstrated, but the air of transcendence about him is portentous.

Still one more delay: the soldiers, Odysseus says, must eat before going into battle, and Agamemnon takes the opportunity to arrange for the delivery of those unwanted gifts. Achilles, his impatience nearly palpable, defers dealing with the gifts and then goes further:

> "No, but I would now
> drive forward the sons of the Achaians into the fighting
> starving and unfed, and afterwards when the sun sets
> make ready a great dinner, when we have paid off our defilement.
> But before this, for me at least, neither drink nor food shall
> go down my very throat, since my companion has perished
> and lies inside my shelter torn about with the cutting
> bronze, and turned against the forecourt while my companions
> mourn about him. Food and drink mean nothing to my heart
> but blood does, and slaughter, and the groaning of men in the hard work."
> *Iliad* 19. 205–214

Refusing food, sleep, and sex—Achilles also avoids the latter two, as we will see—is another traditional sign of grieving in the culture out of which the *Iliad* comes. The gesture, like the others we have noted, signals a desire to withdraw from the regular flow of nature, in part simply to smart in private, but also as a form of denying what nature has done, of denying death. And stepping back, we observe that Achilles' renunciation is also of a piece with other forms of apartness, playing its part in the larger schema of the second-self motif.

But though appropriate, the gesture is impractical, even for Achilles—he too must have strength to fight. Zeus prompts Athena to remedy this. Has she abandoned her favorite? How will he fight without nourishment? She must go and "distill nectar inside his chest, and delicate ambrosia" (*Iliad* 19. 347–348). Athena has been a steady supporter of the Greek cause, but Zeus seems to imply something more here in her affection for Achilles, almost a parental solicitude. This would be consistent with the gesture she makes, in that her intervention parallels Thetis' preservation of Patroclus' corpse with the same two substances. And here too the intervention interrupts the regular flow of nature. In both cases the female protector gives support which helps Achilles continue to stay apart from the process that ultimately defines him as human, continue to postpone confronting the issues he must inevitably negotiate, sooner or later.

Athena's intervention has two other dimensions. First, it represents in a particularly unsettling way the intensity of the relationship between Achilles and Patroclus: when Patroclus dies, a part of Achilles dies as well; the nectar and ambrosia will nourish Achilles, but, as the embalming agents for Patroclus, are also emblems of his own mortality. Second, and paradoxically, the nourishment is of course divine, the food of the gods. At this point, we may begin to feel overpowered by the density of Homer's presentation: the nectar and ambrosia symbolize both Achilles' mortality and his divinity. This is true to Achilles' uncanny nature, part god, part mortal, but there is more. In course of the vengeful rampage leading up to Hector's death, there is a sense in which he seems to transcend normal human bounds. This transcendence is especially vivid in book 21, in his challenging of the river god, Skamandros.

Revenge as Self-Loathing: The Pursuit of Hector

Hacking his way toward Hector, Achilles at one point begins killing Trojans and throwing them into the river Skamandros. The pace is such that the river becomes clogged, cannot flow. A protest from the river god, who calls Achilles' acts "greater . . . more violent than all men's" (*Iliad* 21. 214–215), leaves him undeterred: he will stop only after he has tracked down

Hector; the dumping of corpses continues, as the avenger "like something more than mortal swept down on the Trojans" (*Iliad* 21. 227).

Stopping the river flow, Achilles continues to oppose the regular order of nature. But then Skamandros assumes the offensive—Zeus has ordered the gods to keep Achilles from taking Troy—by overflowing and attacking Achilles. There follows an extraordinary battle, with Skamandros on one side, Achilles, Poseidon, Athena, and then Hephaestus on the other. Now the river becomes the agent of disorder, while Achilles slips, rather uneasily, into the traditional role of the hero who faces the Chaos Monster, defending or even establishing civilization. Hephaestus finally stems the flow with fire—appropriately enough, since Achilles himself has been increasingly associated with fire in the poem—and order is restored.

Agent of both order and chaos, Achilles is "something more than mortal" here, but exactly *what* he is remains unclear; he transcends ordinary categories, but seems to be defined by nothing more precise than the fact of transcendence. He remains a hero, testing boundaries for other mortals, but is not very convincing in the role suggested here of savior of civilization. In some respects his behavior is like a god's, powerful and impatient of opposition, removed from the worries attendant on mortals—his pitiless treatment of various suppliants who approach him in books 20-22 has about it the cruel indifference of deities. In some unsettling way, he is moving away from the mortal part of his nature toward the divine.

But if Achilles approaches godliness, it is an increasingly savage, almost bestial kind of divinity—nothing like what is displayed in the comic battling of the Olympian deities that brings book 21 to a close. To be like an animal in the *Iliad* can be a symbol of physical traits useful to the warrior, strength, swiftness, fortitude, but not of any quality that Achilles lacks—Patroclus, unlike Enkidu, does not represent an unreflective oneness with the rhythms of the wilderness. Identification with the world of animals is not, then, an emblem of Achilles' renewed contact with his second self, but a sign at best of his continuing espousal of the heroic values that keep him from this contact, at worst of his estrangement from humanity as a whole.

Slinging Lykaon's corpse negligently into the river prompts this:

> "Lie there now among the fish, who will lick the blood away
> from your wound, and care nothing for you, nor will your mother
> lay you on the death-bed and mourn over you, but Skamandros
> will carry you spinning down to the wide bend of the salt water.
> And a fish will break a ripple shuddering dark on the water
> as he rises to feed upon the shining fat of Lykaon.
> Die on, all; till we come to the city of sacred Ilion,
> you in flight and I killing you from behind; and there will not
> be any rescue for you from your silvery-whirled strong-running
> river, for all the numbers of bulls you dedicate to it

and drown single-footed horses alive in its eddies. And yet
even so, die all an evil death, till all of you
pay for the death of Patroklos and the slaughter of the Achaians
whom you killed beside the running ships, when I was not with them."

Iliad 21. 122–135

The savagery evident here crescendos in Achilles' final exchanges with
Hector. After the great chase around the walls of Troy, after he is
tricked by Athena into facing Achilles, Hector tries to bargain: let it be
agreed that the victor will give back his victim's corpse for burial. Nothing
doing:

"Hektor, argue me no agreements. I cannot forgive you.
As there are no trustworthy oaths between men and lions,
nor wolves and lambs have spirit that can be brought to agreement
but forever these hold feelings of hate for each other,
so there can be no love between you and me, nor shall there be
oaths between us, but one or the other must fall before then
to glut with his blood Ares the god who fights under the shield's guard."

Iliad 22. 261–267

Having now openly assumed the role of beast, Achilles invokes what he
sees as the inflexible laws of nature to sanction his savagery—ironic behavior for one who has persistently tried to oppose the natural flow of the
cosmos. Like Gilgamesh, Achilles has been led by his heroic but myopic
perspective to misapprehend his place in the larger order of things.
Only when he makes contact with Patroclus again will he be able to re-
focus.

The duel is brief. Hector, doomed from the start, finally sees that he
must die, and true to the heroic vision, vows to do so gloriously. As Achilles
draws near, Homer takes the opportunity to remind us of the suicidal
nature of this last killing:

He was eyeing Hektor's splendid body, to see where it might best
give way, but all the rest of the skin was held in the armour,
brazen and splendid, he stripped when he cut down the strength of Patroklos;

Iliad 22. 321–323

The fatal opening found, Achilles drives home the spear, and taunts his
victim—killing Patroclus, Hector thought himself safe, forgetting the
avenger waiting by the ships—and ends by calling forth the dogs and vul-
tures that "shall feed and foully rip you" (*Iliad* 22. 335) while the Achaians
bury Patroclus.

Hector is dying, but—impossible not to think of opera here—he can still
speak, and he asks once more for humane, or in the circumstances, human,
treatment. Achilles is far beyond this:

"No more entreating of me, you dog, by knees or parents.
I only wish that my spirit and fury would drive me
to hack your meat away and eat it raw for the things that
you have done to me. So there is no one who can hold the dogs off
from your head, not if they bring here and set before me ten times
and twenty times the ransom, and promise more in addition,
not if Priam son of Dardanos should offer to weigh out
your bulk in gold; not even so shall the lady your mother
who herself bore you lay you on the death-bed and mourn you:
no, but the dogs and the birds will have you all for their feasting."

Iliad 22. 345–354

Now Hector is himself a dog, as if dragged into the animalistic world of Achilles' excess. In any event, the threat of cannibalism might seem to take Achilles as far into bestiality and as far from divinity as he can go. And yet (to Hera):

Deeply troubled, Zeus who gathers the clouds answered her:
"Dear lady, what can be all the great evils done to you
by Priam and the sons of Priam, that you are thus furious
forever to bring down the strong-founded city of Ilion?
If you could walk through the gates and through the towering ramparts
and eat Priam and the children of Priam raw, and the other
Trojans, then, then only might you glut at last your anger."

Iliad 4. 30–36

It may be that the animal savagery of Achilles ought not to be set apart from his divinity after all. In him, anyway, the two extremes coexist in lethal solution, whatever we may say about Homeric gods in general. We have circled back yet again to Homer's opening lines, to that specter of "delicate feasting" (*Iliad* 1. 4).

Achilles' Dark Side as a Reflection of His Divinity

Another major movement in the story is complete, and we may pause to consider where Achilles is in his spiritual journey. A second "suicide" has allowed him to work off, perhaps, some of the guilt from the first, while sustaining the anger that seems to motivate him; his apartness has taken on several new dimensions, a simultaneous movement upward toward the gods, downward toward the world of animals, inward to some private, numbing darkness. There is no real analog in the Gilgamesh epic for this place in the evolution of Achilles, because the earlier work has no elaboration on the killing of the second self. The anger, so central to the characterization of Achilles, has reached a kind of peak—turned, as we have said, both outward and inward at the same time—but it is not yet finished.

By making the journey into darkness an internalized one, as opposed to Gilgamesh's externalized trip to the underworld, Homer also causes us to reflect both on the uncanny nature of divinity in general and on its peculiar manifestation in Achilles. Patroclus' death brings out the dark side of Achilles, a self-imposed hell into which he descends in denial of that death and his own. That movement is characterized as a separation from humanity and a surging toward some kind of unworldly, godlike status, itself a mix of exalted power, cold detachment, and debased savagery. I have suggested that the unsavory aspects of divinity in Achilles are not confined to him, and we may note that his rampage offers the opportunity to assess the brutal indifference of the Homeric gods in a context where these qualities can have real consequences. At the same time, all of this has special relevance to Achilles. Achilles is part god, and to move toward the divine is for him to realize something of his true nature. And yet the same impulse is characterized as a manifestation of his dark side. Oppositions float in uneasy solution here; resolution will only come at the end of Achilles' journey, in the rich and mysterious encounter with Priam at the edge of the sea.

Patroclus' Ghost: The Stirring of the Second Self

His vows fulfilled—Hector's corpse lies ready to feed the dogs, twelve young Trojans are at hand to fuel the funeral fires—Achilles can now bury Patroclus. As book 23 opens, preliminaries proceed briskly: the wood is to be gathered on the following day, a "gloomy feast" is held, and all go off to bed. Achilles is, as usual, alone by the seashore. He drifts off to sleep, and the ghost of Patroclus appears, accusing his friend of forgetting him, begging to be buried so he may cross the river into Hades and find what rest he can. The specter sees it all from the other side of the great chasm still dividing Achilles from the finality of death—the life they two had together is over—and makes one final request, that their bones be buried together, foreshadowing perhaps the reintegration to come in book 24.

Patroclus is impatient, his words conveying some feeling that Achilles has delayed his final rest unnaturally—a parallel, in our perspective, to the gestures of Thetis and Athena. We have noted that withholding the body from burial can be seen as a gesture of denial, not only of Patroclus' death but also of Achilles'. But now Achilles seems eager to complete the rites, and we might expect to see an end to this denial. Not so, in the event.

Achilles, still in a dream state, asks for an embrace, but grasps only air, prompting the following when he awakes:

> "Oh, wonder! Even in the house of Hades there is left something,
> a soul and an image, but there is no real heart of life in it."
>
> *Iliad* 23. 103–104

The relationship between physical remains and spiritual essence that Achilles touches on here, already familiar from the battle over corpses, will become increasingly important in the story. The issue is natural enough in the context of grieving, and indeed one important function of the funeral service even today is to help the living let go of the dead person *as a physical presence*, making room for whatever sort of spiritual relationship might evolve. In the case of Achilles, where grieving for a friend has an unusually personal dimension, the transition is especially crucial.

Cremation and burial take place the next day, followed by funeral games. Achilles' demeanor during the latter suggests some renewed impulse in him to end his isolation from the other Greeks — he is a relatively genial master of ceremonies, generous to winners and losers, never making his own honor an issue. This behavior contrasts strongly with the previous versions of Achilles, solipsistic and volatile. Now that Patroclus is buried and avenged — and Achilles' conscience eased — we look for evidence of some kind of shift in perspective toward, perhaps, more humility, less self-aggrandisement, and the games seem to provide it.

Savagery Revisited: The Last Stages of Denial

The opening of book 24 belies our expectations. Once again, Achilles is alone:

> And the games broke up, and the people scattered to go away, each man
> to his fast-running ship, and the rest of them took thought of their dinner
> and of sweet sleep and its enjoyment; only Achilleus
> wept still as he remembered his beloved companion, nor did sleep
> who subdues all come over him, but he tossed from one side to the other
> in longing for Patroklos, for his manhood and his great strength
> and all the actions he had seen to the end with him, and the hardships
> he had suffered; the wars of men; hard crossing of the big waters.
> Remembering all these things he let fall the swelling tears, lying
> sometimes along his side, sometimes on his back, and now again
> prone on his face; then he would stand upright, and pace turning
> in distraction along the beach of the sea, nor did dawn rising
> escape him as she brightened across the sea and the beaches.
> Then, when he had yoked running horses under the chariot
> he would fasten Hektor behind the chariot, so as to drag him,
> and draw him three times around the tomb of Menoitios' fallen
> son, then rest again in his shelter, and throw down the dead man
> and leave him to lie sprawled on his face in the dust. But Apollo
> had pity on him, though he was only a dead man, and guarded
> the body from all ugliness, and hid all of it under the golden
> aegis, so that it might not be torn when Achilleus dragged it.

Iliad 24. 1–21

Sleeplessness now takes its place beside other emblems of grieving—no eating, no washing (cf. *Iliad* 23. 44–47)—and we see that Achilles has not yet accepted the death of Patroclus. Notice also the connection between this denial and the desecration of Hector's corpse: though Achilles has let Patroclus' body go, he clings to Hector's, as if it were a substitute— doubling in the second-self motif continues. What, then, does this gesture signify? First, continuing anger at both his enemy *and himself*— killing Hector seems not to have been enough to quell the wrath; second, following the linkage established between Patroclus, Hector, and Achilles, continuing denial of Patroclus' death and his own. As we enter the final scenes in the story, then, potential for reintegration in the second-self motif is still unrealized. The "problem" of Achilles persists, carried in the story by his anger, which continues to have a life its own. The games in book 23 now look like an interlude rather than a sign of progress in Achilles.

And yet, there is a difference. As Achilles stalks Hector, his denial takes an increasingly expansive, at times even cosmic, form, peaking in his savage behavior while killing his prey. The atmosphere of book 23, by contrast, is subdued, reflecting a kind of exhaustion from the enormous tension of the preceding five books; Achilles appears burnt-out now, beyond caring enough to feed the anger. That tone persists in the opening lines of book 24, so that though Achilles' actions show him to be still far from peaceful, his unease now seems to have collapsed inward. Compressed now into a terrible soul-sickness, it is manifested outwardly in the obsessive and futile dragging of the corpse, around and around.

Divine Intervention: The Return of the Second Self Begins

This savagery is too much even for the gods. Remembering all the sacrifices Hector dutifully performed, Zeus takes action, sending Iris to summon Thetis. The latter's reception on Olympus is carefully orchestrated:

> She sat down beside Zeus father, and Athene made a place for her.
> Hera put into her hand a beautiful golden goblet
> and spoke to her to comfort her, and Thetis accepting drank from it.
>
> *Iliad* 24. 100–102

In the symbolic language of early Greek literature, to offer a seat and a drink to someone grieving is to urge him or her to rejoin the community of the living, to accept consolation for loss, to bring an end to grief, while acceptance of the tokens shows compliance. Thetis, then, seems to be accepting consolation here, not for Hector, not for Patroclus, important as he is to her son, but for Achilles. The proleptic nature of this response is consistent with the strong linkage between the fates of Patroclus, Hector, and Achilles. At the same time, Thetis' acceptance of her son's mortality foreshadows his own—significantly enough, as she represents the divine part of Achilles' nature. It is typical of Homeric poetry that major events or movements in the story are confirmed variously and gradually, rather than all at once. Thetis' consolation marks only one of many indications, beginning as early as book 23, that Achilles is finally coming to the end of his denial, is on the brink of a new understanding of his place in the world.

Zeus delivers an unambiguous message: the gods are angry—and most of all *he* is angry—at Achilles for mistreating Hector's corpse; he is to give the body back to Priam, whom Zeus is also bestirring to bring ransom. The missions of Thetis and Iris (to Priam) begin a significant parallelism between Achilles and Priam as grieving survivors. To accept consolation is part of what Achilles must do to achieve spiritual regeneration; to give it is another part. From now until the end of the poem, Achilles and Priam will be increasingly drawn together, effecting a mysterious bond that becomes the vehicle for the final thematic synthesis of the *Iliad*.

We may profitably pause to consider the implications of the gods' intervention. The gesture might tempt us to see some kind of divine sanction for the spiritual evolution of Achilles. But here, even more than in the Gilgamesh epic, the gods follow their own private agenda—Apollo champions his favorite, Hector; Hera's stormy rebuttal is prompted by her personal attachment to Thetis; Zeus is as usual at pains to mollify his spouse, and so grants Hera's debating point, but remembers too that the Trojan hero "never failed of gifts to my liking" (*Iliad* 24. 68). The end result is to push Achilles toward fruitful change, but the gods' motives remain "personal"— indeed, the famous "plan of Zeus" that informs the entire story is generated by a similar mix of familial bonding and private markers called in. As we move toward the climactic scenes of reconciliation, the notion that humans ought to look to any divine behavior as a model is in fact rejected with increasing force: the gods do what they wish, and mortals do what they can. As Paris puts it: "Never to be cast away are the gifts of the gods" (*Iliad* 3 .65). Here, as in the Gilgamesh epic, the pattern of self-realization that Achilles embodies is part of the authorial perspective, outside the naturalistic world of the story.

Thetis relays the message promptly, prefacing it with some motherly solicitude:

> "My child, how long will you go on eating your heart out in sorrow
>   and lamentation, and remember neither your food nor going
>   to bed? It is a good thing even to lie with a woman
>   in love. For you will not be with me long, but already
>   death and powerful destiny stand closely above you.
>   But listen hard to me, for I come from Zeus with a message.

He says that the gods frown upon you, that beyond all other
immortals he himself is angered that in your heart's madness
you hold Hektor beside the curved ships and did not redeem him.
Come, then, give him up and accept ransom for the body."

Iliad 24. 128–137

As usual, Achilles' impending death is on Thetis' mind. But notice too that
her first expression of concern takes a form especially relevant to the process of grieving — indeed, this is the first explicit mention of Achilles' self-
enforced celibacy. Now Thetis, who before has supported her son without
question, even in his more self-destructive attitudes, pushes him toward a
new perspective. In this, we see reflected her new acceptance of Achilles'
death, and we have another confirmation of the movement underway
within Achilles himself. At the same time, there is reflected the letting go
that her consolation on Olympus signified: having accepted the coming loss
of her son, Thetis can acquiesce in becoming the agent of the *father's* hard
wisdom, represented for the moment by Zeus' initiative.

The reply is stunning in its brevity:

"So be it. He can bring the ransom and take off the body,
if the Olympian himself so urgently bids it."

Iliad 24. 139–140

We may be pardoned for feeling a certain sense of anti-climax here. After
all that bloodshed, all that pain, Achilles apparently gives up the struggle
with what amounts to a shrug. But here again, Homer's narrative strategy
can mislead: this is only one confirmation among many of Achilles' progress. And in any event, we have seen that Achilles' words are not always a
complete reflection of his state of mind. If we watch what he does from
now until the end of the interview with Priam, we see a less decisive man.

Iris is equally persuasive, and Priam begins immediately to prepare for
his journey to the Greek camp. Hecuba is alarmed, and begs him to stay at
Troy, to "sit apart in our palace / now, and weep for Hector" (*Iliad* 24.
208–209). But like Achilles, Priam has been prompted by Zeus to break the
cycle of isolation and pain, to act in the world rather than "sit apart." Still,
the process is just beginning, and we see evidence that Priam's pain over
Hector continues to isolate him. Impatient to set out for the Greek camp,
driven by pain and anger, he curses his children and the other Trojans,
beating them with a stick.

Both Priam and Achilles have been led by their grief to cling to the dead
and push away the living. Achilles has been able to realize this attitude
more concretely, keeping with him the bodies of Patroclus and Hector in
succession, but Priam's preoccupation with the sons lost to him has the
same effect, causing him to drive away those still living. The end of grief
for both will entail reversing this dynamic, letting go of the dead and
rejoining the living. Integral to this process in turn is the role of memory.

The Greek verb *mimneskomai* has approximately the same semantic range as our English word, "to remember." In the *Iliad*'s world of battle, the word is often used to rouse fighting spirit in a way that makes its meaning of "bring to mind again" especially vivid:

> "Trojans, Lykians, Dardanians who fight at close quarters,
> be men now, dear friends, remember your furious valour
> while I am putting on the beautiful armour of blameless
> Achilleus, which I stripped from Patroklos the strong when I killed him."
>
> *Iliad* 17. 184–187

Hector urges his men to "recall" their valor as if it were in reserve like fresh troops, to make it come alive and be useful. The "remembering" that Achilles and Priam do in grief has this same sense of *conjuring up, reanimating* those lost to them. As the two men struggle with their loss and reach out to each other, the process of "remembering" will be ever present.

Priam's Embassy: The Hero's Renewed Contact with His Second Self

The lonely night journey of Priam and his herald sets the tone for his encounter with Achilles. Homer hints that we are to have in our minds the *katabasis*, or trip to the underworld—Priam travels in the dark, crosses a river, passes a tomb; his subjects say goodbye to him "as if he went to his death" (*Iliad* 24. 328). Priam is cast in the role of the epic hero, awake while others sleep, who goes to the land of the dead to bring back a loved one. Achilles, in turn, would seem to be the Death God who must be placated. How prominent this mythical paradigm is meant to be in the story is hard to judge, but its implications are tantalizing. Achilles, doomed to an early death, is in this paradigm *already resident in the land of the dead*; a new kind of divinity, more serene, less self-involved than the brutal version on display in books 20–22, is suggested as the source for the magisterial detachment he shows in responding to Priam: he is once again *transcendent*, but in a more positive way.

Priam's first words to Achilles prompt remembrance:

> "Achilleus like the gods, remember your father, one who
> is of years like mine, and on the door-sill of sorrowful old age.
> And they who dwell nearby encompass him and afflict him,
> nor is there any way to defend him against the wrath, the destruction.
> Yet surely he, when he hears of you and that you are still living,
> is gladdened within his heart and all his days he is hopeful
> that he will see his beloved son come home from the Troad.
> But for me, my destiny was evil. I have had the noblest

of sons in Troy, but I say not one of them is left to me.
Fifty were my sons, when the sons of the Achaians came here.
Nineteen were born to me from the womb of a single mother,
and other women bore the rest in my palace; and of these
violent Ares broke the strength in the knees of most of them,
but one was left me who guarded my city and people, that one
you killed a few days since as he fought in defence of his country,
Hektor; for whose sake I come now to the ships of the Achaians
to win him back from you, and I bring you gifts beyond number.
Honour then the gods, Achilleus, and take pity on me
remembering your father, yet still I am more pitiful;
I have gone through what no other mortal on earth has gone through;
I put my lips to the hands of the man who has killed my children."
   So he spoke, and stirred in the other a passion of grieving
for his own father. He took the old man's hand and pushed him
gently away, and the two remembered, as Priam sat huddled
at the feet of Achilleus and wept close for manslaughtering Hektor
and Achilleus wept now for his own father, now again
for Patroklos.

Iliad 24. 486–512

Priam urges Achilles explicitly to remember the living (Peleus, Priam) and
let go of the dead (Hector). The immediate effect is more weeping, though
at least Achilles' attention is now focused on Peleus as well as Patroclus.
Priam's suggestion that Achilles think of Peleus and himself together, as
fathers grieving for their sons, is significant. To do so requires Achilles
to realign his perspective radically: the two old men go from mortal enemies to fellow sufferers, united by their pain. And by directing Achilles'
attention to his father, Priam encourages another critical shift in the
hero, away from the comforting support of his mother and toward an accommodation with certain hard but necessary truths that only his father
can provide.

   Achilles' reply, one of the great speeches in the poem, shows the new
perspective already broadened:

                        "Ah, unlucky,
surely you have had much evil to endure in your spirit.
How could you dare to come alone to the ships of the Achaians
and before my eyes, when I am the one who have killed in such numbers
such brave sons of yours? The heart in you is iron. Come, then,
and sit down upon this chair, and you and I will even let
our sorrows lie still in the heart for all our grieving. There is not
any advantage to be won from grim lamentation.
Such is the way gods spun life for unfortunate mortals,
that we live in unhappiness, but the gods themselves have no sorrows.

There are two urns that stand on the door-sill of Zeus. They are unlike
for the gifts they bestow: an urn of evils, an urn of blessings.
If Zeus who delights in thunder mingles these and bestows them
on man, he shifts, and moves now in evil, again in good fortune.
But when Zeus bestows from the urn of sorrows, he makes a failure
of man, and the evil hunger drives him over the shining
earth, and he wanders respected neither of gods nor mortals.
Such were the shining gifts given by the gods to Peleus
from his birth, who outshone all men beside for his riches
and pride of possession, and was lord over the Myrmidons. Thereto
the gods bestowed an immortal wife on him, who was mortal.
But even on him the gods piled evil also. There was not
any generation of strong sons born to him in his great house
but a single all-untimely child he had, and I give him
no care as he grows old, since far from the land of my fathers
I sit here in Troy, and bring nothing but sorrow to you and your children.
And you, old sir, we are told you prospered once; for as much
as Lesbos, Makar's hold, confines to the north above it
and Phrygia from the north confines, and enormous Hellespont,
of these, old sir, you were lord once in your wealth and your children.
But now the Uranian gods brought us, an affliction upon you,
forever there is fighting about your city, and men killed.
But bear up, nor mourn endlessly in your heart, for there is not
anything to be gained from grief for your son; you will never
bring him back; sooner you must go through yet another sorrow."

Iliad 24. 517-551

This is an astonishing turnabout. Gone is the obsessive preoccupation with
the dead, replaced by apparently genuine solicitude for both Peleus and
Priam—the old man's plea has already made an impact; paternal wisdom
leads the way to a new understanding. But Achilles has gone beyond the
personal, leaping from the particular to the universal. As in the Gilgamesh
epic, so here the focus shifts from one set of boundaries to another: instead
of viewing the world as divided between mortal friends and enemies, Achilles now—in a detached perspective commensurate with his elusive transcendence—sees a more fundamental divide, between the gods who live at their
ease and humans, who can hope for at best a mix of prosperity and catastrophe, at worst unrelieved misery. There is recognition here of the basic
fact of human existence that Achilles has been unable to accept: all humans,
Hector and himself included, are united by their mortality.

So Achilles, much in need of consolation himself, offers it to Priam. The
old man is not ready:

In answer to him again spoke aged Priam the godlike:
"Do not, beloved of Zeus, make me sit on a chair while Hektor

lies yet forlorn among the shelters; rather with all speed
give him back, so my eyes may behold him, and accept the ransom
we bring you, which is great. You may have joy of it, and go back
to the land of your own fathers, since once you have permitted me
to go on living myself and continue to look at the sunlight."

Iliad 24. 552–559

Reference to sitting in this context invokes the themes of grieving and consolation — apparently Priam cannot let go of his grieving for Hector until he has the body. Indeed, though Priam will eventually join Achilles in gestures that seem to signal acceptance of consolation, it will not be over entirely for him until he buries Hector, in the last passages of the poem, serene and splendid.

Meanwhile, Achilles is not pleased. He warns the old man not to "stir (him) up" (*Iliad* 24. 560), using the same words Agamemnon did way back in book 1 when threatening the priest of Apollo — a significant parallel, as we will see. Though he knows that Priam cannot have gotten unharmed into his quarters without the help of some god, further provocation may drive him to act in defiance of Zeus' commands and harm Priam. Achilles hints that his anger is still within reach, and the warning reminds us that Priam is always in danger, that the new detachment is fragile. As if to head off any further slippage, Achilles moves immediately:

He spoke, and the old man was frightened and did as he told him.
The son of Peleus bounded to the door of the house like a lion,
nor went alone, but the two henchmen followed attending,
the hero Automedon and Alkimos, those whom Achilleus
honoured beyond all companions after Patroklos dead. These two
now set free from under the yoke the mules and the horses,
and led inside the herald, the old king's crier, and gave him
a chair to sit in, then from the smooth-polished mule wagon
lifted out the innumerable spoils for the head of Hektor,
but left inside it two great cloaks and a finespun tunic
to shroud the corpse in when they carried him home. Then Achilleus
called out to his serving-maids to wash the body and anoint it
all over; but take it first aside, since otherwise Priam
might see his son and in the heart's sorrow not hold in his anger
at the sight, and the deep heart in Achilleus be shaken to anger;
that he might not kill Priam and be guilty before the god's orders.
Then when the serving-maids had washed the corpse and anointed it
with olive oil, they threw a great fair cloak and a tunic
about him, and Achilleus himself lifted him and laid him
on a litter, and his friends helped him lift it to the smooth-polished
mule wagon. He groaned then, and called by name on his beloved companion:
"Be not angry with me, Patroklos, if you discover,

though you be in the house of Hades, that I gave back great Hektor
to his loved father, for the ransom he gave me was not unworthy.
I will give you your share of the spoils, as much as is fitting."

Iliad 24. 571–595

There is much here that signals closure. These will be Achilles' final words
to Patroclus, attentive, characteristically for the poem, to concrete, objective symbols of inner worth. But acts, even more than words, signify a
change in Achilles. Though underlings attend to the preparation of the
corpse, Achilles himself lifts the body onto the wagon, balancing with this
gentleness the earlier desecration. By doing so, he seems to finalize separation from the physical remains, to let go of this inert thing that has taken
the place not only of Hector, but also Patroclus. The way is now clear for
Patroclus to be present for Achilles in a different way.

One other small detail repays attention. Describing Achilles as he springs
to action, Homer is careful to mention that he is accompanied by two
henchmen. In the symbolic art language of Homer, this piece of information is not as trivial as it might seem. The Greek phrase which is translated
as "nor went alone" here, *ouk oios*, regularly introduces situations in which
the one accompanied is prominently "in charge." Achilles relinquishes that
status in book 1 as he storms from the Greek camp after his quarrel with
Agamemnon, slamming to the ground the scepter, symbol of authority in
the Greek assembly. Since then, he has been in self-imposed exile from the
society of warriors, has been, consequently, *displaced*. Giving up the body
allows Achilles to return to his natural position of authority in the Greek
army: he is "not alone."

Releasing the corpse seems finally to free Achilles as well:

"Your son is given back to you, aged sir, as you asked it.
He lies on a bier. When dawn shows you yourself shall see him
as you take him away. Now you and I must remember our supper.
For even Niobe, she of the lovely tresses, remembered
to eat, whose twelve children were destroyed in her palace,
six daughters, and six sons in the pride of their youth, whom Apollo
killed with arrows from his silver bow, being angered
with Niobe, and shaft-showering Artemis killed the daughters;
because Niobe likened herself to Leto of the fair colouring
and said Leto had borne only two, she herself had borne many;
but the two, though they were only two, destroyed all those others.
Nine days long they lay in their blood, nor was there anyone
to bury them, for the son of Kronos made stones out of
the people; but on the tenth day the Uranian gods buried them.
But she remembered to eat when she was worn out with weeping.
And now somewhere among the rocks, in the lonely mountains,
in Sipylos, where they say is the resting place of the goddesses

who are nymphs, and dance beside the waters of the Acheloios,
there, stone still, she broods on the sorrows that the gods gave her.
Come then, we also, aged magnificent sir, must remember
to eat, and afterwards you may take your beloved son back
to Ilion, and mourn for him; and he will be much lamented."

Iliad 24. 599–620

Achilles' universalizing perspective continues, as he now recasts both his
and Priam's experience as mourners against the backdrop of myth: even
Niobe remembered to eat; so must they. The speech, like so much of what
passes between Achilles and his suppliant, encapsulates central themes in
the poem: the jealousy and awful power of gods, the dangers of human
pride, the love of parents, sometimes unwittingly destructive of their children, the suffering of the innocent, the horror of unburied corpses. And
finally, that recurrent image: tears flowing across cold, hard rock. Achilles'
immediate intent is to console Priam, to urge an end to grief; the form of
his overture, delivered from the position of detachment he has assumed,
makes his message carry a heavy symbolic load: by taking care of each
other, he and Priam create, almost embody, a thematic synthesis for the
entire poem. We may even say that Achilles assumes another magisterial
role here, that of the poet, who takes the raw material of experience and,
by shaping it in a certain way, makes sense out of — or at least achieves a
kind of closure for — what appears senseless, endless.

The meal follows, described in the deliberate, measured, and largely
traditional language that dominates the last scenes of the poem. The mysterious union of Priam and Achilles reaches here its zenith:

But when they had put aside their desire for eating and drinking,
Priam, son of Dardanos, gazed upon Achilleus, wondering
at his size and beauty, for he seemed like an outright vision
of gods. Achilleus in turn gazed on Dardanian Priam
and wondered, as he saw his brave looks and listened to him talking.

Iliad 24. 628–632

The process drawing the two enemies together has come to fruition. From
hatred to simple acceptance is, in the world of the *Iliad*, a lengthy journey.
There remain some issues to be worked out, sleeping arrangements, how
long the truce is to last, but in effect the big work is done. The very last
glimpse we have of the two strips their relationship down yet further, to
companionable silence:

Then these two,
Priam and the herald who were both men of close counsel,
slept in the place outside the house, in the porch's shelter;
but Achilleus slept in the inward corner of the strong-built shelter,
and at his side lay Briseis of the fair colouring.

Iliad 24. 672–676

This parallel slumber, with everything it symbolizes in the context of grieving, is a moment of rest, not from the war, but from the relentless surge of aggression, created by the heroic perspective, embodied and carried to frightening lengths by Achilles. A different world, however fragile, has been created in Achilles' quarters. The moment will pass, the war will resume, but Homer allows his hero, and us, some respite. Priam's sleep will soon be interrupted—the funeral remains; Achilles we will not see again. This last picture of him in particular, with Briseis finally back at his side, recalls, perhaps disquietingly, the only comparably tranquil moment in the story:

> Zeus the Olympian and lord of the lightning went to
> his won bed, where always he lay when sweet sleep came on him.
> Going up to bed he slept and Hera of the gold throne beside him.
>
> *Iliad* 1. 609–611

The Hero's Integration of a Lost Self

The story seems, in one sense, to have circled to its beginnings. Momentary rest has been achieved, relief from the inexorable march of fate. Against that circularity is traced the piercing trajectory of Achilles' journey, informed by the motif of the second self, the focus of our attention here. To finish the journey, to reach manhood in the complex sense that Homer envisions, Achilles must reintegrate those parts of himself embodied in the second self—Patroclus, having died, must live again in Achilles. In the thematic density of the *Iliad*, this rebirth is embedded in various other movements in the poem, is reflected variously. We have seen that Patroclus represents a compassion for others, a self*less*ness that Achilles has forfeited in pursuit of various forms of transcendence over other humans. This urge isolates him from the beginning of the poem—he is *apart*—but the manifestation of it changes over the course of the story. In the beginning, it is a desire to be recognized as the best of the Achaian warriors; after Patroclus is sacrificed to this demand—or, to put it in the language of the second self, after Achilles "kills" the compassion in himself—the movement away from the community of humans takes other, more drastic forms: downward, upward, inward.

We have seen that all these movements are reversed in book 24: gentleness and compassion for Priam counterbalance the brutal indifference to suffering in books 20 to 22; personal handling of the corpse of Hector replaces savage desecration; a divine transcendence characterized by cruelty and myopic attention to his own needs gives way to a magisterial detachment that allows Achilles to see all of humankind as united by a powerlessness before the capricious gods; clinging to the dead and driving away the living is replaced by genuine solicitude for those around him and a final releasing of the dead; refusing to partake of food, sex, and sleep, emblems of human culture, is balanced by a shared meal and a final return of Briseis to Achilles' bed.

Central to all of this is the renewed presence of Patroclus. Those qualities most prominent in him, compassion for the suffering of others and a self-lessness uncharacteristic of the heroic ethic, are precisely what we see in Achilles as he consoles Priam. While living, Patroclus' compassion is di-rected solely at his Greek companions; resident again in Achilles, it expands in a way characteristic of the latter's increasingly cosmic perspective, but the root impulse, to humility, is constant. Achilles, like Gilgamesh, learns finally to focus not on what separates him from other mortals, but rather what he shares with them. By letting go of the desire to keep Patroclus with him, even in death, Achilles finds again the part of his friend that did not die.

Conclusion: Love and Death

Because the exchange in Achilles' quarters is the vehicle for an overall thematic synthesis, its larger implications reveal much that Homer has to tell us about human life and death. There is a relentless attention through-out the poem to physical objects, armor, booty, corpses, as representative in the heroic society of less tangible qualities, honor, shame, and so forth. It is sometimes suggested that this perspective ought to be taken as the norm for the poem, that Agamemnon's offer of gifts in book 9 ought to be considered sufficient recompense for whatever wrongs he has done to Achilles, because the world of the *Iliad* does not make the distinction that we do (or profess to do) between material and nonmaterial realities. Per-haps, but Achilles' evolution in the story, and in particular his behavior in book 24, suggests an alternative. In the place of the desire to *possess* things, as a symbol of one's inner worth, of the clinging to corpses as the only available essence of a person, there is offered a glimpse of another world, in which spiritual things endure as material things do not, in which the ultimate expression of love is letting go of what one supposes he cannot live without.

Likewise, the dominant perspective in the first twenty-three books of the poem is heroic in the conventional sense I have suggested above: self-worth is dependent on competing successfully with one's fellow mortals; to be the swiftest, the strongest, the wisest, ensures status in the society of warriors. Certainly Achilles is admirably equipped, like Gilgamesh, to prosper in this kind of system. And yet Achilles does not prosper—indeed, it is precisely this heroic perspective that drives him to destroy a part of himself, to range far from the community of his fellows and suffer from the isolation that entails. Homer's vision of fully evolved, mature manhood, like Sîn's, im-plies a critique of the heroic system of values: rather than taking pride in

one's ability to bend others to one's own desires, honor is given to accepting
one's place in a larger scheme, over which no real control is possible—pain
and death come for us all; humility, not self-assertion, is finally the emblem
of maturity.

One further critique is implied here. Throughout the *Iliad*, the life of the
gods is held up as an ideal, carefree, unchanging—to be particularly excellent in the heroic mode is to be "like the gods." The semi-divine hero, then,
is in this view more fortunate by nature, closer by birth to ultimate happiness than other ordinary mortals. But again, the end of the poem suggests
some revision. If one is a god, then life is unassailably good—nothing more
is necessary; to aspire to godliness if one is not divine, just what the heroic
view seems to urge, turns out to be disastrous. Worst of all is to be semi-
divine, to know something of the terrible power of the gods, but be finally
subject to the death sentence awaiting all mortals. How exactly to sum up
the message here is not clear, but certainly it has to do with the most
conspicuous of all pieces of Greek wisdom: know thyself.

Stepping back a little from Homer's exquisite synthesis, we may observe
that the dynamic of the second self, stripped down to its essentials, is much
the same in the *Iliad* as in the Gilgamesh epic. Patroclus represents parts of
Achilles unrealized. When confronted with these qualities, Achilles pushes
them away, "kills" them by sending Patroclus into battle. Though this loss
makes Achilles acutely *aware* of his own mortality, he does not yet *accept*
it. Rather, denial increases, pushing Achilles into a darkness, variously
characterized, where he confronts basic truths about himself and his place
in the world. This encounter finally allows him to reclaim what was always
his, to reintegrate the parts of himself that have been projected out onto
the second self.

A useful summary, but finally reductive. Homer's realization of the basic
motif is, as we have seen, more complex than what we find in the Gilgamesh
epic. And most subtle of all is the hero himself, vivid and powerful, yet
elusive, difficult to categorize; part culture hero, part Chaos monster. By
doubling the second self, Homer provides a way of maintaining the driving
anger but rechanneling it so as to effect a complex motivation, giving us a
glimpse of the hero from the inside. We feel that Achilles ultimately
achieves some measure of reintegration, with his fellow mortals, with his
own lost self. And yet, by the mere hinting at a mythical paradigm, the trip
to the underworld, Homer complicates even this, suggesting that Achilles
can assume a detached perspective only because he is in some way already
beyond human life, transcendent still.

Transcendent, but for the moment at least, not alone. Amid the sometimes dizzying richness of the *Iliad*, nothing, as I have said, is more compelling to me than what Homer has to tell us about self-knowledge and the
nature of love. Achilles, out of touch with a part of himself and thus
blinded by pride, withdraws into isolation; in his loneliness, he keeps Pa-

troclus, the embodiment of what he has lost, close by. The motive for this is, in the frame of the story, love; the result is further loss of contact with his own true nature and increased isolation, both dramatized simultaneously in the death of Patroclus. As he tries to express his love in the aftermath of this loss, paradox proliferates: the more he clings to Patroclus, the more estranged they become; the more attention he pays to holding on to himself, the more alienated he becomes from the fullness of his true nature. To regain what he has lost, understood both as the man he loved and a part of himself, he must learn to let go. In selflessness he regains both himself and the ability to love:

> let it go — the
> smashed word broken
> open vow or
> the oath cracked length
> wise — let it go it
> was sworn to
>   go
>
> let them go — the
> truthful liars and
> the false fair friends
> and the boths and
> neithers — you must let them go they
> were born
>   to go
>
> let all go — the
> big small middling
> tall bigger really
> the biggest and all
> things — let all go
> dear
>   so comes love
>   e.e. cummings

4

Deserts of the Heart:
The Aeneid *(1)*

**If you bring forth what is in you, what you bring forth will save
you. If you do not bring forth what is within you, what you do
not bring forth will destroy you.**

Gospel of Thomas 45

Coming to the *Aeneid* from earlier epic, we enter an uncanny world. There
is much here that seems familiar, and yet somehow alien in ways difficult to
fix in words. Virgil's mastery of his predecessors' work—especially Homeric
epic—is evident; what he makes in response is at times frustratingly elusive:
Aeneas speaks and recalls Achilles; we begin to home in on the Homeric
passage, it suddenly melts away, and we find ourselves stranded. Pursuing
the motif of the second self in the *Aeneid* will at times create this experience, taking us down trails that turn cold, up blind alleys. Potential candi-
dates for the second self appear, then fade; integration seems possible, but
is denied. All of this is part of Virgil's design, a somber and profound
reworking of the second-self motif that thrusts the hero's search for spiritual wholeness into an entirely new milieu.

Divine Anger

Juno's anger dominates the poem's opening:

> I sing of warfare and a man at war.
> From the sea-coast of Troy in early days
> He came to Italy by destiny,
> To our Lavinian western shore,
> A fugitive, this captain, buffeted
> Cruelly on land as on the sea

> By blows from powers of the air — behind them
> Baleful Juno in her sleepless rage.
> And cruel losses were his lot in war,
> Till he could found a city and bring home
> His gods to Latium, land of the Latin race,
> The Alban lords, and the high walls of Rome.
> Tell me the causes now, O Muse, how galled
> In her divine pride, and how sore at heart
> From her old wound, the queen of gods compelled him —
> A man apart, devoted to his mission —
> To undergo so many perilous days
> And enter on so many trials. Can anger
> Black as this prey on the minds of heaven?

Aeneid 1. 1-11

Virgil, like Homer in the *Iliad*, makes anger his leitmotif. But this is *divine* anger: a goddess, nursing old grudges, initiates a major movement in the story; the poet's imagination is fixed on the frightening enormity of Juno's rage — can such a thing exist? The model here is Poseidon in the *Odyssey*, pursuing Odysseus across the sea, but that vendetta is not so prominent in the story as this one, not fueled by an anger so cosmic in its magnitude and reach. All of this suggests a subtle shift in perspective from earlier epic, a changing of the balance between human and divine initiative in the story to come. Divine will is always a part of hero stories — nothing new about that. But usually it is the hero's self-assertion that first brings the gods into play — Odysseus is harried by Poseidon because he hurt Polyphemus. Aeneas, by contrast, is paying for someone else's transgressions. So it will be throughout the story: the acts and suffering of mortals are overshadowed in the *Aeneid*, to a degree unprecedented in the tradition, by larger forces, divine will, fate, and history. In such a perspective, the definitive struggle of the hero for self-knowledge and self-acceptance, perilous in any event, is rendered yet more problematical.

Juno's anger is striking not only in its scope but also in its strongly *sexual* motivation. This is true to the tradition of Jupiter's jealous wife, but Juno's rage serves other ends in the poem beyond consistency. We might infer from a passing mention in book 24 of the *Iliad* that the judgment of Paris was taken by Homer to be in some sense the first act in a chain of events leading to the Trojan War, but the incident plays no part in the poem, carries no thematic significance. Not so in the *Aeneid*. After the prologue comes report of Juno's long affection for Carthage, and of the prophecies that foretell the defeat of Carthage by descendants of the Trojans. Next comes the old wound, right up front:

> In fear of this, and holding in memory
> The old war she had carried on at Troy
> For Argos' sake (the origins of that anger,

> That suffering, still rankled: deep within her,
> Hidden away, the judgment Paris gave,
> Snubbing her loveliness; the race she hated;
> The honors given ravished Ganymede),
> Saturnian Juno, burning for it all,
> Buffeted on the waste of sea those Trojans
> Left by the Greeks and pitiless Achilles,
> Keeping them far from Latium. For years
> They wandered as their destiny drove them on
> From one sea to the next: so hard and huge
> A task it was to found the Roman people.
>
> *Aeneid* 1. 23–33

By his careful modulations, Virgil implies that all the suffering and death visited on the Greeks, the Trojans, and eventually the native Italians, can be traced back to a jealous female. Now Paris' choice becomes the first in a series of sexually motivated acts, forming a continuous arc extending seamlessly through the cycle of Trojan stories to the founding of Rome. This insistent focus on sexuality is unusual in ancient epic, a genre ordinarily characterized by restraint when it comes to this topic. In this, one of antiquity's most restrained works, the realignment of our perspective affords not titillation, but rather an introduction to one of Virgil's' major themes, the relationship between power and gender.

Power and Gender

The boundaries of masculine and feminine experience are so firmly fixed in the male-dominated world of the Gilgamesh epic or the *Iliad* as to be rarely if ever at issue. The roles that men and women play in their culture, the inner qualities of temperament and intellect upon which these roles are assumed to be based, all are taken more or less for granted. Nothing in the *Aeneid* suggests that Virgil sought to modify these parameters — men and women go about their business in much the same way as we would expect from our knowledge of the epic tradition. And yet, as we will see, Virgil brings the role of gender in the distribution of power to our attention insistently so as to make it an issue in the story. This innovation is crucial in turn for the working-out of one part of the second-self motif.

Juno's malignant rage carries us beyond the prologue and into the story. Aeneas and his men, having left a band of fainthearted exiles in Sicily, press on for Italy. Juno, "never free / of her eternal inward wound" (*Aeneid* 1. 36), moves to head them off:

> The goddess made her way to the stormcloud country,
> Aeolia, the weather-breeding isle.

Here in a vast cavern King Aeolus
Rules the contending winds and moaning gales
As warden of their prison. Round the walls
They chafe and bluster underground. The din
Makes a great mountain murmur overhead.
High on a citadel enthroned,
Scepter in hand, he mollifies their fury,
Else they might flay the sea and sweep away
Land masses and deep sky through the empty air.
In fear of this, Jupiter hid them away
In the caverns of black night. He set above them
Granite of high mountains — and a king
Empowered at command to rein them in
Or let them go. To this king Juno now
Made her petition:
　　　　　　"Aeolus, the father
Of gods and men decreed and fixed your power
To calm the waves or make them rise in wind.
The race I hate is crossing the Tuscan sea,
Transporting Ilium with her household gods —
Beaten as they are — to Italy.
　　　　　　　　Put new fury
Into your winds, and make the long ships founder!
Drive them off course! Throw bodies in the sea!
I have fourteen exquisite nymphs, of whom
The loveliest by far, Deïopëa,
Shall be your own. I'll join you two in marriage,
So she will spend all future years with you,
As you so well deserve,
And make you father of her lovely children."
　　　　　　　　　　　　Aeneid 1. 51–75

Certain polarities begin to emerge here. On one side, Juno, a jealous, angry female, using female sexuality as a tool to undermine the regulation of natural forces, to foster disorder; on the other, Aeolus, the first of several paradigms of masculine authority we will meet in the opening scenes of the poem. He rules the winds with *imperium,* "sovereignty," a strong word in Latin with specific connotations in the Roman culture of Virgil's time — only a few of the highest political office holders in Rome had such authority, which included the power of life and death over citizens; he is called a *rex,* "king," the word for the kind of absolute monarch the Romans were proud to have overthrown when founding their oligarchic republic centuries before; his reply to Juno is calm in the face of her excitement, as obedient to established hierarchies as her offer is subversive:

> "To settle on what you wish
> Is all you need to do, your majesty.
> I must perform it. You have given me
> What realm I have. By your good offices
> I rule with Jove's consent, and I recline
> Among the gods at feasts, for you appoint me
> Lord of wind and cloud."
>
> *Aeneid* 1. 76–80

A bargain is struck, the winds are loosed, and the Trojans are engulfed. The damage is terrible, but Aeneas and his men are saved from total annihilation by Neptune, roused from the depths by the commotion. Though majestically calm, the god is angered, sensing — Virgil does not tell us how — the hand of his "angry" sister. We have moved up a notch in the male power structure — Aeolus has overstepped his bounds and must be brought into line. Neptune quiets the winds instantaneously, then glides majestically off across the waves in his chariot. Meanwhile, the polarities persist: male, order, calm versus female, disorder, excitement. Lest we miss the political significance of all this, Virgil provides a simile:

> When rioting breaks out in a great city,
> And the rampaging rabble goes so far
> That stones fly, and incendiary brands —
> For anger can supply that kind of weapon —
> If it so happens they look round and see
> Some dedicated public man, a veteran
> Whose record gives him weight, they quiet down,
> Willing to stop and listen.
> Then he prevails in speech over their fury
> By his authority, and placates them.
> Just so, the whole uproar of the great sea
> Fell silent, as the Father of it all,
> Scanning horizons under the open sky,
> Swung his team around and gave free rein
> In flight to his eager chariot.
>
> *Aeneid* 1. 148–156

The day ends with a glimpse at the highest level of authority, as Jupiter, calming the fears of Venus, reaffirms the fate of the Trojans, to rule Italy. Virgil's deities, like Homer's, are guarantors of cosmic order; though "fate" is a separate entity, divine will is consonant with it, and both are always fulfilled. Here again, female agitation is met by male serenity, cosmic order is preserved by "the father of gods and men" (*Aeneid* 1. 254), who backs up his assurances with action, sending Mercury down to Carthage to make the Phoenicians and their queen, Dido, receptive to the Trojans.

Finally, hovering somewhere offstage is Virgil's contemporary referent, Augustus, who was consolidating his own position as absolute ruler of the Roman state even as the *Aeneid* was being written. He will surface more explicitly later in the story, when Virgil places the mission of Aeneas in the larger context of Roman history.

The Hero's "Problem"

Amid these three divine models of male authority, Aeneas makes his first appearance. They are gods, he is only a man, and so perhaps we ought not to compare—the distance between mortals and deities is, after all, one of Virgil's themes. But heroes are usually defined by their pushing against the boundaries of human existence, and Aeneas *is* a male authority figure, so some consideration of his leadership qualities seems to be appropriate here. The results are mixed at best. Beset by the storm, he cries out:

> "Triply lucky, all you men
> To whom death came before your fathers' eyes
> Below the wall at Troy! Bravest Danaan,
> Diomedes, why could I not go down
> When you had wounded me, and lose my life
> On Ilium's battlefield? Our Hector lies there,
> Torn by Achilles' weapon; there Sarpedon,
> Our giant fighter, lies; and there the river
> Simois washes down so many shields
> And helmets, with strong bodies taken under!"
>
> *Aeneid* 1. 94–101

Another Homeric model lies behind this passage, Odysseus braving a storm, but it is not the Greek hero's debut in the poem, as it is for Aeneas, who enters the action wishing he were dead. Serenity in the face of a howling tempest may be too much to ask of any hero, but the contrast implied between Aeneas' response and Neptune's is striking nonetheless. Our next encounter with Virgil's hero comes after the ships have washed ashore in Libya. Having provided food, he tries to encourage the survivors:

> "Friends and companions,
> Have we not known hard hours before this?
> My men, who have endured still greater dangers,
> God will grant us an end to these as well.
> You sailed by Scylla's rage, her booming crags,
> You saw the Cyclops' boulders. Now call back
> Your courage, and have done with fear and sorrow.
> Some day, perhaps, remembering even this
> Will be a pleasure. Through diversities

Of luck, and through so many challenges,
We hold our course for Latium, where the Fates
Hold out a settlement and rest for us.
Troy's kingdom there shall rise again. Be patient:
Save yourselves for more auspicious days."

Aeneid 1. 198–207

The content of the speech is appropriately upbeat, and Aeneas seems more authoritative here. But Virgil gives him away in the lines immediately following:

So ran the speech. Burdened and sick at heart,
He feigned hope in his look, and inwardly
Contained his anguish.

Aeneid 1. 208–209

The split between brave outward confidence and inner doubt is not typical of epic heroes, who may show anger, fear, disbelief, or doubt, but always genuinely. To feign in this way is new to the tradition. The Latin translated here as "inwardly/Contained his anguish," *premit altum corde dolorem*, might also be rendered, "he pressed the sorrow/anguish deep down into his heart," suggesting an effort at control analogous to Aeolus', a taming of disorderly, inappropriate emotions. The thrust of Virgil's coda to the speech is to suggest that though Aeneas has grasped the substance of what is required of him as a leader, he is not being entirely true to his own nature: he is in the right place, but is the wrong man. This incongruity lies at the heart of Virgil's complex realization of the second-self motif. Like Gilgamesh and Achilles, Aeneas is not in touch with fundamental aspects of himself. In response to this "problem," two different versions of a second self appear in the story as potential guides for him in his evolution toward spiritual integration. So far, the pattern runs true. Virgil's innovation is to add a further complication: to fulfill the mission given him by the gods, Aeneas must do a job that requires him to betray his own fundamental nature.

The Hero and His Mother

Aeneas' next heroic gambit gives further evidence of his problematical situation. He spends the night of the storm turning events over in his mind while the rest of the crew sleeps, a common role for the hero who is about to embark on some notable exploit. Eager to explore, he sets out with his henchman, Achates, and encounters a stranger:

Then suddenly, in front of him,
His mother crossed his path in mid-forest,
Wearing a girl's shape and a girl's gear —

A Spartan girl, or like that one of Thrace,
Harpalyce, who tires horses out,
Outrunning the swift Hebrus. She had hung
About her shoulders the light, handy bow
A huntress carries, and had given her hair
To the disheveling wind; her knees were bare,
Her flowing gown knotted and kirtled up.

She spoke first:
                    "Ho, young fellows, have you seen —
Can you say where — one of my sisters here,
In a spotted lynx-hide, belted with a quiver,
Scouting the wood, or shouting on the track
Behind a foam-flecked boar?"
                                   To Venus then
The son of Venus answered:
                                   "No, I've heard
Or seen none of your sisters — only, how
Shall I address you, girl? Your look's not mortal,
Neither has your accent a mortal ring.
O Goddess, beyond doubt! Apollo's sister?
One of the family of nymphs? Be kind,
Whoever you may be, relieve our trouble,
Tell us under what heaven we've come at last,
On what shore of the world are we cast up,
Wanderers that we are, strange to this country,
Driven here by wind and heavy sea.
By my right hand many an offering
Will be cut down for you before your altars."

                                   Aeneid 1. 314–334

The address-to-deity-in-disguise is a recurrent scene in ancient literature, with certain conventions attached. Those familiar with Homeric poetry will, however, recognize a specific precedent from the *Odyssey*, itself a clever parody of the standard encounter, Odysseus sweet-talking the young virgin, Nausicaa:

"Mistress: please: are you divine, or mortal?
If one of those who dwell in the wide heaven,
You are most near to Artemis, I should say —
great Zeus' daughter — in your grace and presence.
If you are one of earth's inhabitants,
how blest your father, and your gentle mother,
blest all your kin."

                                   Odyssey 6. 149–155

The emphasis here is on the hero's masterful manipulation of an innocent girl, turning her vulnerability to his own advantage. Against this backdrop, Aeneas appears distinctly at a disadvantage, uneasy rather than masterful — manipulating *this* female would not be easy, even if he wanted to.

The exchange continues. She denies her divinity, tells the history of Dido — about which more below — then asks about him; he begins to respond, she cuts him off and urges that he go to Carthage, then finally reveals herself:

> On this she turned away. Rose-pink and fair
> Her nape shone, her ambrosial hair exhaled
> Divine perfume, her gown rippled full length,
> And by her stride she showed herself a goddess.
> Knowing her for his mother, he called out
> To the figure fleeting away:
>   "You! cruel, too!
> Why tease your son so often with disguises?
> Why may we not join hands and speak and hear
> The simple truth?"
>
>   *Aeneid* 1. 402–409

Two more antecedents from the *Odyssey* surface here, both of them Odysseus talking to a disguised Athena, once as a young girl (*Odyssey* 7. 14–36), once as a young man (*Odyssey* 13. 221–310). In the first, Odysseus asks the virgin for information on how to get to the royal palace of the Phaeacians, and she complies, adding some advice on how to behave when there; in the second, the hero again asks for information, this time about his native Ithaka, which the goddess has also disguised so that he fails to recognize it. She tells him where he is, he responds with a lying story about his own history, and she shows her appreciation, praising his prodigious capacity for falsehood, for manipulating others with his intelligence, something that makes him a kind of mortal counterpart to her divinity.

The thrust of all these allusions is to portray Aeneas as tentative, slightly obtuse, even inept — far from the easy air of command that characterizes Aeolus, Neptune, and Jupiter. The moment of epiphany is particularly poignant. Instead of Odysseus' nimble falsehoods, admired even by a goddess, we have a man who realizes that his own mother, ordinarily the source of unfailing support for the hero, has been deceiving him — and not for the first time — apparently to no real purpose except her own amusement.

Not only is Aeneas presented, then, as less than masterful, he is also in an uneasy relationship with his own mother. Venus clearly cares for her son — she intervenes with Jupiter, she plots ostensibly to ease his way in the world — but finally, she is unreliable, she may trick him. Indeed, there is a very real sense of cruelty in her epiphany, and possibly even some flirting. All of this is consistent with Venus' essential nature as guileful goddess of love, but this is not just anyone she is playing with, and her behavior only emphasizes Aeneas' vulnerability in the role that the gods and fate have chosen for him—if he cannot count on his mother to tell him the truth, whom *can* he rely on?

Notice that Venus' impact on her son might not be entirely inconsistent with the tradition of the hero story. Both Gilgamesh and Achilles are helped by their mothers in ways that, though showing great love and loyalty, finally do not forward their progress toward maturity. Likewise, Venus' efforts to foster his romance with Dido might be seen as another case of the hero's mother giving him what he wants even though it might not be good for him: staying with Dido means forsaking his heroic mission; she is a "detaining woman," as Calypso and Circe are for Odysseus.

Against this interpretation run two countercurrents. First of all, Venus, above all other deities, is set on Aeneas fulfilling his heroic mission. She will send her other son, the god Amor, to enslave Dido—in her eyes the agent of Juno—precisely so that Aeneas will *not* fall prey permanently to her charms, so that she, Venus, will be able to control the outcome of the romance. And second, Virgil's use of the second-self motif throws, as I have said, real doubt on whether fulfilling his mission will help Aeneas to achieve spiritual integration. We may say, in fact, that Venus' treatment of Aeneas, far from showing a mother's special love for her son, is only an especially painful example of the indifference of the gods in the *Aeneid* toward the welfare of mortals. Here, as elsewhere, Virgil declines to resolve complexity.

What have we learned about Aeneas and his situation so far? He is on a heroic journey something like Odysseus', but different in that the Greek hero struggles to get back home, while he must leave home and found a new city, start a new life; the gods have a stake in how the mission comes out, giving the Trojans support or opposition accordingly; in particular, Juno opposes them, Venus works for them, though in a way that sometimes casts doubt on her motives; Aeneas himself struggles to carry out his assignment, but lacks the confident, self-assertive nature that usually characterizes heroes in this kind of story; indeed, the poet is at pains to show how Aeneas is unsuited to the role of masculine leader. Perhaps the most striking aspect of this portrait is the reluctance of Aeneas—he did not choose to lead the Trojans, and would rather have died at Troy. Passive rather than active, dutiful, not a troublemaker, he trudges along toward a future that does not hold out any prospect of personal satisfaction for him. Both Gilgamesh and Achilles hurt the community by their arrogant solipsism; Aeneas sacrifices himself to ensure the establishment of a community he will never even see.

Aeneas Enters Carthage

Into the life of such a man comes Dido. Aeneas and Achates, secreted away in a cloud of Venus' making that lets them see what is around them while going undetected, soon reach the outskirts of Carthage and find there a busy scene. The locals are hard at work building a city, enacting laws, choosing a senate. All are as busy as, Virgil tells us, bees, humming around in a field, and the sight evokes envy in the erstwhile hero: "How fortunate these are/Whose city walls are rising here and now" (*Aeneid* 1.437). Dido presides over what Aeneas hopes to achieve, a new, thriving city.

The two men proceed to the middle of the town, there to gaze at some arresting works of art, representations—Virgil does not say what kind—on the walls of a temple being built for Juno. There are images of the Trojans' own past, the war at Troy, Hector's death, even Aeneas himself in battle, all eliciting a complex response. Here is a fixed record of human suffering, transformed through art into something that can, in some way, nourish those who look at it:

> "What spot on earth,"
> He said, "what region of the earth, Achatës,
> Is not full of the story of our sorrow?
> Look, here is Priam. Even so far away
> Great valor has due honor; they weep here
> For how the world goes, and our life that passes
> Touches their hearts. Throw off your fear. This fame
> Insures some kind of refuge."
>
> *Aeneid* 1. 459–463

The import of this scene is elusive. Aeneas sees himself and his comrades as part of the heroic past, as *historical* figures. At the same time, they appear in a work of art, which, as I have said, transforms their suffering, raw and painful in the event, into something distanced, and this distance allows them to be nourished by their own suffering, to draw some comfort from it. But then Virgil seems, characteristically, to undercut the validity of the experience:

> He broke off
> To feast his eyes and mind on a mere image . . .
>
> *Aeneid* 1. 464

The Latin for "mere," *inanis*, is a favorite word of Virgil's, and is often translated "empty," denoting something that contains nothing nourishing. So the existence of Aeneas and his past is rendered problematic—can history nourish in any form? Are its lessons only a mirage? Does art provide a valid perspective on what it depicts, or is it inherently compromised in a way that makes it deceptive? What is said about Aeneas' judgment here? Is he once again deceived? Virgil provides many more questions than answers, but the issues raised here, the meaning of history, the role of art, will surface again as a part of the portrait of both Aeneas and Dido.

Dido and Her Antecedents

As they gaze, Dido appears:

> Now, while these wonders were being surveyed
> By Aeneas of Dardania, while he stood
> Enthralled, devouring all in one long gaze,
> The queen paced toward the temple in her beauty,
> Dido, with a throng of men behind.
>
> As on Eurotas bank or Cynthus ridge
> Diana trains her dancers, and behind her
> On every hand the mountain nymphs appear,
> A myriad converging; with her quiver
> Slung on her shoulders, in her stride she seems
> The tallest, taller by a head than any,
> And joy pervades Latona's quiet heart:
> So Dido seemed, in such delight she moved
> Amid her people, cheering on the toil
> Of a kingdom in the making. At the door
> Of the goddess' shrine, under the temple dome,
> All hedged about with guards on her high throne,
> She took her seat. Then she began to give them
> Judgments and rulings, to apportion work
> With fairness, to assign some tasks by lot . . .
>
> *Aeneid* 1. 494–508

Once again, allusions layer the scene with meanings. Dido is clearly a commanding figure, giving laws and assigning tasks, like the queen of the Phaeacians, Arete, whom Odysseus meets in book 7 of the *Odyssey* after his encounter with her daughter, Nausicaa. Virgil's simile adds to the air of authority, comparing Dido to the austere virgin goddess of the hunt. But the simile also echoes closely Homer's comparison of Nausicaa and her maiden friends to Artemis and her band of virgins in book 6 of the *Odyssey*, just before they meet Odysseus, the handsome hero who has appeared unexpectedly on the shore near them after surviving a storm sent by a deity. Regal, even godlike, Dido also has, Virgil suggests, a certain naivete that will make her vulnerable to the hero appearing suddenly from the sea.

This vulnerability has its analog in yet another paradigm, the young virgin Medea, overwhelmed by Eros' power and Jason's beauty, in the Hellenistic poem by Apollonios of Rhodes, the *Argonautica*. Virgil refers frequently to the meeting and subsequent tryst of Jason and Medea in his portrait of Dido and Aeneas: Aphrodite and Athena plot together to have Medea fall in love with Jason, sending the boy Eros to infect her with passion for the visiting hero; Hera covers Medea's hometown with a mist so that Jason and his henchmen can approach with impunity; the assignation takes place in a cave; Medea herself is conversant with magic; Jason will finally desert Medea, though this part of the legend is beyond the scope of Apollonios' poem, and Virgil alludes instead, as we will see, to Euripides' version of this part of the story.

To this dense amalgam Virgil adds one more layer. The landing near Carthage of the Trojans in their battered ships is modeled on the visit, in book 10 of the *Odyssey*, of Odysseus and the remnants of his crew to the island of Circe, witch goddess, who turns the advance party of Greeks into pigs. Odysseus, protected by a special charm from the gods, resists the spell and subdues the witch by drawing out his sword. Circe immediately capitulates, offers sex, and the Greeks spend a pleasurable year on the island before sailing on toward Ithaka. Complementing what Venus has told us there now swirls around Dido when we meet her another dizzying package of traits, covering a wide range of roles traditionally associated with women by the ancient Mediterranean cultures: virgin, witch, queen, goddess—maybe even *mother*, in that Venus is disguised, we remember, as a virgin huntress. The allusions also prime the reader for the meeting to come, forecasting pleasure and success for Aeneas, a somewhat less promising future for Dido. Aeneas, like Odysseus and Jason, is "charmed," thanks to the interventions of Jupiter and Venus; he will spend a pleasant vacation with the queen and then press on toward his destination. Dido, like Nausic Arete, and Circe, will be left behind. Against this traditional background, Virgil paints a strikingly unique portrait of the hero's interlude in Carthage.

The Hero's Epiphany

The other Trojans have their own advance party, the crew of a ship blown off course and separated from the main group. They approach the queen just after she arrives, and are observed by the still-invisible Aeneas and Achates. The vantage point affords Aeneas the opportunity to listen in secret to both his lieutenant's description of him and Dido's response. Both prove heartening: Aeneas is admired by his men, famous among the Carthaginians. Dido, meanwhile, shows none of the Circean trickery we might expect. On the contrary, she is apparently welcoming and open—Mercury has done his work — even going so far as to offer half of her new kingdom to the Trojans. So far, none of the negative Homeric paradigms seem to be active.

Aeneas bursts on this scene precipitously. Achates remarks on how well things appear to be going, and then:

> He barely finished when the cloud around them
> Parted suddenly and thinned away
> Into transparent air. Princely Aeneas
> Stood and shone in the bright light, head and shoulders
> Noble as a god's. For she who bore him
> Breathed upon him beauty of hair and bloom
> Of youth and kindled brilliance in his eyes
> As an artist's hand gives style to ivory,
> Or sets pure silver, or white stone of Paros,
> In framing yellow gold.
>
> *Aeneid* 1. 586-593

We note here how the simile makes Aeneas into Venus' work of art, and recall the "mere pictures" on the bronze doors, with their ambiguous import. At the very least, Virgil makes us think about the *authenticity* of what Venus presents, and perhaps about the effect of her artifact on Dido — can the queen be nourished by the man she sees, or is it all empty?

Aeneas has greeted Dido, identifying himself, praising her generosity, and asking about her origins. She is stunned by the epiphany, but recovers to assure him that she knows the story of Troy's fall, then ends with another generous gesture:

> "Come, then, soldiers, be our guests. My life
> Was one of hardship and forced wandering
> Like your own, till in this land at length
> Fortune would have me rest. Through pain I've learned
> To comfort suffering men."
>   She led Aeneas
> Into the royal house. . . .
>
> *Aeneid* 1. 627-632

Dido's sympathy and good will are evident, and yet Virgil still hedges: the invitation into the palace and feasting echo Circe's welcome to the doomed sailors who become pigs.

Aeneas, an anxious parent, sends Achates to fetch his son, Ascanius, while he and the rest proceed within. At this point, Venus intervenes again, snatching Ascanius away to hiding, substituting her other son, Amor, disguised. Her intentions toward Dido are malevolent in the casual way of deities: "brother Aeneas" has been tossed around on the seas by Juno, and

Dido may be her agent; why not trap the queen with her own passion, so she can be kept in line? Amor, Venus goes on to say, must impersonate Ascanius, worming his way into Dido's affections and infecting her with a powerful passion for Aeneas. Dido is to be a tool of Venus' ambitions for her son, one of many mortals to be sacrificed to the march of Rome's destiny. We wonder too at the maternal solicitude that prompts Venus to arrange a doomed love affair for her widowed son, lonely and vulnerable, because she wants to protect him.

Book 1 draws to a close with a great banquet in the royal palace. Amor does his work, making Dido forget her former spouse as she is increasingly drawn to Aeneas. Irony hangs heavy as the queen prays to the gods, Jupiter, Bacchus, and most ominously, "kindly Juno," to bless the festive event. The book ends with Aeneas preparing to tell the story of Troy's fall. The meeting of Dido and Aeneas has been carefully orchestrated within the story by the gods, from without by Virgil. We may pause to consider the implications of these elaborate preparations: what, if anything, have they to do with the motif of the second self?

Dido and the Second-Self Motif

We return to Dido's debut in the poem, the description of her history by Venus to Aeneas in their unsettling encounter before he reaches Carthage: she is the leader of a band of exiles, forced from their homeland by enemies, now settled in a new city that is flourishing under her guidance; she has lost a spouse she loved dearly, again through no fault of hers—indeed, the ghost of her husband came to her to urge flight. The resemblance to Aeneas' life is, of course, startling—book 2 will fill in some more details—and we wonder what Virgil's purpose is in presenting the hero with what is, in effect, a finished version of his own proposed mission. It may have something to do with Carthage's role as false candidate for a new Troy—book 3 will show us that Aeneas has been prone to err in this way. Dido, in this sense, embodies another false future for Aeneas. But this would not require such a detailed correspondence between the two characters. Dido's history is what it is because we are to compare her to Aeneas, and then to think about how she differs from him. She is to be a second self for the hero, representing parts of himself unrealized, holding out the prospect of a richer, more complete life. Like Enkidu and Patroclus, she will die as a result of her contact with the hero; that he cannot in turn complete the normal pattern of the motif by reintegrating what she represents is part of Virgil's meditation on the interaction between the larger forces of fate, history, and divine will on one side, and individual lives on the other.

Treating Dido this way marks a departure in more than one sense. The Carthaginian queen has usually been understood as another example of the "detaining woman," who keeps the hero from his true mission—the allusions to Homer support this—but not as representing a part of the hero. Virgil seems to be pushing the traditional contours of the hero story, and we wonder why, to what end. From our perspective, putting Dido in the role of the second self makes the entire sojourn in Carthage a central part of Aeneas' spiritual evolution—or lack of it. At the same time, the imperfect fit between Aeneas and his mission, hinted at earlier in the poem, is realized more concretely in Dido's death. It is not only she who is sacrificed on the altar of Rome's future greatness.

Dido is also the first example in the epic tradition of a second self of the opposite sex. Pursuing the implications of this innovation will raise some new issues, and will require rethinking some parts of the motif we have been exploring up to this point. Virgil takes pains, as we have seen, to bring the relationship between power and gender to the foreground early in the poem. In that context, Aeneas seems to be found wanting as a male leader. At the same time, Dido's conspicuous success as a leader would appear to run counter to the polarities suggested in book 1—is she a heroic creator of order from chaos, or a female bent on disruption? As is often the case in the *Aeneid*, the gods will finally decide the issue.

It might be objected that I am building an elaborate case for a heretical interpretation when Virgil provides a much more obvious candidate for the second self in "faithful Achates," who plays the role of Aeneas' sidekick throughout the poem. When Aeneas goes hunting to feed his men after the shipwreck near Carthage, Achates goes along to carry the weapons; venturing forth the next day to explore, Aeneas takes one man, Achates; the two enter Carthage incognito and watch the reception of the advance party side-by-side; when someone is needed to fetch the precious Ascanius, Achates is the man; Achates is the first to see Italy; walking fearfully into the underworld, Aeneas has Achates with him; later in Italy, Achates fights stoutly with his leader; throughout the poem, only Achates is called Aeneas' *comes*, "companion."

That Virgil means us to think of Achates as a special companion to Aeneas seems clear; whether he plays the role of the second self is less obvious. Achates is, in fact, a very opaque figure, doing errands and saying little. His presence in Aeneas' life and the role he plays there are never explained; his character is never developed so as to be complementary to Aeneas' in any significant way, and his relationship to the hero has none of the intensity we expect from the second self. And finally, Achates fails to do the one thing always required of the second self as I have defined it here: he does not die as the result of the hero's denial.

Dido, by contrast, fits the model we have been developing rather well.

We may explore this further by considering her role in the light of Keppler's categories.

1. *The first and second selves are not identical, but complementary; each possesses what the other lacks.*
Though Virgil urges us to see Aeneas and Dido as initially playing similar roles, they are not identical. At the same time, Virgil establishes her character rather vividly from the outset, making her strong presence potentially complementary to Aeneas' opacity. The complementarity of Aeneas and Dido is dramatized within the context of Virgil's preoccupation with power and gender, so that Dido's being a woman becomes an important part of her function in Aeneas' life.

2. *The intrusion of the second self cannot be entirely accounted for by "the facts."*
Dido's advent is, within the context of the story, the result of Juno's malevolence; her feelings for Aeneas are, in that same context, at least partly Venus' doing. She is a tool of the gods, as is Enkidu, and like him is used to fulfill aims unconnected to the second-self motif, which is imposed as an ideative structure from without. While Achates is simply there, Dido's entrance into Aeneas' life is carefully prepared.

3. *The second self always appears when the first self is most vulnerable to its influence.*
Dido appears at a critical time in Aeneas' life. We will learn in book 3 that just before the Trojans landed in Carthage, Aeneas' father died. The hero is now bereft of all those closest to him who might give advice and support—his first wife died at Troy, where he left all of his other relatives except for an infant son; his mother, though loving, is unreliable to say the least. At this moment, Dido comes into his life.

4. *There is an instant, strange, and inexplicable affinity between the two selves.*
Divine initiatives blur our consideration of Dido here. Both Jupiter and Venus intervene to secure her good will before she meets Aeneas. Certainly the first meeting between the two shows them to be powerfully drawn to each other.

5. *Whatever the feelings between the two, they are always* **intense.**
Again, Dido's behavior is affected from the start by divine influence, but the intensity of her feelings for Aeneas is clear from the start and grows throughout the first four books. Aeneas' feelings, on the other hand, are rarely shown to us. This latter trait is an issue in the working out of the second-self motif.

6. *The feelings and reactions of the first self are always in the foreground, those of the second in the background.*

The relationship between Aeneas and Dido does not fit easily into this category. Aeneas is, as we have said, remarkable among epic heroes for his relative lack of expressiveness—he is, in many ways, the least vivid of all the major characters in the poem. Dido's feelings are much more accessible to us than Aeneas', particularly in book 4, which is presented in great part from her perspective. On the other hand, one aspect of the "problem" of Aeneas that the second self might address is epitomized by his lack of definition in the story—by the time he reaches Carthage, he has lost everything which and everyone who could help to define who he is.

7. *The encounter with the second self is always at least potentially therapeutic.*

It remains for me to argue the relevance of this characteristic to the *Aeneid*. The clash between Aeneas' personal development and the requirements of his mission is central to my understanding of him. If Rome is to be founded, then Dido must be left behind (to her death). She embodies qualities that Aeneas lacks, or has lost touch with, and reintegrating these traits would, as I will argue, lead Aeneas to a higher level of spiritual wholeness.

And finally, as I have said, in the motif as we have been defining it here the second self must die in order to be integrated or reintegrated into the hero. At poem's end, Dido is long dead, killed as we expect by Aeneas' denial of his own essential nature. That Aeneas does not find Dido again is part of Virgil's unique realization of the motif.

Returning for a moment to Achates, we are left with a question: why does Virgil set up Achates in the role associated with the second self in earlier epic, and then underinvest the character? A companion to Aeneas in name only, Achates provides little except ready obedience. He resembles in this respect the Patroclus of *Iliad* 1–9, and never reaches any higher level, either of visibility in the poem or influence on the development of Aeneas. There is only so much we can do here, arguing from silence, but one explanation might be that by creating a hollow realization of such a standard figure in the hero story, Virgil only emphasizes how atypical both his hero and his story are: Achilles and Gilgamesh achieve a higher level of self-knowledge and self-acceptance from the intense relationship with a companion; Aeneas is not the same kind of hero, and must look elsewhere.

Another question: if Dido is a second self to Aeneas, what are we to make of the complex pattern of allusions Virgil uses to introduce her? Some of the allusions are to models that appear negative in their new context: naive Nausicaa, Circe the witch; Arete, wise queen of the Phaeacians, is more positive. And then there is Diana, austere goddess of the hunt, patroness of virgins, certainly no supporter of romantic liaisons between the sexes. Finally—and I do not insist on this—if the simile of Diana and her nymphs recalls Venus' false persona, then Virgil may, as I have said, even be suggesting something *maternal* about Dido in relation to Aeneas, a disquieting note, especially in light of the strained relations between Aeneas and his mother.

Note first of all that the allusions are all at the beginning of Virgil's portrait, before we know much beyond Venus' version of Dido's history. The effect is to prime us for the queen's appearance, to load up the character with significance even before she arrives. Given the mixed import of the allusions, we wonder too how we are to understand their relationship to the woman we see—are the allusions meant to foreshadow events? Are we to expect Dido to resort to witchcraft, to coquettish flirting? Or do the references imply qualities of character, in which case we might wonder which Dido will emerge, the shy ingenue or the commanding queen?

In the event, nearly all these attributes will surface in one way or another. Dido will resort to magic; though she is not, we suppose, a virgin, her innocent, open acceptance of the Trojans and especially their leader will be her undoing; at the end, she displays a vengeful anger toward Aeneas and a regret for her love of him that is true to Diana's example; and certainly Dido is noble throughout her story, playing out a fate that shows her to be not only regal like Arete, but tragic in a way that finally reminds Virgil of Sophocles' Ajax. The allusions at first seem contradictory, but as Dido lives out their promise, we see that they only mark a complexity of motivation and response to life that is true to the corresponding complexity of adult human beings.

One further element of Dido's portrait is germane to our particular project. As we recognize the import of the various allusions, we need also keep in mind that she is, before the Trojans ever arrive, programmed by the gods to be vulnerable to Aeneas. Though the allusions to Circe and Nausicaa portend the role of "detaining woman" for Dido, she is herself the tool of forces she never understands, is herself "detained" from completing the mission of founding and ruling over Carthage that she has begun so well. Likewise, the nobility and firm leadership so prominent as the Trojans approach will be overwhelmed by the combined powers of Jupiter, Venus, and Juno, so that she becomes another mortal sacrificed to the relentless surge of Roman fate. The manipulation of Dido by the gods, against the background of allusion, adds an ironic tonality to her portrait. The negative models are realized primarily as Dido descends, already destroyed by the gods, into suicidal despair; as we watch that final disintegration, what holds us is the use to which Dido puts some of her best qualities, nobility, courage, unflinching acknowledgment of the truth as far as she can see it. Admirably equipped to be a heroic creator and guardian of order, she is unwittingly, and to some extent unwillingly, made by the gods into an agent of disorder, all finally in the service of a yet higher cosmic plan.

The Hero's Past: Troy

But I anticipate. Aeneas becomes the narrator in books 2 and 3 of the
poem, telling to an already captivated Dido the story of his past, the fall of
Troy and the wanderings that brought the Trojans to Carthage. Again
Virgil works with a Homeric model, Odysseus entertaining the Phaeacians
with tales of his journey, and again we are struck by the difference in
temperament between the Greek and Trojan heroes. The former, faced
with monsters and dangerous women, escapes each time through his own
wit and skill, pressing on inexorably for home; Aeneas, by contrast, would
have preferred to stay and die in his home city, and must be prompted
more than once to take up the burden that the gods and fate have chosen
for him.

The story begins with the Trojan horse, how the Greeks fool the trusting
and good-hearted Trojans into accepting the lethal icon, how they fan out
into the city while their victims sleep innocently. Aeneas himself slumbers,
and is visited by the ghastly image of Hector, torn and bloody:

> "Ai! Give up and go, child of the goddess,
>   Save yourself, out of these flames. The enemy
>   Holds the city walls, and from her height
>   Troy falls in ruin. Fatherland and Priam
>   Have their due; if by one hand our towers
>   Could be defended, by this hand, my own,
>   They would have been. Her holy things, her gods
>   Of hearth and household Troy commends to you.
>   Accept them as companions of your days;
>   Go find for them the great walls that one day
>   You'll dedicate, when you have roamed the sea."
>   *Aeneid* 2. 289–295

Here is the mission, stated plainly. The greatest of Troy's defenders has
given up, sees that Troy is doomed, and urges flight in order to save something of the civilization. With this sanction, there would be no shame in
fleeing, one supposes. Aeneas does the opposite:

> "To arm was my first maddened impulse — not
>   That anyone had a fighting chance in arms;
>   Only I burned to gather up some force
>   For combat, and to man some high redoubt.
>   So fury drove me, and it came to me
>   That meeting death was beautiful in arms."
>   *Aeneid* 2. 314–317

He plunges into the burning city, reckless in the face of certain death,
urging his companions to a heroic last stand:

> "Soldiers,
> Brave as you are to no end, if you crave
> To face the last fight with me, and no doubt of it,
> How matters stand for us each one can see.
> The gods by whom this kingdom stood are gone,
> Gone from the shrines and altars. You defend
> A city lost in flames. Come, let us die,
> We'll make a rush into the thick of it.
> The conquered have one safety: hope for none."
>
> *Aeneid* 2. 348–354

Pursuit of heroic death takes Aeneas to Priam's palace, there to see the old king butchered by Achilles' degenerate son, Pyrrhus. Horrified, anxious about his own family, alone, he suddenly sees Helen, and is determined to kill her. A second supernatural intervention dissuades him: his mother appears to add her voice to those urging flight. Venus, like Hector, knows the future—Troy is finished and any effort to save the city is in vain. To convince her son, she allows him a rare glimpse at the world as from the perspective of a god. Now he can see that other deities are busy toppling the city, that it is the gods who finally will raze the citadel. The strategy is effective, turning the maddened hero around.

Aeneas rushes to protect his family, Anchises, his aged father, his wife, Creusa, and infant son Ascanius. But Anchises, like his son, refuses at first to leave the city, preferring to stay and die at home. Aeneas' fragile resolve is shaken again—he will go back to fight rather than leave his father, making a last ditch, futile stand against the Greeks. His foot is on the threshold when Creusa plays her trump, holding up the infant Iulus (another name for Ascanius)—what will become of *him* after Aeneas dies? Before he can decide, the gods again prompt their reluctant hero, sending a miraculous portent, harmless flames shooting from the boy's head. Anchises, joyful but cautious, prays to Jupiter for further confirmation and is rewarded with a shooting star. This is enough; Anchises is converted and will leave Troy. Released, the family struggles toward the city gate, Aeneas carrying Anchises on his shoulders, holding Iulus by the hand, Creusa (ominously) following behind.

Creusa disappears, separated from the rest in the chaos of burning Troy. Leaving his family and some other exiles in a secluded spot outside the city, Aeneas plunges back into the flames one more time. The journey is literally hellish—Virgil would now have us see Troy as akin to the dark underworld, Creusa as Eurydice to Aeneas' Orpheus—and Aeneas sees for the last time the smoldering ruins of his former life. Once more a supernatural visitation brings him up short: his worst fears are confirmed as the ghost of Creusa looms before him. Aeneas' wife, like all the others, urges flight. She too knows the future, that her husband is fated to found a new civilization, to remarry in Italy. He reluctantly takes up his duty

again, but not before a poignant last attempt to touch what he has already
lost:

> With this she left me weeping,
> Wishing that I could say so many things,
> And faded on the tenuous air. Three times
> I tried to put my arms around her neck,
> Three times enfolded nothing, as the wraith
> Slipped through my fingers, bodiless as wind,
> Or like a flitting dream.
>
> *Aeneid* 2. 790–794

Creusa is the first of many loves that Aeneas will have to forsake to
become the hero he would rather not be. The story Aeneas tells in book 2
serves many purposes. Within the frame of the poem, it further engages
Dido's sympathies, focussing on the pain Aeneas has already suffered; Virgil, meanwhile, is able to deepen the portrait of Aeneas, giving evidence of
his hero's courage and patriotism in a less compromised milieu than book
1, and also underscoring again how little enthusiasm Aeneas has for his
mission; we, finally, come upon a man hardly recognizable from book 1,
passionate, expressive, a natural leader, and ask ourselves what happened
in the interim.

At least part of the answer to our question is offered in book 3, Aeneas'
version of the journey from Troy to Carthage. But before going further,
we may pause to observe how Virgil develops and rather complicates
the polarities associated with gender in book 1. The Trojan horse at first
seems to be associated with things female, pregnant as it is with lethal
progeny. But when it is brought into the city, the image is of sexual inter-
course, with the horse in the masculine role: So we breached the walls/
And laid the city open" (*Aeneid* 2. 234). Later, Pyrrhus, the incarnation of
overbearing masculinity, forces the doors to the inner recesses of Priam's
palace:

> Pyrrhus shouldering forward with an axe
> Broke down the stony threshold, forced apart
> Hinges and brazen door-jambs, and chopped through
> One panel of the door, splitting the oak,
> To make a window, a great breach. And there
> Before their eyes the inner halls lay open,
> The courts of Priam and the ancient kings,
> With men-at-arms ranked in the vestibule.
> From the interior came sounds of weeping,
> Pitiful commotion, wails of women . . .
>
> *Aeneid* 2. 479–488

The word translated as "courts" here is *penetralia*, also used to describe the insides of a human being — this is a rape. Now we rethink the association of masculinity with order, as Virgil seems to be showing us another side of male power, one that might be seen as part of a larger plan — the fall of Troy as the prelude to the founding of Rome — but which certainly disrupts an order associated in the immediate context with females. There are orders and orders, Virgil seems to be saying, not all preserved by males, not all disrupted by females. The poet will reinvoke all of these images, along with their ambiguous import, in book 4 at the moment of Dido's death.

The Hero and His Father:
The Role of Anchises

Book 3 is not the most engaging part of the poem — Virgil's gestures to his Homeric antecedent provoke some rather grotesque adventures with monsters. From our perspective, two things stand out: first, a general air of misapprehension, false starts at founding a new city, the misreading of prophecies, and second, the prominence of Anchises. Though Aeneas is the nominal leader of the expedition, it is Anchises who makes many critical decisions, who intercedes with the gods when trouble arises. Anchises gives the order to sail away from Troy, while his son weeps; when the Delphic oracle urges the Trojans to seek their "mother of old," Anchises interprets this (incorrectly) to mean that they should settle in Crete, then performs the sacrifice before they sail on; when, after the settlement in Crete fails, the household gods of Troy appear in a vision to Aeneas, telling him to seek Italy, he goes immediately to his father to report; the Harpies attack, and it is Anchises, not Aeneas, who prays to the gods for relief; another prophet has advice for the Trojans in Buthrotum, and delivers it to Anchises; Anchises is the first to recognize Scylla and Charybdis.

As he tries one abortive settlement after another, Aeneas leans on his father, and book 3 helps us understand Virgil's hero more clearly, how tentative, discouraged, vulnerable, and most of all alone he is by the time the expedition reaches Carthage. In the context of the traditional hero story, Aeneas' dependence could be seen as positive, in that fathers are normally the source of wisdom for their heroic sons. This aspect of the relationship will certainly be evident later when Aeneas visits the underworld. And the strong tradition of paternal authority within Roman culture also surfaces here. But finally there is also a disquieting aspect to Aeneas' dependence, in light of what we have seen of him in book 1. Passivity and unease in the role of leader are established in the poem's opening scenes as problems for Aeneas as he struggles with his assignment; book 2 shows us a different man, more passionate, more engaged; book 3 reverses this, as Aeneas is shown to be initially miserable, then tentative and confused, always ready to defer to his father when decisions are to be made. Aeneas is renowned within the story and in the literary tradition as a man admirable for his devotion to duty, for his willingness to serve his family, the state, and the gods. Books 1 to 3 support this, but also suggest a darker side to these qualities, showing him in situations where deference and dutiful allegiance appear less admirable. In Gilgamesh or Achilles, both in need of humility, the achievement of what Aeneas has in abundance is counted as gain; for the Roman hero, deprived of so much that defines him as a person, self-assertion, not self-effacement, is required. But the gods have plans for Aeneas that preclude what Gilgamesh and Achilles finally achieve.

The Second Self as Detaining Woman

Book 4 belongs to Dido. The voice in books 2 and 3 is, ostensibly, Aeneas'; as book 4 opens, Virgil is back, and invites us to observe the growing passion of the queen:

> The queen, for her part, all that evening ached
> With longing that her heart's blood fed, a wound
> Or inward fire eating her away.
> The manhood of the man, his pride of birth,
> Came home to her time and again; his looks,
> His words remained with her to haunt her mind,
> And desire for him gave her no rest.
>
> *Aeneid* 4. 1–5

There are few more noble or more poignant figures in ancient literature than Dido in the throes of her desire. Noble, in the dignity with which she faces her death, in the proud defiance and refusal to be humiliated; poignant, in the picture of such nobility destroyed, almost casually, to suit the jealous machinations of Juno and Venus. Vivid, fierce, powerful, Dido embodies what the denatured Aeneas might recapture—might, if Rome's destiny did not have a prior claim.

Dido struggles briefly against her passion, but when her sister urges her to pursue the pleasures of love and childbearing, she yields, haunting the shrines, reading entrails for favorable signs. Virgil now introduces a major metaphor in his portrait:

> Unlucky Dido, burning, in her madness
> Roamed through all the city, like a doe
> Hit by an arrow shot from far away
> By a shepherd hunting in the Cretan woods—
> Hit by surprise, nor could the hunter see

His flying steel had fixed itself in her;
But though she runs for life through copse and glade
The fatal shaft clings to her side.

Aeneid 4. 68–73

Characteristically, Aeneas is an unwitting agent of destruction. Not so Venus and Juno, who observe Dido's frenzy and calmly decide, each for her own reasons, to turn it to their advantage. The metaphor continues, as the two deities arrange for the lovers to take shelter from a storm in a cave during a hunt planned for the royal entourage and consummate the "marriage," as Juno cynically calls it — the stalking is now overt as the real hunters emerge.

That the two deities, ostensibly opposed in their goals, could move in concert is troubling. Venus is not fooled, we hear, by Juno's proposal, nor is she disinclined. Can this collusion really be in the interests of her son? Only in the long perspective of the gods, looking down the centuries toward the new civilization to be founded by Aeneas' descendants; more immediately, the liaison will bring yet more pain to Aeneas. Again, personal satisfaction is sacrificed to a larger plan; again, Aeneas' mother is a doubtful ally for him.

All is brightness and gaiety as the hunt commences. Dido, lingering in her chambers like a shy bride, emerges resplendent in gold and scarlet; noble Phrygian hunters and their eager horses crowd around; young Iulus takes it all in. But Virgil's attention is on Aeneas especially:

Above the rest, Aeneas walked to meet her,
To join his retinue with hers. He seemed —
Think of the lord Apollo in the spring
When he leaves wintering in Lycia
By Xanthus torrent, for his mother's isle
Of Delos, to renew the festival;
Around his altars Cretans, Dryopës,
And painted Agathyrsans raise a shout,
But the god walks the Cynthian ridge alone
And smooths his hair, binds it in fronded laurel,
Braids it in gold; and shafts ring on his shoulders.
So elated and swift, Aeneas walked
With sunlit grace upon him.

Aeneid 4. 141–150

The grand entrance and striking simile recall Dido's advent in book 1 — Virgil seems almost to be reintroducing his hero, to Dido and to us, in this heightened form. And notice that Aeneas plays the role of Apollo to Dido's Diana. The unusual nature of the two similes — no other mortal characters in the poem are compared so fully to deities — and the strongly marked contexts in which they occur suggest that they are to be taken together: divine siblings are an apt vehicle for representing the special relationship between Aeneas and his second self.

All proceeds according to plan. The tryst occurs with appropriately grand cosmic accompaniment: rolling thunder, lightning as nature's version of the marriage torch, nymphs singing hymns from the mountains. At this charged and presumably joyous moment, Virgil interjects a dark note: "That day was the first cause of death, and first/Of sorrow" (*Aeneid* 4. 169–170). We are reminded of a parallel from the *Iliad*, when Achilles sends Patroclus to inquire after the wounded Machaon:

> At once he spoke to his own companion in arms, Patroklos,
> calling from the ship, and he heard it from the shelter, and came out
> like the war god, and this was the beginning of his evil.
>
> *Iliad* 11. 601–603

Like Patroclus, Dido will be destroyed by the fellow mortal closest to her. But here there is a difference: Achilles sends Patroclus into battle knowingly, to serve his own pride; Aeneas "kills" Dido because the gods intervene to drive him away from her, and he knows nothing of her death until long after the fact.

Virgil presents the aftermath of the assignation rather obliquely. Dido, we are told, calls it marriage, and has no qualms about the liaison being known. Enter Rumor, a personified goddess in Virgil's pantheon, an evil deity who thrives on motion and spreads truth and lies indiscriminately:

> In those days Rumor took an evil joy
> At filling countrysides with whispers, whispers,
> Gossip of what was done, and never done:
> How this Aeneas landed, Trojan born,
> How Dido in her beauty graced his company,
> Then how they reveled all the winter long
> Unmindful of the realm, prisoners of lust.
>
> *Aeneid* 4. 189–194

What is true and what false remains unclear. Rather, the emphasis is on the destructive consequences: one Iarbas, a disgruntled suitor of Dido's, complains to Jupiter of how the effeminate newcomer, a match for Paris in his foppery and his stealing of women, has usurped him in Dido's affections. The prayer reaches Jupiter, who immediately sends Mercury to dislodge Aeneas: he is not living up to his mother's promises; the fate of Rome demands he leave at once, to become the ruler of Italy, to father men to bring the whole world under Roman law; if this stirring future cannot rouse him, what of his duty to his son? Aeneas is to sail for Italy, now.

Divine will has been fragmented up to now in regard to Aeneas' stay in

Carthage, Juno setting snares, Venus pretending to go along, but hiding
her own agenda. All that is swept aside by the father of gods and men:
Aeneas must go. Whatever enjoyment or benefit Dido offers is of no weight
on the scales with Rome's destiny. Notice too that the immediate impetus
behind Iarbas' prayer is sexual jealousy: the momentum from the judgment
of Paris persists.

Mercury finds Aeneas in a telling situation:

> Alighting tiptoe
> On the first hutments, there he found Aeneas
> Laying foundations for new towers and homes.
> He noted well the swordhilt the man wore,
> Adorned with yellow jasper; and the cloak
> Aglow with Tyrian dye upon his shoulders—
> Gifts of the wealthy queen, who had inwoven
> Gold thread in the fabric.
>
> *Aeneid* 4. 259-264

Here is a glimpse at what might have been: Aeneas becoming a city-builder,
but sharing the role and the city with Dido. Details of dress are crucial to
the meaning of this vignette. The decorated sword, the colorful cloak with
its gold inlay, all place Aeneas in the role of exotic *Easterner*, the kind
of male that could make Romans—particularly those enamored of sturdy
Roman virtues—uneasy. Iarbas represents this attitude taken to a negative
extreme, as will Aeneas' Italian opponent, Turnus. And notice that Virgil is
careful to identify the clothing as a gift from Dido—this new, more expansive version of the hero reflects his winter with her. Aeneas seems at this
moment to be emerging from the passive, anxious, lonely man who landed
at Carthage, evolving, apparently under Dido's influence, into someone
more active and assertive.

Mercury crushes this chrysalis with brutal dispatch:

> "Is it for you
> To lay the stones for Carthage's high walls,
> Tame husband that you are, and build their city?
> Oblivious of your own world, your own kingdom!"
>
> *Aeneid* 4. 265-267

If Aeneas is not ashamed for his own honor, the god says indignantly, let
him think of Iulus, to whom the rule of Italy is due. Jupiter's priorities are
clear: Aeneas is not on a journey to build any city, he is to found Rome;
this is not about his personal happiness or anyone else's (even Iulus'), but
about the working out of a national destiny. Mercury is a messenger, and
delivers his message forcefully. But he also adds his own touch, calling
Aeneas *uxorius* in Latin, picking up the contemptuous tone of Iarbas: not

only is Aeneas failing to carry out his mission, he is also becoming soft, letting himself be ruled by a woman!

Encounters with deities are always unsettling, and sometimes frightening, but Aeneas' reaction is striking even in this context:

> Amazed, and shocked to the bottom of his soul
> By what his eyes had seen, Aeneas felt
> His hackles rise, his voice choke in his throat.
> As the sharp admonition and command
> From heaven had shaken him awake, he now
> Burned only to be gone, to leave that land
> Of the sweet life behind.
>
> *Aeneid* 4. 279–282

The new self on display for the instant before Mercury spoke has been blasted out of existence by Aeneas' fear. From now until the end of the poem, he will rarely look back, and never reach again for the "sweet life." The violence of this shift has not, I think, been properly appreciated by students of the poem; its implications for the motif of the second self are profound.

The Lost Aeneas

We have seen that the second-self motif is characteristically realized within the context of other themes. We have also seen how prominent Virgil makes the relationship between power and gender in book 1 of his poem. The particular nature of the encounter between Mercury and Aeneas brings the second-self motif into the orbit of this relationship, focussing several crosscurrents of imagery into a new configuration. Dido has been established at this point as at least potentially a second self for Aeneas, while he has been shown to be uneasy in the role of masculine authority figure that the gods have chosen for him. And he is uneasy in part because, it would appear, he cannot assume the calming air of command over disorder—and disorderly women—that characterizes Aeolus, Neptune, and Jupiter. Now we find him, in the aftermath of his tryst with Dido, assuming a more commanding, less tentative role, finally becoming the agent of order required by his situation. But this new version has some troubling—to Jupiter, Mercury, and Iarbas at least—characteristics: a certain exotic, even foppish air, and, it would appear, a rather excessive accommodation of his *wife's* culture.

What we see here is the beginning of what would be, in our perspective, a reintegration by Aeneas of the qualities within himself that Dido represents. First of all, a more active and more creative response to the world— Aeneas as Mercury finds him resembles no one more closely than Dido in her first appearance in the poem, presiding over the creation of a new civilization, actively directing and shaping the emerging society; second, a more balanced mix of masculine and feminine, a middle ground between the wildly emotional, subversive behavior of Juno and Venus and the excessively unemotional, almost tyrannical masculinity of Jupiter, Neptune, or Iarbas.

It is tempting, though perhaps perilous given the brevity of this vignette, to see the first new trait, a more active stance, as a product of the second. That is, by acknowledging and accommodating a feminine part of himself, Aeneas taps into energies previously unavailable to him, can be more assertive because he is more at home with himself. Such an interpretation would parallel a modern psychological metaphor, the confrontation by a man of what Jung calls the anima, or "soul-image," a representation, like the Shadow, of archetypal material from the unconscious. Typically, the anima, a personification of unrealized feminine part of a man's unconscious, and reflecting the influence of the first important woman in his life, his mother, is projected onto a woman by the conscious mind, so that a man may choose to pursue as a partner a woman who corresponds to the character of his own unconscious femininity. Being able to accept the anima on the conscious level produces an access of creative energy, as a man taps resources of which he was previously unaware. So Aeneas is drawn to Dido as a projection of his own unconscious femininity—and maybe that of his mother, thus the correspondence between the Diana simile and Venus' disguise—and his brief appearance as city-builder represents the creative realization of parts of himself previously untapped.

But there is a difficulty in pushing this modern metaphor very far, in that Jung differentiates between the confrontation of the Shadow and of the anima, making the former a prerequisite for the latter. There is certainly no significant Shadow figure, the integration of which precedes that of Dido, in the *Aeneid*. So if we insist on Dido as anima, then we have a hero who violates the procedures of the analyst, skipping the first step in Jung's four-step process of self-realization. While Virgil is representing something we are now used to describing in the language of psychology, the confrontation of submerged parts of the self as yet unrealized, it seems best not to invoke a modern schema that, though suggestive, requires the imposition of an elaborate template that does not fit the poem very comfortably.

To suggest that a hero reaches a higher level of spiritual development by acknowledging and integrating aspects of himself objectified in a woman may seem a heretical notion in the epic tradition. But Virgil is merely pushing further an element of the second-self dynamic already present, if underplayed, in the Gilgamesh epic and the *Iliad*. Both Enkidu and Patroclus represent in various ways qualities that could be associated, in the cultures out of which the poems emerged, with femininity: Enkidu's long hair and connection to the rhythms of nature, Patroclus' compassion and honoring of attachment.

At the same time, the physical expression between Aeneas and Dido of the erotic potential in the second-self relationship complicates matters. Here we need to be careful not to import our modern notions of romantic love into an alien milieu. Since the nineteenth century at least, the idea that men and women may find a spiritual fulfillment through sexual relations has gained considerable acceptance. This idea was not so prominent a part of Virgil's culture, which often made a clear distinction between, say, the devotion of married couples to each other and sexual attraction. Dido and Aeneas have a physical relationship and presumably this bond creates its own dimension of intimacy. But from our perspective here, Dido is important primarily because of the potential self that she holds up to Aeneas, not because she offers sexual fulfillment.

As usual, we run the risk of being reductive in making these kinds of distinctions when thinking about Virgil's poetry. The boundaries between sexual intimacy, romantic love, and spiritual integration are blurred enough at any time in any context, and Virgil is not adverse to a certain opacity where earlier poets have been limpid. Allowing ourselves to speculate nevertheless, what we may see in the relationship of Aeneas and Dido is that rarity in ancient literature, a man and woman who love each other physically but also as do Achilles and Patroclus or Gilgamesh and Enkidu, having a bond encompassing not only physical sexuality, not only respect and affection, but also a merging of souls usually reserved for the bonds between men in the heroic literature of antiquity.

But if Aeneas has already begun to integrate the qualities that Dido represents before Mercury arrives, then we have a significant departure from the dynamic of the second self as we have been defining it. In previous versions, there is a central paradox: the second self must die before the qualities he represents are available to the hero, the death itself resulting from the hero's denial of traits in himself that the second self held up to him. There follows then further denial, characterized by a journey into darkness, understood on one level as a retiring into the deepest recesses of the unconscious, often represented as a trip to the underworld. Out of this latter journey comes a new perspective and understanding, which in turn allows for the reintegration of the qualities of the second self.

Much of this process appears to be present in the *Aeneid*: Dido will die, Aeneas will travel to the underworld and learn new things, and yet no reintegration occurs, no spiritual wholeness is achieved: the "sweet life" that Dido held out is gone forever. As with Achates, so here the form is not realized as we would expect. And here too the reason lies in the peculiar nature of Virgil's hero: Aeneas is on a heroic mission, but the energy fueling the journey comes not from him, but from the gods. Rather than being a problem for the divine order because he is too assertive, pushing against the normal bounds of human existence, he is instead not aggressive enough, not masculine enough, not driven to achieve the goals the gods have chosen for him—so it is that the second selves in the poem are more vivid and active than the hero; the denial of Dido and what she represents is not Aeneas', but the gods'—denial is driven by the impulse to heroism, and in the *Aeneid* this comes from the gods, not the hero—and what Aeneas will learn in the underworld is not about himself, but about his part in a larger plan to which his own self is systematically sacrificed.

The Death of the Second Self

Mercury wafts away, and the Aeneas that might have been is dead—how dead is evident in the gruesome exchange between himself and Dido that follows. The queen has discovered Aeneas' secret preparations to leave, and true to her bold character, confronts him in a powerful speech, veering between abject pleading and bitter denunciation. It would be difficult to give a satisfactory answer to this magnificent soul-baring, but Aeneas' attempt is hideously inadequate by any standard. Attempts have been made to rehabilitate Aeneas, to uncover hidden messages of love and support for Dido, but in the end these arguments seem contrived, and cannot stand up to the brutal weight of what he says. He begins stiffly, granting his love for her but then moving on quickly to a repellent set of arguments, tricked out with rhetorical flourishes: *he* never called it marriage, and in any event if fate had permitted him to do what he wanted—now we expect some concession to Dido's feelings, and are even more stunned by what follows—he would never have left Troy; now he must go to Italy: "there is my love, there is my country"—if she is so fond of Carthage, why does she begrudge him *his* new lands? He finishes with mention of his responsibilities to Ascanius, the frightening message of Jupiter, and finally with a plea:

> "So please, no more
> Of these appeals that set us both afire.
> I sail for Italy not of my own free will."
>
> *Aeneid* 4. 360–361

The final lines seem to make some concession to her feelings, but given what he has just said, not a very large one.

Virgil has a model for Aeneas here, Jason in Euripides' *Medea*, who tries to explain to his foreign wife why he must abandon her in favor of a more politically advantageous marriage. As it happens, Aeneas too will make a dynastic marriage in Italy, to a woman he does not know or care about, as far as we can tell. But once again the contrast is between the Greek hero, self-confident, and self-important, looking out for himself at all costs, and Aeneas, who has just been told that he may not attend to himself in any way that impedes the destiny of Rome, a city he will never see. Self-knowledge is at least partly the product of observed choice: I am, it appears, the sort of

man who chooses *this* over *that*, and so forth. Aeneas, since he left Troy
and everything that helped define him, has rarely been allowed to choose
according to his own wishes, and, when he has, the gods have intervened to
smash any satisfaction that might have followed. Perhaps Aeneas' speech is
not so hard to understand if we see it as the desperate improvisation of a
man who has lost all track of who he is.

As Aeneas fades, Dido grows yet more vivid. Her reply to him is more
searing than her first attack. No pleading here, no concessions, only curses,
promises to haunt Aeneas after her death. The opening verses recall
Patroclus' angry denunciation of Achilles, reminding us perhaps of the
parallels between the two as second selves:

> "No goddess was your mother. Dardanus
> Was not the founder of your family.
> Liar and cheat! Some rough Caucasian cliff
> Begot you on flint."
>
> *Aeneid* 4. 365–367

> "Pitiless: the rider Peleus was never your father
> nor Thetis was your mother, but it was the grey sea that bore you
> and the towering rocks, so sheer the heart in you is turned from us."
>
> *Iliad* 16. 33–35

Dido's angry words are her last to Aeneas. As she leaves, we see one final
glimmer of his feelings for her:

> Duty bound,
> Aeneas, though he struggled with desire
> To calm and comfort her in all her pain,
> To speak to her and turn her mind from grief,
> And though he sighed his heart out, shaken still
> With love of her, yet took the course heaven gave him
> And went back to the fleet.
>
> *Aeneid* 4. 393–396

Once closed, this door is never opened again; whatever Aeneas might have
been is lost. He hurries to obey the gods, but not fast enough. Mercury
appears to him in a dream, to frighten him once more and drive him out
of Carthage ignominiously, under cover of night. The god's last words
and Aeneas' response to them are true to the brutal indifference to Dido
and all she means to Aeneas that the gods have forced upon their chosen
hero.

> "Woman's a thing
> Forever fitful and forever changing."

*   *   *

> He pulled his sword aflash out of its sheath
> And struck at the stern hawser.
>> *Aeneid* 4. 569–570; 579–580

The rest of book 4 shows us Dido doing what Aeneas cannot do, choosing to die, to end her life on her terms, like the Greek tragic heroes she is modeled on. As she falls on Aeneas' sword, we think of Ajax, an association that will surface again in book 6. At the same time, Virgil makes the moment emblematic of her fundamentally compromised position:

> Amid these words her household people saw her
> Crumpled over the steel blade, and the blade
> Aflush with red blood, drenched her hands. A scream
> Pierced the high chambers. Now through the shocked city
> Rumor went rioting, as wails and sobs
> With women's outcry echoed in the palace
> And heaven's high air gave back the beating din,
> As though all Carthage or old Tyre fell
> To storming enemies, and, out of hand,
> Flames billowed on the roofs of men and gods.
>> *Aeneid* 4. 663–671

The simile tells us how important Dido is to Carthage, her creation: when she dies, it is as if the city were destroyed. But it also reminds us of her victimization. The obvious analog to the simile is Troy, the burning of which is still fresh in our minds, a city destroyed because its inhabitants were taken in by a fraudulent work of art, the Trojan horse. And the analog to *that* is Venus' deceptive work of art, Aeneas, who enters Carthage and destroys it from within. Now the sexual imagery in the description in book 2 of Troy's violation comes into play again. Carthage, embodied for the moment in Dido, is raped—remember that it is Aeneas' sword that kills the queen—by a destructive masculine force that serves a larger plan. Playing Dido's death against that background only reinforces the ambiguous nature of the imperatives generated by Rome's destiny; putting Aeneas in the role of the Trojan horse only emphasizes his own manipulation by the gods—he is an unwitting and unwilling tool for the destruction of a city he has helped to plan, a woman he loves, and finally, a version of himself.

Book 4 ends with one more illustration of Dido's inability to escape the imperatives of divine will. Mortally wounded, she cannot make the final passage to death. Now comes an intervention the inappropriateness of which can only be called grotesque:

> Almighty Juno,
> Filled with pity for this long ordeal
> And difficult passage, now sent Iris down

Out of Olympus to set free
The wrestling spirit from the body's hold.
For since she died, not at her fated span
Nor as she merited, but before her time
Enflamed and driven mad, Proserpina
Had not yet plucked from her the golden hair,
Delivering her to the Orcus of the Styx.
So humid Iris through bright heaven flew
On saffron-yellow wings, and in her train
A thousand hues shimmered before the sun.
At Dido's head she came to rest.
                                   "This token
Sacred to Dis I bear away as bidden
And free you from your body."
                                   Saying this,
She cut a lock of hair. Along with it
Her body's warmth fell into dissolution,
And out into the winds her life withdrew.

Aeneid 4. 693–705

The beauty of this passage may at first distract us from its horrors, but the final effect is to obscure the bold outlines of Dido's choice, to subject her one last time to the whims of the gods. She has been their puppet all through the encounter with Aeneas, and has never been allowed to know enough to protect herself.

The Meaning of Dido's Death

The destruction of one as worthy as Dido is painful enough to witness. But the motif of the second self plays another film for us simultaneously, the story of a man groping to recover himself in the ruins of his former life, reaching for a new and richer version of himself only to be torn away by forces beyond his power to understand or control. Virgil's use of the motif departs markedly from earlier versions, but the full impact of his innovation is only felt if we understand him to be working, as he always does in his references to earlier literature, against familiar norms. The outlines are, as we have seen, all in place: the hero is out of touch with some parts of himself; he confronts these qualities objectified in another person, his second self; denial follows from that confrontation, leading to the killing of the second self; this death is in turn followed by a journey into the darkness, out of which comes new knowledge.

In previous realizations of the pattern, as we have seen, a struggle is posited within the hero between the imperatives generated by traditional heroic values, success in competition with others, distinction from the rest of humankind as a result of this success, and so forth, and a different perspective reflecting a different set of values. This struggle is dramatized by the objectification of the new values, understood as being at least potentially a part of the hero, in a separate person, with whom the hero interacts. The drive toward traditional heroic goals comes, then, from within the hero, in turn fueling the denial that "kills" the second self and pushes the hero off into the darkness. The will of the gods is always prominent in these stories, generally as one of a set of imperatives against which the hero pushes defiantly until events bring him to a new attitude of acceptance. The "problem," in this way of telling the story, resides in the hero's hubristic unwillingness to accept limitations that are an unalterable part of the human condition; the solution entails adopting a new perspective, tempering the heroic drive by seeing oneself as part of a larger system, which in turn brings an appreciation not of how one is different from others, but of what one shares with them. It is, finally, the projecting outward of an inner, private struggle.

Virgil's great innovation is to locate the drive for heroic goals not in the hero, but in the gods, who in turn protect and forward the progress of a destiny that transcends any individual life, the fated founding of Rome. This fundamental shift generates an entirely new kind of struggle, an entirely new kind of hero, an entirely new realization of the second-self motif. Aeneas might, we suppose, have succeeded in reintegrating the qualities of his second self if the opposing drive for heroic achievement—the will to found Rome—had been a product of his own self, temporarily out of touch with the complementary traits of the second self. As it is, the heroic impulse is backed by forces that he is by nature unable to overcome or rechannel. The alternate self that Dido embodies is opposed as usual to the destructive heroic drive, but can never supersede it; the struggle of Aeneas for a richer life is over before it starts. The problem for Aeneas is not how to rechannel or temper his own self-assertion so as to live fruitfully in a larger community, but rather how to preserve any vestiges of a self while pursuing a mission on behalf of a future community that requires behavior contrary to his most fundamental nature.

The death of Dido ends Aeneas' first encounter with a second self—there will be no reintegration. Driven out to sea again, he is, for the moment, the dutiful servant of Rome's destiny. The price of this status has been another possible self, more assertive, more creative, happier. Now we wonder what is left, what sort of creature the gods have in fact sent off to found Rome.

5

Another Achilles:
The Aeneid *(2)*

Blessed are the solitary and the chosen, for you will find the Kingdom.

Gospel of Thomas 41

Book 5 opens with Aeneas characteristically torn:

> Cutting through waves blown dark by a chill wind
> Aeneas held his ships firmly on course
> For a midsea crossing. But he kept his eyes
> Upon the city far astern, now bright
> With poor Elissa's pyre.

Aeneid 5. 1–4

The gods have yanked him back on course, he holds to it firmly, but still he looks back. The tableau might well sum up Aeneas' behavior throughout the first four books, the picture of a man being slowly dismantled by his own admirable sense of responsibility and the imperatives of forces far beyond his control. Those forces, as we have seen, have a firm agenda, one that finally includes neither Dido nor the potential Aeneas that burns with her before his eyes. The heroic drive has, as usual, "killed" the second self, and our experience with the motif breeds further expectations: denial, realized through grief; journey into darkness; revelation; acceptance. All will appear in their time, but refracted through the prism of Virgil's unique vision of the hero's quest, so that nothing will be as we found it in previous realizations of the motif. Aeneas will grieve, but not for Dido; the gods, in whom the heroic will resides, will indeed push Aeneas further away from what Dido reflected back at him; they will drive him into the Underworld, they will, using Anchises, reveal deep truths; and Aeneas will, on some level, accept what is shown him. But none of this is about him or what he might become. Rather, it is about Rome, and what *it* will become.

Displaced Grief and the Second Self

Meanwhile, a "new" Aeneas, chastened by his encounter with Dido and with the gods, would seem to be on display—what sort of man is he? The second-self motif leads us to expect something *less* than the flamboyant co-regent seen building Carthage, someone diminished for the moment at least by his loss, and here again our expectations are met, but in a curiously skewed way. Book 5 is a relatively serene sequel to the preceding turmoil, an interlude before the momentous *katabasis* in 6; Aeneas too is quiet, tamped down, but not by grief for Dido—characteristically, he is unaware of her death, is unable to decipher the meaning of the distant flames. Into the space we reserve in our minds for Dido's funeral, Aeneas puts memorial games for his father, dead now one year. The displacement is revealing. Instead of grieving for Dido, and in the context of the second self absorbing and coming to accept what the lost self represented, Aeneas trains his feelings on an object more acceptable to the gods' agenda. Thinking about Anchises channels Aeneas' energies away from self-scrutiny and reengages his famous *pietas*—loyalty to family, the state, the gods—while at the same time priming him for the revelations to come in the underworld.

Virgil puts his Homeric precedent for book 5, the funeral games for Patroclus in *Iliad* 23, to excellent use. Achilles there is burnt out by grief for his lost friend; after the rampage and killing of the previous three books, the games provide some relaxing of tension, lowering of energy. As host for the games, Achilles is genial and low-key, focussing on what others do rather than his own agenda. The Iliadic games themselves have a parallel function in the larger context of the poem. The murderous and potentially tragic competition of the battlefield is recast in a safer milieu, the deadly struggle for dominance now denatured into athletic competition. This affords the chance to see the norms of heroic conduct in a more favorable light, to appreciate the importance of fair play, to share the victor's joy but avoid contemplating any lasting pain in the losers.

All of this applies to Virgil's games as well. The drive for dominance, so corrosive in the world of battle, is here safely on display; Aeneas, like Achilles, is attentive to others rather than himself. But of course it all has a different meaning in this new context. Achilles takes a rest from the searing pain of losing Patroclus by putting on games that deflect the feelings onto new objects, but the games are at least in memory of Patroclus, and are preceded by a wrenching description of Patroclus' burning and Achilles' pain; Aeneas too in effect avoids pain by deflection, but his ignorance of Dido's death makes the gesture reveal not a conscious choice to turn from raw feelings, but an unwitting substitution of one grief for another. And the contrast in the *Iliad* between the aggressively solipsistic Achilles of books 20 to 22 and his later, more subdued self also has a new import when transferred to the Roman hero: being attentive to the feelings of others is a step toward humility and spiritual growth for the Greek hero; in Aeneas, already self-effacing to a fault, the same gestures signal only the prospect of spiritual renewal receding yet further into the distance.

Enlarging the Hero's World

Aeneas' retreat into ignorant opacity, significant in itself, also makes room for a new element in the story, Roman history. As the various contests unfold, names from the Rome of Virgil's time parade past, glorified by association with founding fathers:

> Mnestheus' eager oarsmen drove the Seabeast —
> Mnestheus of Italy he soon would be,
> From whose name came the clan of Memmius.
> Then Gyas captained the Chimaera, huge
> In length and weight, big as a town afloat,
> Which Dardan oarsmen in three tiers drove onward,
> Surging together at three banks of oars.
> Then he for whom the Sergian house was named,
> Sergestus, rode the great Centaur. Cloanthus,
> From whom your family came, Roman Cluentius,
> Rode in the sea-blue Scylla.
>
> *Aeneid* 5. 116–123

Similar advertisements appear sprinkled throughout the games, capped by an equestrian finale performed by Trojan boys under the leadership of Ascanius. This latter exercise is generally thought to be Virgil's attempt to provide an origin for an old ceremony reinstituted by the emperor Augustus, the *lusus Troiae*, "Trojan Games." As the maneuvers draw to a close, their later "history" is made explicit:

> This mode of drill, this mimicry of war,
> Ascanius brought back in our first years
> When he walled Alba Longa; and he taught
> The ancient Latins to perform the drill
> As he had done with other Trojan boys.
> The Albans taught their children, and in turn
> Great Rome took up this glory of the founders.
> The boys are called Troy now, the whole troop Trojan.
>
> *Aeneid* 5. 596–602

This sort of anachronism was probably a part of the genealogies of the *Iliad* as well, but we cannot know for sure, lacking any written information about the history of the period apart from the poem. As it is, we have perforce gotten used to reading the Homeric poems—and the Gilgamesh epic as well, apart from some speculation on the case for some kind of historical king named Gilgamesh—as an almost purely self-contained literary document, drawing on mythical patterns paralleled elsewhere, but divorced from the dynastic history of, say, the eighth century B.C. in Chios. Not so the *Aeneid*, because we know more Roman history, and because Virgil insists on reading that history back into the Aeneas legends, making it a part of the hero's burden. What does this new feature have to do with the motif of the second self? Primarily, it adds a new context for Aeneas' mission, one that further diminishes the prominence of the *hero's* personal evolution in favor of the progress toward *Rome's* founding and eventual glory. As Aeneas struggles along toward Italy, his acts and suffering appear in the long shadow cast backwards by Roman civilization. And because we know how it will all come out centuries later, what now happens to him in particular is further devalued. The images on Juno's temple in Carthage have already established Aeneas and his men as historical figures, their past recorded and preserved for the edification of those who follow; from now until the end of the poem, the focus will be on these men as forerunners of something destined to be realized centuries hence.

The Hero's Further Testing

While the men amuse themselves at the games, the women lament by the sea, worn out from wandering. Juno, seeing another opportunity to disrupt the march of fate, sends Iris down in disguise to urge the women to burn the ships and bring the search for a new Troy to an end in Sicily. The disguise is only effective momentarily, but the women give way to their longings anyway and set the ships aflame. Word reaches the men, Ascanius arrives first and denounces the burning, followed by Aeneas, who prays to Jupiter, who in turn sends rain to put out the fires. All but four of the ships are destroyed.

Notice the familiar pattern here: emotional females foster disorder, mobilizing in response the hierarchical chain of male authority which restores order. Notice too that the ultimate sources of order *and disorder* are divine—Juno, still angry, starts the process; Jupiter finishes it. Here, as so often in the *Aeneid*, mortals are manipulated by deities to serve ends they do not understand. This is itself is not peculiar to the *Aeneid* or even Roman literature—omniscient deities and mortals blind to their fate are a staple of Greek and Near Eastern literature. What is new, particularly in the tradition of heroic epic, is the degree to which movement is initiated by the gods, not by assertive mortals who provoke a divine response.

Also new is the prominence of Ascanius, now inserted in the male chain of authority. His high visibility in the midst of the crisis signals a change in his status. Barely one year before, he could be fondled in Dido's lap, a silent and inconsequential boy; now he assumes a position of authority over the women:

> First to act, Ascanius,
> As he had led his troop rejoicing, now
> Whipped on his horse to reach the mutinous camp—
> And winded trainers could not hold him back.
>
> "What unheard-of madness!" the boy shouted.
> "Where now, where do you intend to go?
> Poor miserable women of our city,
> Not the enemy, not the Argive camp,
> But your own hopes are what you burn! Look here,
> I am your own Ascanius."
>
> *Aeneid 5. 667–673*

The speech has no discernible effect on the situation, but serves notice that Ascanius has entered on his inheritance as a male. And as his son increases in stature, Aeneas' own position is rendered yet more problematical. As the story progresses, it will become clear that the future lies with Ascanius, not Aeneas, that the father is expendable in a way that the son is not.

Aeneas is again at a loss in the wake of this latest catastrophe:

> Aeneas had been stunned by the mischance
> And could not rest, turning this way and that
> Within him, coping with momentous questions:
> Should he forget the destiny foretold
> And make his home in Sicily, or try
> Again for Italy?
>
> *Aeneid 5. 700–703*

Nautes, "an older man," comes to his aid, advising him to leave in Sicily those who have no stomach for the rest of the journey, taking in the remaining vessels only those hardy enough to see it through. Sensible advice, but:

> . . . still
> Aeneas wondered, all the more torn between
> Anxieties of all kinds.
>
> *Aeneid 5. 719–720*

Only his real father will do, it seems. Anchises appears in a vision, seconds the advice of Nautes, and adds a further set of imperatives:

In Latium you must battle down in war
A hard race, hard by nurture and by training.
First, however, visit the underworld
The halls of Dis, and through profound Avernus
Come to meet me, son. Black Tartarus
With its grim realm of shades is not my home,
But radiant gatherings of godly souls
I have about me in Elysium.
To that place the pure Sibyl, after blood
Of many black sheep flows out, will conduct you.
Then you will hear of your whole race to come
And what walled town is given you. Farewell . . .

Aeneid 5. 730–738

Anchises calls Aeneas to the next stage in his mission; the interlude is over.

The entire episode of ship-burning may be seen as a replay of the poem's opening: angry Juno sending trouble, prayerful Aeneas at a loss, male deities intervening. That this pattern precedes a surge forward in the march of Roman destiny should not surprise us—we have seen how often heroic action in the *Aeneid* is driven by the imposition of male order on female disorder. At the same time, the repetition prompts reflection on Aeneas' performance as hero: has the suppression of Dido and what she embodied moved him closer to the kind of leader the gods require? The evidence is not encouraging. Faced with hard decisions, Aeneas is still immobilized by doubt, and must be prompted once again by father figures. On the eve of his great descent, he is not yet fully transformed into the instrument of divine will required for the assignment given him.

Nevertheless, Aeneas moves forward dutifully. He lays out yet another surrogate Troy, chooses his band of explorers, makes the requisite gestures to the gods, and sails, leaving another piece of his past behind. Book 5 closes with a telling vignette. Venus, seeing Juno's hand in the burning, anxiously approaches Neptune to arrange safe passage for the Trojans. Majestically calm as usual, he reassures her: the Trojans will reach Italy, with just one life as payment. As the ships slip quietly through the night, Palinurus the helmsman stays awake at his post while others sleep, the role usually reserved for heroes on the brink of decisive action—he is, at this moment, a surrogate for Aeneas, the man in control of the expedition. Though he fights gamely and will not let go of the tiller, Neptune's agent, Sleep—a deified abstraction—prevails, pushing him over the side to a quiet death, and the gods steer the ship. The last lines of the book show Aeneas back at the helm, steering we are told, though how he does so without a rudder is not clear. But then again, Aeneas is *never* really in control, and

Virgil's inconsistency may represent aptly the nature of the entire journey, the voyage of a hero who thinks he is steering when it is the gods who guide the ship.

The Hero's Journey into Darkness:
Preliminaries

Finally, as book 6 begins, the Trojans reach Italy. Here Aeneas will get to the business of securing a homeland, here he will prepare the way for Ascanius, founder of Alba Longa, the city from which in turn the settlement of Rome itself will proceed in the distant future. But first, the ultimate heroic adventure: a trip to the underworld. We have already seen how this kind of episode can figure in the evolution of the hero, taking him into a primordial darkness that may be understood in various ways. It is a journey to the land of the dead, and so can represent the hero confronting his own mortality; as a journey to inner darkness, it can be a macrocosmic version of the hero's delving into his own deepest recesses; and, in the context of the grieving process, it can allow the hero to follow a lost love as a way of postponing the final separation that death seems to present to survivors in the throes of grief. The first two metaphors suggest the opportunity to discover — or uncover — deep truths ordinarily hidden from mortals; the third serves the denial that characterizes the hero's response to losing the second self.

The presence of such a fertile construct dead center in the poem prompts curiosity: how will the metaphors be realized in the context of Virgil's unique revision of the heroic journey? Aeneas has already been driven away from one source of enlightenment, his own growth not being on the gods' agenda except as it prepares him to take up the burdens they have reserved for him. What then will be the nature of the truths imparted? How will the process of grieving be transfigured? The episode is carefully prepared — entry into the land of the dead demands extensive preliminaries. How these are presented reflects Virgil's ongoing thematic priorities, and here is where we begin to look for answers.

Aeneas, following his father's instructions with care as usual, seeks out Apollo's prophetess, the Sibyl. This remarkable creature lives in a cave near to Lake Avernus, a traditional entrance to the underworld. The cave is apparently part of a temple complex dedicated to Apollo by Daedalus, legendary Cretan artist and craftsman, who flew to Cumae — near the modern city of Naples — to escape punishment for helping either Ariadne and Theseus to flee the labyrinth and the resident Minotaur, or Pasiphae to indulge illicit lust for a bull. These latter two subjects are pictured in reliefs on the doors of the temple, along with the murder of Androgeos, Minos' son, an act bringing retaliation from the Cretan king in the form of a yearly sacrifice of Athenian youths to the Minotaur. As he did in Carthage, Aeneas pauses to look at these works of art, and we in turn pause to consider their import. The themes are dark: murder, blood sacrifice, unnatural lust leading to the birth of a monster. There is also, in the stories of Androgeos and Icarus, the common theme of fathers unable to help their sons. And finally, there is the central image of the labyrinth, dark and mysterious artifact with a deadly monster at its very core. The overall impact of all these various images is elusive, but certainly they provide a troubling overture for a trip into primordial darkness, ending with a meeting between father and son.

After appropriate sacrifices, the god draws near to his instrument:

> The Sibyl cried out:
> > "Now is the time to ask
> Your destinies!"
> > And then:
> > "The god! Look there!
> The god!"
> > And as she spoke neither her face
> Nor hue went untransformed, nor did her hair
> Stay neatly bound: her breast heaved, her wild heart
> Grew large with passion. Taller to their eyes
> And sounding now no longer like a mortal
> Since she had felt the god's power drawing near . . .
> > > *Aeneid* 6. 45–51

As the audience continues, Apollo's possession takes on a by-now familiar character. Aeneas prays to the god for guidance, but the response must be forced from the Sibyl:

> > But the prophetess
> Whom the bestriding god had not yet broken
> Stormed about the cavern, trying to shake
> His influence from her breast, while all the more
> He tired her mad jaws, quelled her savage heart,
> And tamed her by his pressure. In the end
> The cavern's hundred mouths all of themselves
> Unclosed to let the Sibyl's answers through:
> > > *Aeneid* 6. 77–82

Once again, the progress of destiny, of the heroic mission, requires the imposition of male order on female disorder. Apollo's breaking of the Sibyl is, from this perspective, aligned with the quelling of the winds by Neptune, the driving of Aeneas from the clutches of Dido—and perhaps the taking of Troy by the Greeks. After the prophecy, the nature of Apollo's intervention is even more explicit:

> These were the sentences
> In which the Sibyl of Cumae from her shrine
> Sang out her riddles, echoing in the cave,
> Dark sayings muffling truths, the way Apollo
> Pulled her up raging, or else whipped her on,
> Digging the spurs beneath her breast. As soon
> As her fit ceased, her wild voice quieted . . .
>
> *Aeneid* 6. 98–102

The imagery here is of horsebreaking, but sexual dominance is also im-plied—having stirred overpowering energies in the Sibyl for his own pur-poses, the god now channels the forces into an acceptable form. The strug-gle to preserve the male cosmic order continues.

Virgil seems here to be pushing the polarities of gender as they custom-arily appear in his story further than anywhere else in the poem so far: the Sibyl embodies the female potential for disorder in a particularly pure, almost savage form; the god's response is more explicitly repressive than anything we have yet seen. In one sense, this is only to be expected: the most momentous part of the male heroic mission requires a vivid and pow-erful envoi. But Apollo's violence has another dimension: because the Sibyl is to be not only Aeneas' adviser, but also his guide through the underworld, guaranteeing his safe passage to Anchises and the deep truths always avail-able to heroes when they make this journey, she must be broken to the proper perspective before the expedition departs, she must be Apollo's sur-rogate, not a renegade female.

Which brings us back to psychological metaphors. Jung and his followers have usually identified the female guide for a male hero as an anima figure, the projection of an archetype from the unconscious, embodying powerful images associated with femininity within the hero. One task of the process for males of *individuation*, as Jung called the evolution of adults into emotional and spiritual maturity, is to liberate the anima from the uncon-scious in such a way as to tap its creative powers. I have already suggested that Dido might be seen as corresponding to an anima figure for Aeneas, though this paradigm brings with it some knotty problems of interpreta-tion. In any event, the anima often appears as a guide in heroic journeys, especially those to the underworld. This is appropriate, in that such jour-neys have on their itinerary dark places in which the nonrational, intuitive nature of the anima would be especially helpful to the hero.

But not welcome to the male order in this poem—the parts of the hero to which the anima corresponds have been systematically repressed by Virgil's gods; the very order of the cosmos appears to rest on such repression. So we ask ourselves why Aeneas' guide is to be such a potentially ambivalent figure: can she lead the hero without tapping dangerous qualities unsuitable to the new kind of leader he must be—Dido, as we have seen, could not be trusted. There is, as usual with Virgil, no clear answer. We may speculate, however, that Apollo's repression has the effect of coopting the energies of the anima for ulterior motives, letting the female be a guide as long as she has been suitably disarmed—or realigned, perhaps. Because the Sibyl is Apollo's creature, she can be broken; Dido, heroic figure that she is, cannot, and so must be destroyed.

Circling back, we note the content of the Sibyl's prophecy, which is to serve as a kind of overture for the rest of the story:

> "You, sir, now quit at last of the sea's dangers,
> For whom still greater are in store on land,
> The Dardan race will reach Lavinian country—
> Put that anxiety away—but there
> Will wish they had not come. Wars, vicious wars
> I see ahead, and Tiber foaming blood.
> Simois, Xanthus, Dorians encamped—
> You'll have them all again, with an Achilles,
> Child of Latium, he, too, goddess-born.
> And nowhere from pursuit of Teucrians
> Will Juno stray, while you go destitute,
> Begging so many tribes and towns for aid.
> The cause of suffering here again will be
> A bride foreign to Teucrians, a marriage
> Made with a stranger.
>   Never shrink from blows.
> Boldly, more boldly where your luck allows,
> Go forward, face them. A first way to safety
> Will open where you reckon on it least,
> From a Greek city."

Aeneid 6. 83–97

The Odyssean part of the mission appears to be drawing to a close, to be replaced by some kind of replay of the *Iliad*—as he moves into the Italian future, Aeneas will simultaneously relive a Trojan past. Two aspects in particular of the prophecy tantalize: the "foreign bride," and "another Achilles"—the Latin text has *alius*, "another," with the Greek hero's name. The Sibyl, looking from her long perspective both backward and forward, creates for us two categories of being, the Foreign Bride, and the Achilles figure. Once created, these categories prompt us to look forward and backward as well. As he did with the references to Roman history, so here again Virgil offers a different perspective from which to view his story, generating a ripple of implications for our understanding of Aeneas.

Dido, to the gods a "detaining woman," to us a second self for Aeneas, now becomes in retrospect a counterpart of Helen, a woman foreign to the Trojans, though encountered on her own soil. Playing opposite her is Aeneas, an updated version of Paris. This latter persona is not new. Iarbas, we recall, has compared Aeneas to Paris, but his ravings could then be discounted as the distortions of a jealous man. Now Apollo himself weighs in, and we wonder whether the pairing signifies anything further. Could, for instance, Carthage be considered Aeneas' "home," destroyed by his own self-indulgence? Did Aeneas in any sense sacrifice the Trojans to his own desires? Neither of these questions is very helpful on the naturalistic level— Carthage is only a potential home for Aeneas; the Trojans are not noticeably harmed by the interlude—but both highlight the conflicting perspectives from which everything is viewed in the *Aeneid*. The gods see Aeneas as potentially harmful to the Trojans, his search for self-fulfillment keeping them from their destined new home, though we have another slant: we can see Carthage as a home for the Aeneas who might have been; Juno, meanwhile, would have Aeneas settle anywhere but Italy, while the rest of the gods cannot abide him anywhere else.

Looking forward, we wonder about the new bride. Will she threaten the destiny of Rome, will the gods destroy her too? And what of the other Achilles? Aeneas has already been in the role of Achilles, conducting the memorial games. But the new version is to be a native of Latium, suggesting that Aeneas is not the man the Sibyl at least has in mind. Instead, we expect this version to be hostile to the Trojans, not only another Achilles, but also part of another *Iliad*. If so, where will Aeneas fit in? As, presumably, the major Trojan protagonist, is he to be another Hector? Or perhaps Paris, destroying the new home he is to create? Answers, as usual, are scarcer than questions—Virgil uses Homeric models just as subtly in the last six books as in the first six. Aeneas, we will learn, can be at times Achilles, at others Hector, and even Paris again, depending on what the scene is and who is doing the casting. These shifting personae are the key to understanding Virgil's realization of the second-self motif in the second half of the poem.

Descent into the Past:
Dido's Abortive Return

All of this awaits the outcome of the *katabasis*, the pivot between past and future, Troy and Italy. Like the Sibyl's prophecy, Aeneas' journey into the darkness has a Janus-like quality, summing up and sometimes refiguring the past, previewing and preparing Aeneas for the rest of his assignment. The actual descent cannot in fact begin until Aeneas buries his former trumpeter, Misenus—cleaning up the past—and secures the Golden Bough, the mysterious talisman owed to Proserpina and available only to those fated to enter and return from the underworld—preparing the future. These done, and animals duly sacrificed, he begins, the Sibyl at his side.

Dreadful abstractions, Cares, Diseases, Old Age, Toil, Death, Sleep,

come first, then monsters, and on to the river Styx; now a crowd of pitiful
ghosts, denied crossing because they are unburied, and among them, Palinurus. Aeneas lingers to talk, but the Sibyl pushes him on, denying passage
to Palinurus. Now across the river, past those dead before their time, in-
fants, those falsely accused, suicides, and finally the "Fields of Mourning,"
where roam those whom "pitiless love" consumed. Among these, Dido—a
delayed reckoning is now at hand. The confrontation, if addressing a mute
ghost can be called that, is rich and suggestive, bringing to a close and
commenting on the entire relationship, all in a few lines.

Dido's farewell, like all of her previous appearances, is carefully prepared, embedded in a context that layers the scene with meaning. The
episode is modeled on Odysseus' encounter with Ajax in the underworld
(*Odyssey* 11. 543-567), when the Greek hero, enraged at losing a contest
for Achilles' arms, refuses to speak to Odysseus when the latter tries for a
reconciliation. Dido, we recall, has already been associated with Ajax in
her death scene, but now Virgil pushes the implications further. Ajax embodies the self-destructive aspect of Greek heroism in an especially stark
form. In contrast to the mercurial Achilles, Ajax in the *Iliad* seems massive,
slow but inexorable, a defensive bulwark rather than a swift pursuer. His
speech to Achilles in *Iliad* 9 captures his essence: short, blunt, sincere beyond question, and radiating a certain *austerity* alien to more expressive
heroes; the famous simile in *Iliad* 13, comparing his grudging retreat before
overwhelming numbers of Trojans to a donkey beaten by children, rounds
out the portrait. These qualities endured in Greek literature, so that Sophocles could make Ajax represent an old-fashioned heroism seen in the fifth
century B.C. as already outmoded, his suicide motivated by shame at appearing weak before his fellow warriors.

Seen through this lens, Dido's response to Aeneas' pleading takes on a
rich coloration:

> Aeneas with such pleas tried to placate
> The burning soul, savagely glaring back,
> And tears came to his eyes. But she had turned
> With gaze fixed on the ground as he spoke on,
> Her face no more affected than if she were
> Immobile granite or Marpesan stone.
> At length she flung away from him and fled,
> His enemy still, into the shadowy grove . . .
> *Aeneid* 6. 467-473

Crushed as she is by loss, we might expect Dido to appear vulnerable, her
anger covering a wound. Yet as an Ajax figure, she takes on a certain
grandeur, her burning silence showing not only anger, but disdain for Aeneas' rather feeble attempts to explain himself—the gods forced him to

leave, he went unwillingly. The Trojan hero, so often an object of sympathy in his subjection to divine manipulation, comes for this moment under an older, sterner standard of judgment than the one we have been using, one in which intentions count less than results. And when Dido leaves we feel that Aeneas loses touch with more than his personal relationship with her: as he struggles to become a new kind of hero, he begins to distance himself — or better, is driven — from the older sort of heroism embodied by Ajax.

The emotional leverage in the encounter is, as it was in book 4, all with Dido. All the more curious, then, that the echoes of that scene here reverse the emotional dynamic of the earlier exchange: Aeneas pleads, Dido remains aloof — now it is she who resembles rocky cliffs. The point is that Dido's power comes not from anything in particular that she says or does, but from an *emotional authenticity* usually lacking in Aeneas. He often seems in a false position when dealing with her because he is so seldom acting out of his own true self. In this case, the frustration and anguish in him ring true, but he is saddled with explaining his past behavior, which, dictated by the gods, is not really defensible because it is false to his essential nature.

Here we return to a crucial aspect of Dido as a second self. As I have said, she seems to represent, in her fierce determination to preserve her own autonomy even in the face of death, an older kind of heroism — *she*, not Aeneas, is in this sense the true heir to Achilles or Gilgamesh. And this quality also marks an important element of her *complementarity* as a second self in relation to Aeneas, one part of himself that he seems to have lost touch with. But then Rome's destiny seems to require a new kind of hero, in whom loyalty is more prized than autonomy. So we are reminded again that Aeneas' self-fulfillment runs counter to the gods' agenda.

One other aspect of Dido's complementarity may be hinted at in the passage. The exemplar immediately preceding her in Virgil's catalogue of women destroyed by love is Caenus, a woman seduced by Apollo, then at her own request turned by the god into a man until his/her death, when he/she became a woman again in the underworld. Given the alternating shape of Dido's life, as a widow taking on a leadership role usually reserved for men, then falling in love and losing the authority that role brought her, then killing herself in a way reminiscent of Ajax, then reverting in the underworld to the role of wife to her first husband, the Caenus paradigm is tantalizing. Love destroyed Dido because it made her give up an authority she had won by integrating into herself masculine qualities, and so forming a fruitful blend of masculine and feminine that apparently made her a successful leader. When she died, Aeneas' chance to achieve a similarly fruitful balance, glimpsed in its first flowering as Mercury arrived, died with her.

As Aeneas moves on, frustrated and guilty but ever dutiful, we may pause to consider how this powerful vignette functions in Virgil's realization of the second-self motif. First, there is the element of grief. Both Achilles and Gilgamesh give full vent to their grief at the loss of a second self, and this process leads each to a deep truth within himself that in turn allows the grief to subside and the second self to return. Aeneas only discovers that Dido has died at the moment he sees her ghost, well over a year after the fact; a dismal few seconds pass, she vanishes, and he is left to absorb the implications of what he has learned. Like the preemptive intervention of Mercury in book 4, this encounter is terminated with brutal abruptness; once again, Aeneas is told something that forces a complete reappraisal of the world as he has learned to see it. As it happens, he is in the place that functions in other hero stories as a metaphor for the inner recesses to which grief characteristically drives us. But—here the irony in Virgil's revision of the traditional motif is especially strong—he is not there because of Dido, and he is not allowed to process the grief. He is in the underworld to serve the destiny of Rome, not himself, and the truths he will be shown teach nothing that would address his loss.

We also note that Virgil did not, as we might expect, put Dido in the category of famous suicides. To do so would emphasize her autonomy even more. As it is, she embodies a tension between the fierce independence that enabled her to lead her people from exile and the pathetic dependence on Aeneas forced on her by the gods—thus the significance of her return to her first husband in the underworld: the last we see of her, after she defies Aeneas with stony silence, is at the side of Sychaeus. This clash of personal autonomy and divine will is always at the heart of the hero story. That Virgil plays it out in the figure of the second self indicates how unusual his hero is.

The Hero and His Father:
The Future Previewed

Other dead heroes crowd around, prolonging Aeneas' contact with the past. Most are only named, but Deiphobus, Helen's second Trojan mate, gets special notice as he recalls the last night of his life. Once more the sneaky Greeks, the loathsome Ulysses (the Roman name for Odysseus); once more Helen's fickle treachery—just before the revelation of Rome's glorious future, a reminder of how dangerous unchecked female passion can be. Now the Sibyl pushes again:

> "Night comes on, Aeneas,
> We use up hours grieving. Here is the place
> Where the road forks: on the right hand it goes
> Past mighty Dis's walls, Elysium way,
> Our way; but the leftward road will punish
> Malefactors, taking them to Tartarus."

Aeneid 6. 539–543

So much for the past, for grief; the future, with its wonders and burdens, demands attention.

Stepping quickly past exemplary sinners and their punishments, Aeneas and his guide reach the Blessed Groves, to fulfill the purpose of the *katabasis*. Like the tourists they are, Aeneas and the Sibyl ask for directions from Musaeus, legendary first poet especially prominent among the resident souls — Virgil appears to associate creativity with spiritual fulfillment here — and are shown the way. As promised, Anchises waits to enlighten his son:

> Now Aeneas' father
> Anchises, deep in the lush green of a valley,
> Had given all his mind to a survey
> Of souls, till then confined there, who were bound
> For the daylight in the upper world. By chance
> His own were those he scanned now, all his own
> Descendants, with their futures and their fates,
> Their characters and acts. But when he saw
> Aeneas advancing toward him on the grass,
> He stretched out both his hands in eagerness
> As tears wetted his cheeks.
>
> *Aeneid* 6. 679–685

After an affectionate exchange, and Aeneas' futile effort to embrace the ghost, a remarkable scene:

> Aeneas now saw at the valley's end
> A grove standing apart, with stems and boughs
> Of woodland rustling, and the stream of Lethe
> Running past those peaceful glades. Around it
> Souls of a thousand nations filled the air,
> As bees in meadows at the height of summer
> Hover and home on flowers and thickly swarm
> On snow-white lilies, and the countryside
> Is loud with humming. At the sudden vision
> Shivering, at a loss, Aeneas asked
> What river flowed there and what men were those
> In such a throng along the riverside.
> His father Anchises told him:
>   "Souls for whom
> A second body is in store: their drink
> Is water of Lethe, and it frees from care
> In long forgetfulness. For all this time
> I have so much desired to show you these
> And tell you of them face to face — to take

> The roster of my children's children here,
> So you may feel with me more happiness
> At finding Italy."
>   "Must we imagine,
> Father, there are souls that go from here
> Aloft to upper heaven, and once more
> Return to bodies' dead weight? The poor souls,
> How can they crave our daylight so?"
>   "My son,
> I'll tell you, not to leave you mystified,"
> Anchises said, and took each point in order.
>
> *Aeneid* 6. 703–723

We have left traditional epic notions of the underworld and afterlife behind. Everything up to this point has been recognizable: the squeaking, insubstantial ghosts, the wretched sinners and heroic victims. What Anchises goes on to describe in detail, a system of reincarnation that synthesizes Stoic, Platonic, Orphic, and Pythagorean models of eschatology, is something entirely new in heroic poetry, a fittingly bold departure to match Virgil's revision of the heroic story. All of this leads up to the parade of reincarnated souls who will effect the Roman *imperium*, from the immediate descendants of Aeneas to heroes of the Republic to Augustus himself, a grand vision toward which the entire *katabasis* moves. Here is the deep truth to which Aeneas has been led. What does it tell us about him as a hero?

If the conventions of the *katabasis* motif hold true, then the vision stands in the place of Utnapishtim's message to Gilgamesh and Peleus' (mediated through Priam) to Achilles, the hard wisdom that heroes must learn from their fathers. And there are some superficial resemblances between the new perspective offered these two and what Aeneas sees—in each case, a view of the hero's life as part of a larger scheme is urged. But as we have so often been reminded, Aeneas starts from a different place; he is not in need of more humility but more self-definition, precisely what the march of souls militates against. We may on the other hand see Odysseus as a closer parallel to Aeneas here, learning his future from Tiresias in the underworld, a view of his death that suggests something about the character of his life. Just so, though the two portraits yield very different conclusions. Like other evocations of Roman history in the poem, this panorama has the effect of diminishing yet further any sense of *personal* importance in the dutiful hero. His ultimate function, Anchises seems to say, will be to get in line with the other nameless souls, purged of all vestiges of a personal identity from the past, and ascend to an entirely new life, the meaning of which is determined by how it serves the higher destiny of Rome. Having plumbed the deepest recesses of his being, penetrated to the core of himself,

Aeneas finds an invitation to personal oblivion. Much has been made of
the fact that Virgil ends his catalog with mention of the young Marcellus,
shining hope of the Principate, dead before his time. True enough, but the
very nature and context of the entire catalog marks a more immediate loss,
of Aeneas' very self.

Pushing this line of thought further, we can see the parade of souls as on
one level a metaphor for the process dramatized throughout the *Aeneid*,
the systematic purging from Aeneas of all vestiges of his former life and
former self, in preparation for the new role that the gods have chosen for
him. The overtly *didactic* function of the *katabasis* that this perspective
suggests prepares us for what follows in books 7 and 8.

Aeneas' journey into the dark ends with his departure through the Gate
of Ivory, exit point for false dreams. The import of this has been debated
by scholars endlessly, with no definitive conclusions reached. The issues
raised are essentially of authenticity — does Virgil really mean to undermine
our confidence in the visions he has offered? Is he commenting indirectly
on the genuineness of Aeneas himself as a hero? Our particular perspective
here leads us to focus on the second question, to ask whether Virgil is
raising doubts, even after what looks like a potent initiation rite, about
Aeneas' fitness for the mission. Supposing that were so, further questions:
by what criteria is Aeneas found wanting; is he not yet fully evolved into
the new hero the gods require, or is he being judged by old standards of
heroic behavior? These are not trivial distinctions, as they point beyond the
story to issues of authorial tone — does Virgil align himself with the gods'
imperatives, seeing the founding of Rome as a higher good than the integrity of any individual life? But as with most such questions, answers finally
depend not on clues from Virgil — he gives none that are decisive — but on
how each reader in turn weighs these two goods for him or herself.

Arrival in Italy: Carthage and Latium

Book 7 opens with notice of the death of Aeneas' faithful nurse, another
piece of his past life left behind and forming with Misenus' funeral a sacrifi-
cial frame around the *katabasis*. The pilgrims sail on past the island of
Circe — Virgil reminding us that Aeneas is not Odysseus, that this is not
Homer's poem — and innocently into the mouth of the Tiber. Now the poet
steps downstage:

> Be with me, Muse of all Desire, Erato,
> While I call up the kings, the early times,
> How matters stood in the old land of Latium
> That day when the foreign soldiers beached
> Upon Ausonia's shore, and the events

That led to the first fight. Immortal one,
Bring all in memory to the singer's mind,
For I must tell of wars to chill the blood,
Ranked men in battle, kings by their own valor
Driven to death, Etruria's cavalry,
And all Hesperia mobilized in arms.
A greater history opens before my eyes,
A greater task awaits me.

Aeneid 7. 37–44

The import of this gesture, a part of epic poetry since Homer at least, is unmistakable: high poetic style announces elevation of subject matter; Virgil's Iliad is to be, like Homer's, part of a grander genre than his Odyssey; as the Sibyl has predicted, war, not journeying, impends. And so alerted, we look for another Achilles.

But before the battling begins, we are given a glimpse of what Italy was before the Trojans. We meet Latinus, aging king of the Laurentines, living in the area known to Virgil and his contemporaries as Latium. The king has a problem: lacking a male heir, he must marry his only child, Lavinia, to a suitable man. Many suitors come forward, most impressive among them Turnus of the neighboring Rutulians, whom Latinus' queen, Amata, especially favors. But troubling portents give the king pause: bees swarm in an ancient laurel tree, and the soothsayers foresee a foreign stranger coming to attack; Lavinia's hair bursts into flame, a sign that she will have glory in the future, but also bring a great war on her people. Is this, we ask, the new Helen, Aeneas' foreign bride? Himself perplexed, Latinus goes to the oracle of his divine forebear, Faunus, who urges caution:

"Propose no Latin alliance for your daughter,
Son of mine; distrust the bridal chamber
Now prepared. Men from abroad will come
And be your sons by marriage. Blood so mingled
Lifts our name skyward. Children of that stock
Will see all earth turned Latin at their feet,
Governed by them, as far as on his rounds
The Sun looks down on Ocean, East or West."

Aeneid 7. 96–101

No mistaking this description. Now the Italian part of Aeneas' mission begins to be shaped by prophecy: Lavinia is to be the foreign bride, the Trojans the men from abroad, Rome's empire the final product of a dynastic marriage. But who then is to be the foreigner who attacks the city? Aeneas, a son-in-law at the gates? This latter configuration seems unlikely, but that is to underestimate Juno.

Meanwhile, we shift back to Aeneas and his men, dining in the grass by the banks of the Tiber. They use wheat cakes to hold their food and unwittingly fulfill the conditions of a prophecy given them in book 3, that they would be at their destination when they had "eaten their tables." Aeneas makes the connection, rejoices, and prays to the local gods of the land. The next day, an advance party, led by Ilioneus, travels to the city of Latinus, to present Aeneas' compliments and ask for peace. The expedition is successful, with Latinus recognizing Aeneas as the foreigner meant for Lavinia, and offering her to him along with an alliance. The envoys are returned, laden with gifts.

At this point, we note that the structure of the story is familiar: the Trojans arrive in a strange place; the local inhabitants, informed ahead of time about Aeneas and his men and predisposed by supernatural intervention to be hospitable, welcome the advance party led by Ilioneus and offer to share their kingdom; among the natives is a foreign mate, already marked for Aeneas. Virgil seems to be replaying the beginning of the Carthage episode with a new set of natives, his grand invocation of the muse paralleling the prologue to the poem in book 1.

We have seen that structural and thematic repetition is part of Virgil's narrative technique in the *Aeneid*, and that such devices usually signal important comparisons and contrasts. The position of this particular set of repetitions, right after the seminal *katabasis*, suggests that Aeneas may again be on trial as a hero, that we might look to see if the lessons of the underworld have made an impact on his performance. Is he more decisive, more able to see the way to complete his mission? Does he appear any more at home in his new role, having seen how he fits into the larger scheme of Roman destiny? Like the allusions to the *Odyssey* in books 1 through 4, these repetitions suggest a certain set of norms, create expectations, against which Virgil will work in telling the rest of his story.

If the arrival in Italy recalls the beginning of the Carthaginian episode, we wonder whether the later, less cheerful elements are also to be repeated: will the local civilization eventually be destroyed by the seemingly well-intentioned foreigners; is Lavinia to be sacrificed to Rome's destiny; will her betrothal bring forth another frustrated suitor who sees Aeneas as nothing more than an updated Paris? With things going so well for the Trojans at present, it would take, we suppose, a major intervention to derail Roman destiny again. Familiar as we are with Virgil's narrative rhythm, we look for Juno, and are not disappointed.

Juno's Anger Revisited: Allecto

Despite all her plotting, Juno has not been able to keep the Trojans from Italy. She now admits that she cannot prevent the fulfilling of Rome's destiny. And yet:

> " . . . to drag it out, to pile delay
> upon delay in these great matters — that
> I can do: to destroy both countries' people,
> That I can do. Let father and son-in-law
> Unite at that cost to their own! In blood,
> Trojan and Latin, comes your dowry, girl;
> Bridesmaid Bellona waits now to attend you.
> Hecuba's not the only one who carried
> A burning brand within her and bore a son
> Whose marriage fired a city. So it is
> With Venus' child, a Paris once again,
> A funeral torch again for Troy reborn!"
>
> *Aeneid* 7. 315–322

The gratuitous nastiness of this resolve, the desire to inflict pain for its own sake, shows Juno's malevolence to have escalated as if to fit the grander subject of books 7 to 12. So too the instrument she chooses is commensurately darker:

> When she had said all this, she dropped to earth
> In a shuddering wind. From the dark underworld
> Home of the Furies, she aroused Allecto,
> Grief's drear mistress, with her lust for war,
> For angers, ambushes, and crippling crimes.
> Even her father Pluto hates this figure,
> Even her hellish sisters, for her myriad
> Faces, for her savage looks, her head
> Alive and black with snakes.
>
> *Aeneid* 7. 323–329

There are Furies in Greek literature, are agents of evil there and in Roman literature before Virgil, but nothing as close to pure evil as Allecto. When Juno destroys Dido, she effects evil to forward her plans; now those plans, as she herself admits, are doomed to fail, and yet she persists. In taking this further step, her motives seem to transcend any discernible or even comprehensible set of desires other than to foster evil for its own sake, for the pleasure it gives her. As the wife of Jupiter, Juno occupies, as it were, the center of the universe in the traditional perspective of ancient epic. Her summoning of Allecto raises personal malevolence to a genuinely cosmic level, recalling the troubling question with which Virgil began: "Can anger/ Black as this pray on the minds of heaven?" (*Aeneid* 1. 11).

The creature, goaded to her worst by Juno, goes to work immediately:

> Without delay Allecto,
> Dripping venom deadly as the Gorgon's,
> Passed into Latium first and the high hall

Of the Laurentine king. She took her place
On the still threshold of the queen, Amata.
Burning already at the Trojans' coming,
The plans for Turnus' marriage broken off,
Amata tossed and turned with womanly
Anxiety and anger. Now the goddess
Plucked one of the snakes, her gloomy tresses,
And tossed it at the woman, sent it down
Her bosom to her midriff and her heart,
So that by this black reptile driven wild
She might disrupt her whole house. And the serpent
Slipping between her gown and her smooth breasts
Went writhing on, though imperceptible
To the fevered woman's touch or sight, and breathed
Viper's breath into her. The sinuous mass
Became her collar of twisted gold, became
The riband of her head-dress. In her hair
It twined itself, and slid around her body.
While the infection first, like dew of poison
Fallen on her, pervaded all her senses,
Netting her bones in fire — though still her soul
Had not yet responded fully to the flame —
She spoke out softly, quite like any mother,
Shedding hot tears at the marriage of her child
To a Phrygian . . .

Aeneid 7. 341–358

Like Dido, Amata is to be sacrificed to Juno's anger. So infected, she pleads unsuccessfully with Latinus to retract his offer to the Trojans, arguing for Turnus, portraying Aeneas as another Paris set to abduct their innocent daughter. Failing there, driven to a greater frenzy by the poison, she feigns Bacchic possession, dragging Lavinia into the woods to hide her, inciting other Laurentine wives to abandon their homes and take to the woods.

Next, Allecto goes to Turnus. Disguised as an old woman, she urges him to declare war on the Trojans. He is unmoved, scornfully dismissing the old crone. Her response is a dreadful epiphany:

Being so dismissed, Allecto blazed in wrath,
And sudden trembling ran through the man's body
Even as he spoke, his eyes in a rigid stare,
For now the Fury hissed with all her serpents,
All her hideous faces. Glancing round
With eyes of flame, as the man's faltering tongue
Tried to say more, she threw him back and raised
A pair of snakes out of her writhing hair,

Then cracked and cracked her whip and railed at him:
"Look at me now, sunk in decay, see how
Old age in me is too far gone for truth,
Deluding me with battles between kings
And dreams of fear! Look at these dreams of mine!
I come to you from the Black Sisters' home
And bring war and extinction in my hand."

With this she hurled a torch and planted it
Below the man's chest, smoking with hellish light.
Enormous terror woke him, a cold sweat
Broke out all over him and soaked his body.
Then driven wild, shouting for arms, for arms
He ransacked house and chamber. Lust of steel
Raged in him, brute insanity of war,
And wrath above all . . .

Aeneid 7. 445–462

The infection spreads. Entering as we are into Virgil's *Iliad*, we note that a desire for war is equated here with insanity, that Homer's view of combat as at least potentially ennobling seems far away. This new perspective is yet more sharply focused as the demon completes her work. Now Iulus is to be implicated in the madness, as Allecto drives Trojan hounds to attack a sacred stag, pet of a local Italian princess, and Aeneas' son joins innocently in the hunt. Juno's agent assures that his arrow mortally wounds the stag, then stirs up both the Trojans and the Italians until the first casualties occur: the second *Iliad* begins.

This much accomplished, Allecto reports back, eager to do more:

. . . now the feral goddess
Left Hesperia and veered away
Through airy sky, proud of her feat, to brag
To Juno:
"See your quarrel brought to the point
Of grievous war. Now tell them to be friends,
Tell them to make a pact — now that I've splashed
The Trojans with Ausonian blood! There's more
If I am sure you want it: I can send out
Rumors to stir the border towns to war,
Fire them with lust for the madness of war,
So they'll be joining in from everywhere.
I'll scatter weapons up and down the land."
But Juno said:
"Terrors and treacheries
We have in plenty. All that may prolong
A war is there: they fight now hand to hand

> And arms luck gave are running with fresh blood.
> There is the marriage, there is the ceremony
> Venus' distinguished son and that great king
> Latinus may take joy in! As for you,
> This roving rather freely in high air
> Is hardly as the Father wishes, he
> Who rules highest Olympus. Down with you.
> If any further need to act arises
> I myself will manage."
>
> *Aeneid* 7. 543–560

Allecto's duties end with this chilling exchange—there are, it seems, limits to how much chaos even Juno is prepared to effect. The use of the hunting theme here reminds us again of the parallels with the attack on Dido, of the consistency of Juno's malevolence, of the recurrence in the son of his father's unwitting commission of evil. But as I have said, the scale of this corruption, the unrelievedly dark nature of its agent, and the radical reversals it effects all contribute to a sense that this divine intervention is qualitatively different from what was done to the Carthaginians. Dido was manipulated directly, but what followed, Iarbas' response and complaint to Jupiter, were prompted by the operation of Rumor, an independent force in Virgil's cosmos. Not so in this passage, where Juno orchestrates all of the disorder through Allecto. Likewise, grim as the outcome of Amor's impersonation was, we could perhaps see the feelings stirred as already potential in Dido, feeding a flame that might have broken out anyway. The brutality of Allecto's behavior, on the other hand, draws our attention away from any internal motivation in her victims, emphasizing instead the overwhelming power of the gods to manipulate mortals. This latter point raises questions in regard to the second-self motif to which we will return.

The Hero's Principal Antagonists:
Another Achilles?

Like Rumor, the lust for war takes on a life of its own, and the locals drive Latinus, symbol for the moment of order in Latium, into a self-imposed exile. Into the vacuum steps Turnus, driven by Juno's madness. Virgil now invokes the muse a second time to help him compose a catalog of the native Italian forces. Always the occasion for a virtuoso performance in epic, the form in this case is striking in its lyrical evocation of the rustic, pastoral world that must yield to Roman destiny—the opposition between a primeval Golden Age and the march of human civilization is a central preoccupation in all of Virgil's major poetry. From our perspective here, the listing raises again the question of who the new Achilles will be.

Among the many striking portraits, two in particular draw our attention. First, Turnus, in the penultimate position, painted in vivid tones:

> Turnus himself came on, a mighty figure
> Moving among the captains blade in hand
> And by a head the tallest. His high helm
> With triple plume bore a Chimaera's head
> Exhaling Aetnean fires—raging the more
> With savage heat the more blood flowed, the wilder
> Grew the battle. On his polished shield,
> In gold emblazonry, Io appeared
> With lifted horns and hair grown coarse—that instant
> Changed, in the huge blazon, into a cow.
> There stood her escort, Argus, and her father,
> Inachus, the rivergod, poured out
> A stream from figured urn.
>
> *Aeneid* 7. 783–792

The decoration is telling. Juno's baleful presence is felt here in the story of Io, another one of the goddess' victims; the fire imagery expresses in a general way Turnus' elemental forcefulness, but also suggests a particular allusion to Achilles as he appears in books 18 through 22 of the *Iliad*— here, it would seem, is a strong candidate for the new version of that Greek warrior. Both elements of the portrait are central to the second-self motif.

The catalog and the book end with Camilla, pastoral spirit and woman warrior:

> Besides all these
> Camilla of the Volscian people came,
> Riding ahead of cavalry, her squadrons
> Gallant in bronze. A warrior girl whose hands
> Were never deft at distaff or wool basket,
> Skills of Minerva, she was hard and trained
> To take the shock of war, or to outrace
> The winds in running. If she ran full speed
> Over the tips of grain unharvested
> She would not ever have bruised an ear, or else
> She might have sprinted on the deep sea swell
> And never dipped her flying feet. To see her,
> Men and women pouring from the fields,
> From houses, thronged her passage way and stared
> Wide-eyed with admiration at the style

Of royal purple, robing her smooth shoulders,
Then at the brooch that bound her hair in gold,
Then at the Lycian quiver that she bore
And shepherd's myrtle staff, pointed with steel.

Aeneid 7. 803–817

Here is one of Virgil's most intriguing creations, a magical figure of the pastoral world but also a fierce warrior. In her we hear echoes of Penthesileia, Amazon queen killed by Achilles, whose portrait Aeneas and Achates view on the temple at Carthage, and of Dido, heroic woman in a man's role. Her death occasions one of Virgil's most moving passages; her embodiment of male and female forms part of the ongoing meditation in the *Aeneid* on the relationship between power and gender, and plays a subtle role in the depiction of Aeneas as hero.

The Hero's Education: Aeneas at the Future Site of Rome

Aeneas, apart from the brief description of feasting by the Tiber, has been absent since reemerging from the underworld — as Virgil makes a new beginning in the poem, he keeps his hero to one side. Now Juno's machinations have borne evil fruit, in the maddened enmity of Amata and Turnus, in Latinus' abdication, and in the mobilization of Italian forces in opposition. The question of Aeneas' fitness to combat these forces now arises, but he will not be tested just yet. First, an interlude in another pastoral setting, and further opportunities for learning to be the right kind of hero.

With battle looming, both sides look for allies. The Italians send a delegation to Diomedes, Greek hero of the *Iliad* transplanted to Italy. We find Aeneas, meanwhile, in a familiar state:

Thus affairs
Took shape in Latium. And Laömedon's heir,
Who saw the whole scene, weltered in his trouble,
Wave after wave of it. This way and that
He let his mind run, passing quickly over
All he might do . . .

Aeneid 8. 18–21

Awake while others sleep, Aeneas fills the hero's role, and we look for some heroic initiative to follow; in his quandary, he gets, once again, advice from the supernatural. He drops off to sleep, and the god of the river Tiber rises up to give him two crucial pieces of information. First, a prophecy: when he sees a white sow with thirty piglets sucking, he will know that spot to be the future site of Alba Longa; next, directions to a rustic town peopled by transplanted Arcadians and located in the hills. The name of the town is now Pallanteum; one day—though Aeneas, typically enough, is not told this—it will be Rome.

Setting off for Pallanteum, Aeneas sees the white sow and sacrifices it and its brood to—for all the good it will do him—Juno. He and his select troop slide peacefully up the Tiber, the journey described in some of Virgil's loveliest Latin. They come upon the locals in the midst of a religious exercise, a festival for the god Hercules. They are intercepted by Pallas, son of the local king, and having established their credentials, are welcomed to the feast. As he was in the underworld so here Aeneas is a tourist, taking in sights the whole significance of which he cannot know. His continuing education is, in fact, the major theme of this episode, emphasized most clearly in Virgil's Homeric model, the visit of Odysseus' son, Telemachus, to Nestor's realm in book 3 of the *Odyssey.* There the young man has been sent on a journey to find out what he can about the history and current whereabouts of his father, both the travel and the knowledge being an initiation rite—Telemachus must be mature enough to help his father against the suitors when the time comes. The allusion slants our perception of Aeneas in a striking way, putting him in the role of initiate, in this case into the glorious future of Rome and his place in it.

Part of the learning is in the legend of how Hercules, himself a tourist in the midst of his famous labors, once came through Pallanteum and killed a fire-breathing monster, Cacus, who had stolen some of his cattle. The story, told by the king Evander, has a slight aetiological function, but its main import is as a paradigm for Aeneas. Hercules, we recall, was laboring because of the enmity of Juno (Hera in the Greek version); he freed the humble Arcadian shepherds from the monster's thrall and so fulfilled the first requirement of the hero, to impose order on chaos and ensure the preservation of human culture. The model fits Aeneas rather well, another man driven to labor by the hatred of Juno. And if we remember the prominence of fire in the portrait of Turnus, we have a candidate for the disorderly fire creature who must be defeated in order to ensure the continuance of the settlement Hercules first saved.

The hero's education comes to a glorious climax at the end of book 8, when Venus presents him with a new set of armor made by the smith god, Vulcan. Again Homeric precedent is prominent, taking us back into the *Iliad*, to Achilles receiving from Thetis replacements for the armor Hector stripped from Patroclus. Achilles' shield, crafted by Hephaestus, shows a timeless microcosm placing the battlefield in its larger context; here the shield, described at length in the closing lines of the book, parallels the parade of souls, showing scenes from the future of Roman civilization: the rape of the Sabine women, Tarquin, the evil Catiline and noble Cato, and most prominently, Augustus, now leading Italian allies into battle, defeating Antony at Actium. The latter portrait is slightly ambiguous. The founder of the Empire is shown with twin flames shooting forth from his helmet as he goes into battle. The precedents point two ways: Iulus at Troy and Lavinia have been shown with flaming hair, and the portents have had positive aspects, looking to the founding of Rome, though the latter was also said to be bringing a great war on her people. And closer to this episode are two less reassuring examples, Turnus and Cacus. Since Augustus was associated with Hercules in the Rome of Virgil's time, we seem to have in his presence here a doubleness akin to that of Achilles in book 21 of the *Iliad*—is he a chaos monster or a heroic bringer of order? Virgil declines to choose for us.

Aeneas' last gesture in book 8 is loaded with significance:

> All these images on Vulcan's shield,
> His mother's gift, were wonders to Aeneas.
> Knowing nothing of the events themselves,
> He felt joy in their pictures, taking up
> Upon his shoulder all the destined acts
> And fame of his descendants.
>
> *Aeneid* 8. 729–731

First of all, this shouldering recalls and makes us think again about Aeneas carrying his aged father out of Troy at the close of book 2, trudging into exile against the background of his former life roaring in flames. The emphasis there was on Aeneas' *pietas*, his sense of responsibility to his father, his city, and the gods; now, in what must surely be a purposeful repetition, Virgil redefines and expands these loyalties, with the hero taking upon himself personal responsibility for the future of Rome. Now, we feel, Aeneas has finally learned to accept willingly the burden that the gods have been thrusting on him.

The gesture repays closer examination. Viewed in the perspective of the traditional hero story, it corresponds, we might suppose, to the enlightenment that Gilgamesh experiences after returning from the Land of Dilmun, the fruit of a journey into darkness—certainly the parallels between the shield and the parade of souls encourage such an assumption. But within this structural parallel there are telling differences: out of the darkness comes, for Gilgamesh and Achilles, an altered perspective, allowing them to know themselves and their place in the world anew; for Aeneas, benighted joy; the source of wisdom for the earlier heroes was a father figure, the encounter marking a move away from the sphere of the mother; Aeneas has had such an encounter in the underworld, but he receives *this* guide to heroic maturity from Venus. Taken all together, the signs do point to a new perspective, but not one that draws on traditional symbols of personal enlightenment that can lead to greater self-knowledge and autonomy. Indeed, the trend toward diminished self-knowledge seems to continue—unquestioning acceptance and loyalty are the hallmarks of Aeneas' new disposition.

One other aspect of the Pallanteum episode draws our attention: Aeneas taking on an apprentice, Evander's son Pallas, who will accompany his mentor into battle. The assignment seems natural enough in one sense—a quasi-parental role fits comfortably with our experience of Aeneas in the poem—but is potentially confusing in that the relationship is worked out by Virgil on the model of Achilles and Patroclus in the *Iliad*. What is accomplished by transforming the passionate attachment of the Greek hero into a rather distant, avuncular solicitude? Are we to understand Pallas as in any sense a second self to Aeneas? This latter question will in turn focus our attention on Pallas as one of number of younger figures in the last books of the poem, Nisus, Euryalus, Lausus, Camilla, Turnus. All will die by the end of the poem, sacrificed to the inexorable progress of Roman destiny; all contribute in one way or another to the portrait of Aeneas as hero.

Turnus as Second Self

As book 9 opens, Juno is busy again:

> While all these differing actions were afoot
> In the far distance, Juno from high air
> Sent Iris down to Turnus. As it chanced,
> That day the rash prince rested in the grove
> Of his forebear, Pilumnus, in a valley
> Blest of old. There Iris, rose-lipped child
> Of Thaumas, told him:
>   "Turnus, what no god
> Would dare promise you—your heart's desire—
> The course of time has of itself brought on.
> Leaving his town and ships and followers
> Aeneas journeyed to the Palatine
> Court of Evander. Still unsatisfied,
> He's gone to distant hamlets of Corythus
> To rally and arm the Lydian countrymen.
> Why hesitate? Now is the time to sound
> The call for cavalry and war-cars, now!
> Break off this lull, strike at their flurried camp,
> Take it by storm!"
>   On even wings she rose
> Into the sky, inscribing her great bow
> In flight upon the clouds. He knew her sign,
> And lifting both his hands to starry heaven
> Sent these words after her:
>   "Glory of the sky,
> Who brought you down to me, cloudborne to earth?

What makes the sudden brilliance of the air?
I see the vault of heaven riven, and stars
That drift across the night-sky. I'll obey
This great presage, no matter who you are
Who call me to attack."

Aeneid 9. 1–22

Homeric allusion again seems to point the way: Iris comes to Turnus to urge him into battle as she went to Achilles at the beginning of *Iliad* 18; Turnus, like Achilles, will besiege Trojan battlements. Turnus himself later invokes the parallel, speaking to a Trojan named Pandarus:

"Step forward if you have the heart for it.
Come within range. You will be telling Priam
Achilles has been found again, and here."

Aeneid 9. 741–742

The hint in the fire imagery of the catalog in book 7 would seem to be confirmed here: Turnus is to be the other Achilles. If so, then the Iliadic pattern of the last four books of the *Aeneid* suggests that Aeneas will play the role of Hector. But then again, Aeneas has already been modeled on Achilles as early as book 5, in the memorial games for Anchises. And looking again at the context of Iris' mission, we might also see the Trojan camp as analogous, in its temporary nature in a foreign country, to the *Greek* camp, besieged by *Hector* while Achilles is "away" in books 8 to 16 of the *Iliad*—*this* reading reverses the roles. So who, we ask yet one more time, is the new Achilles?

Here begins a fruitful ambiguity. Though we might see in Turnus' eventual death at Aeneas' hands a sign that Virgil finally modifies the Sibyl's prophecy and crowns Aeneas the new Achilles, this would be reductive. Both the Trojan and the Italian are, at different times, in different ways, in the role of Achilles: we will see that the last four books of the *Aeneid* are modeled with some exceptions on *Iliad* 19 to 22, and in this configuration, Aeneas is the Achilles figure, facing Turnus as Hector; but Virgil also often alludes, in particular contexts, to Achilles in his portrait of Turnus. One further point of confluence: at his most impetuous, most fiery, Turnus resembles no one character so much as the younger Aeneas as we see him in book 2 of the *Aeneid*. Taken all together, these various crosscurrents of allusion and repetition signal that Virgil is not done with the motif of the second self, that Aeneas will face in Turnus yet another alternate, unrealized version of himself. And driven once again by the dictates of Rome's destiny, he will kill that self, but not before Virgil has layered the figure of Turnus, as he did Dido, with associations that give the last act of spiritual suicide a rich and suggestive coloration.

Paradigms for the Second Self: Nisus and Euryalus, Camilla, Pallas

One shade of the palette appears in the Trojans' response to Turnus' siege. Two young warriors, Nisus and Euryalus, volunteer to break through the Italian lines and contact Aeneas. The episode is modeled in a loose way on the covert night raid on the Trojans carried out by Diomedes and Odysseus in book 10 of the *Iliad*. But the dominant themes in this passage, quite different from those of the Iliadic precedent, are established by an exchange between the two young men before they approach their elders. Setting the stage, Virgil invokes the traditional pairing of hero and friend, intimately connected: they are united by one love, and they go into battle side-by-side. And consistent with the traditional dynamic of such relationships, one, Nisus, is older, a mentor as well as a lover for his companion. The ensuing conversation between the two adds other dimensions to their intense relationship:

Nisus is the first to speak:

> "This urge to action, do the gods instil it,
>   Or is each man's desire a god to him,
>   Euryalus? For all these hours I've longed
> To engage in battle, or to try some great
> Adventure. In this lull I cannot rest.
> You see how confident the Rutulians are.
> Their watchfire lights wink few and far between,
> They've all lain down in wine and drowsiness,
> And the whole place is quiet. Now attend
> To a thought I'm turning over in my mind,
> A plan that grows on me. 'Recall Aeneas,'
> Everyone, seniors, all our folk, demand:
> 'Dispatch men to report to him,' Will they
> Now promise the reward I ask for you?
> The glory of the feat's enough for me.
> Below the rise of ground there I can find,
> I think, a way through to Fort Pallanteum."
>
> *Aeneid* 9. 184–196

The tone and subject of the first five lines of this speech recall one of the best known vignettes from the *Iliad*, the musings of Sarpedon, a Lycian ally of the Trojans, to his close friend Glaucus, on the nature of heroism:

> "Glaukos, why is it you and I are honoured before others
>   with pride of place, the choice meats and the filled wine cups
>   in Lykia, and all men look on us as if we were immortals,

and we are appointed a great piece of land by the banks of the Xanthos,
good land, orchard and vineyard, and ploughland for the planting of wheat?
Therefore it is our duty in the forefront of the Lykians
to take our stand, and bear our part of the blazing of battle,
so that a man of the close-armoured Lykians may say of us:
"Indeed, these are no ignoble men who are lords of Lykia,
these kings of ours, who feed upon fat sheep appointed
and drink the exquisite sweet wine, since indeed there is strength
of valour in them, since they fight in the forefront of the Lykians."
Man, supposing you and I, escaping this battle,
would be able to live on forever, ageless, immortal,
so neither would I myself go on fighting in the foremost
nor would I urge you into the fighting where men win glory.
But now, seeing that the spirits of death stand close about us
in their thousands, no man can turn aside or escape them,
let us go and win glory for ourselves, or yield it to others."

Iliad 12. 310–328

Prefacing Nisus' plan in this way lends it a certain archaic tone. Virgil appears to be linking youthful—and naive, as it turns out—enthusiasm for battle with an older kind of heroic view of war and the rewards it can bring, a perspective we have also seen on display in Gilgamesh and Enkidu before the latter's death. As the exchange between the two friends continues, these associations are strengthened:

Taken aback, his love of glory stirred,
Euryalus replied to his ardent friend:

"And me? Are you refusing me my place
Beside you in this great affair? Must I
Send you alone into such danger? Born
For that, was I, and trained for that, amid
The Argive terror, those hard hours of Troy,
By a true fighter, one inured to battle,
My father, Opheltës? Never till now have I
Behaved so at your side, and as a soldier
Pledged to see Aeneas' destiny through.
Believe me, here's a spirit that disdains
Mere daylight! I hold life well spent to buy
That glory you aspire to."
                              Nisus answered:
"Not for a minute had I any qualms
About you on that score. Unthinkable!
Witness great Jupiter—or whoever else

May favor this attempt — by bringing me
In triumph back to you. But if some god
Or accident defeats me — and one sees
Miscarriage of bold missions many a time —
You must live on. Your age deserves more life.
If I am dragged free from a fight or ransomed,
Let there be someone who can bury me.
Or if, as often, bad luck rules that out,
Someone who can carry out the ritual
For me, though I'm not there, and honor me
With an empty tomb.
                         Then too, I would not bring
Such grief on your poor mother, one who dared
As many mothers did not, child, to come
This far with you, taking no care for shelter
Behind Acestes' walls."
                         But the boy said:
"Your reasoning is all a waste of breath.
Not by an inch has my position changed.
Let us be off."

Aeneid 9. 197–221

The preference for a glorious death over an ignominious life mirrors Achilles' choice of a short but glorious life over a long but uneventful one. But we have other precedents closer to hand: Dido's suicide and, most important for our purposes here, the young Aeneas at Troy. These last two links, like a magnet passed over filings, realign the exchange within the larger canvas of the poem, making it a comment on Aeneas' struggle with his lost past and destined future. As we will see, the entire episode is something of an overture for much that follows in the story, its implications rippling through the narrative as it moves toward the final climax in book 12.

The other Trojans accept Nisus' offer, with Ascanius most vocal in his approval of the gesture. The mission goes well, the two men falling on sleeping Italians in their camp and killing them in gory fashion. At Nisus' urging, they prepare to move on, but not before Euryalus takes some booty, medals and a golden belt, which he wears as a trophy. This gesture, reflecting the young man's desire to display proof of his triumph, is his undoing. The ornaments flash in the night, catching the notice of an advance party of Italians that happens to be in the vicinity. Trapped and hunted down, Euryalus faces death as Nisus, having left the woods, returns to find him. Nisus — praying to the Moon goddess, Diana, protectress of young virgins — kills two Italians before an Italian named Volcens finishes Euryalus off. Virgil pauses here to focus on the death:

Euryalus
In death went reeling down,
And blood streamed on his handsome length, his neck
Collapsing let his head fall on his shoulder —
As a bright flower cut by a passing plow
Will droop and wither slowly, or a poppy
Bow its head upon its tired stalk
When overborne by a passing rain.

Aeneid 9. 433–437

In a last suicidal rush, Nisus kills Volcens and dies himself, falling on the
body of his friend. Virgil, speaking in his own voice, ends the story by
eulogizing the two young heroes:

Fortunate, both! If in the least my songs
Avail, no future day will ever take you
Out of the record of remembering Time,
While children of Aeneas make their home
Around the Capitol's unshaken rock,
And still the Roman Father governs all.

Aeneid 9. 446–449

The entire episode has been a digression — nothing that happens is important for the movement of the plot — and yet hardly inconsequential for the
larger themes of the poem. Indeed, the self-contained nature of the story
contributes to its impact. Closed off from the ongoing flow of the narrative, by its setting, by its adolescent and rather unsettling blend of eroticism
and grotesquerie, the episode presents a laboratory for exploring a particular set of heroic attitudes. At the same time, by isolating the story, Virgil
emphasizes its unreality, its quality of anachronism in the midst of the new
Roman order. All of this plays a part in the motif of the second self, adding
nuance to the character of Turnus, who will come to represent in his last
stand much of what appears in the two young men.

The rich complex of associations generated in the Nisus-Euryalus episode
will reverberate through the rest of the story, surfacing in contexts that in
turn add new shadings. Among the most tantalizing of these is the story of
Camilla, young woman warrior introduced so vividly in the catalog. Her
next appearance is in book 11, standing in for Turnus. Much has happened
in book 10, to which we will return: Pallas has died at Turnus' hands;
Lausus, a young Etruscan counterpart to Pallas, has fallen to Aeneas, while
his father, Mezentius, has taken his own life in a memorable scene. Book
11 opens with the funeral for Pallas, modeled on the rites for Patroclus in
the *Iliad*; then comes a lengthy debate in the Italian camp, disrupted by
news of an initiative by Aeneas against the city of Latinus. Turnus, itching
for a fight, rides to meet the Trojans, but is intercepted by Camilla: *she*

will face the Trojan chief; he may attend to other business. He accedes, full
of admiration for the "awesome virgin."

Nearly all the rest of book 11 belongs to Camilla, her moment of glory on
the battlefield, her death and its aftermath. The episode opens in heaven.
Camilla, it seems, is a favorite of Diana, her protector from infancy as the
goddess tells us. Camilla's foray against the Trojans fills Diana with alarm,
and she assigns one of her virgins to watch and avenge any harm that might
come to her ward. Brilliant fighter that she is, Camilla easily dispatches
numerous Trojans, ranging through the ranks with her own band of virgin
women warriors. But then, drawn by his exotic dress and armor, she begins
to stalk one Chloreus. Unbeknownst to her, *she* is in turn being hunted, by
Arruns, a cowardly Trojan who skulks just out of her line of vision, waiting
his chance. The moment comes as Camilla is distracted by Chloreus, and
Arruns delivers the fatal wound, scurrying away immediately. Camilla's
last words are further instructions to Turnus. Virgil lingers over the final
moment:

> Even while speaking she let slip the reins
> And slid fainting to earth. Little by little,
> Growing cold, the girl detached herself
> From her whole body and put down her head,
> Death's captive now, upon her strengthless neck,
> And let her weapons fall.
> Then with a groan for that indignity,
> Her spirit fled into the gloom below.
>
> *Aeneid* 11. 827–831

There is much here that recalls the Nisus and Euryalus episode: the emphasis on virginity, marked by a special connection to Diana; the combina-
tion of youthful energy and naivete; the undermining of heroism by fascination for beautiful ornament; the final moment when sinewy strength gives
way to the languor of death—Camilla's head drooping on her neck might
have occasioned the lovely flower simile that marks the end of Euryalus.
Virgil seems here to be building up a typology for a particular kind of young
heroism. At the same time, the episode radiates out in other directions. The
sneaky Arruns is a clear descendent of Homer's Euphorbos, who finishes
off Patroclus in book 16 of the *Iliad*. But if Camilla is now to be compared
to Patroclus, what of Pallas, in that persona himself from book 8 until his
death in book 10—have we some kind of procession of Patroclus surrogates? And the picture becomes yet more cloudy if we note that the last
two lines of Camilla's death scene reappear verbatim as the last two lines of
the poem, in *Turnus'* death scene. If Camilla and Turnus are linked, and
the latter is a second self to Aeneas, has gender ambiguity reentered the
portrait of Aeneas' heroism? And why should we not think so, since Camilla has much in common—association with Diana, a vital role in what

the world of the poem sees as a man's milieu—with the most prominent vehicle for that ambiguity, Dido? All of these connections hang on delicate threads, and we need to be cautious. But at the very least we can recognize that the figure of Turnus is being embedded in a rich field of associations, his actions resonant with overtones reaching beyond his particular character and circumstances. Before turning to his last hours, we note one further set of associations generated by the figure of Pallas.

The relationship of Aeneas and Pallas is, as I have said, based on Achilles and Patroclus in the *Iliad*. Book 10 tells the story of how Pallas, fighting on his own, away from his more powerful protector, is killed by Turnus. Hearing of this, Aeneas goes into a rather uncharacteristic rage, killing indiscriminately, showing no mercy as he moves inexorably toward a duel with Turnus, intent on avenging Pallas' death. The difficulty in assessing the import of this allusion is in the age gap between Aeneas and his ward. Achilles, though he is the dominant figure in his relationship with Patroclus, is actually younger than his friend; and their bond, if not explicitly sexual, draws on that arena for some of its intensity. No such thing is possible for the Roman hero, who after the death of Dido, has returned to his state of emotional isolation, carrying his burdens alone. In taking on Pallas as his protégé, Aeneas must be drawing on the same reservoir of feelings that feeds his *pietas*—though at times reluctant, he is never one to refuse responsibility. At the same time, there is the sense that Pallas fills the role of surrogate son for Aeneas. We may say that this is hardly necessary, as Ascanius is closeby. But the inexorable destiny of Rome has already begun to thrust itself in between Aeneas and his natural son—the gods have decided that Ascanius is too valuable to be risked in battle, and must be kept sequestered for his later duties. So Pallas can receive the inheritance of Aeneas the warrior, while Ascanius remains safely to one side. Finally, we must keep in mind the connections between Pallas and the other examples of youthful but rash heroism Virgil provides: Nisus, Euryalus, Camilla, and perhaps Turnus.

The anger of Aeneas over Pallas' death does not, as I have said, sit easily with the character we have come to know. Achilles raging gives us no pause, but Aeneas has been marked by a singular lack of overtly expressed emotion throughout the poem, and especially after book 4. We might see this outburst as a sign that Aeneas has entered further into the new heroic perspective urged on him by his role as standard-bearer for the Roman *imperium*. Thus, self-effacing loyalty, the hallmark of the new heroism, fuels the anger: Pallas was entrusted to Aeneas, and Turnus has caused him to violate that trust. Perhaps we ought to allow in this instance for the operation of guilt as well, the anger turned outward toward Turnus rather than inward at himself. All this is plausible, but I have never found it a wholly satisfying explanation. It may be that this is just a weakness in

Virgil's reworking of the Homeric precedent; there may, however, be other kinds of motivation for the anger, triggered by the other aspects of Aeneas' bond to Pallas.

After Pallas' death, Aeneas surges across the battlefield in search of Turnus. Having killed many others, he comes on Mezentius, an Etruscan. The exchange leaves Mezentius wounded, in retreat. Lausus, his son, covers him by challenging Aeneas, who, deep into his vengeful mode, taunts and kills the young man. But after the boy dies, remorse sets in:

> But seeing the look
> On the young man's face in death, a face so pale,
> As to be awesome, then Anchises' son
> Groaned in profound pity. He held out
> His hand as filial piety, mirrored here,
> Wrung his own heart, and said:
> "O poor young soldier,
> How will Aeneas reward your splendid fight?
> How honor you, in keeping with your nature?
> Keep the arms you loved to use, for I
> Return you to your forebears, ash and shades,
> If this concerns you now. Unlucky boy,
> One consolation for sad death is this:
> You die by the sword-thrust of great Aeneas."
>
> *Aeneid* 10. 821–830

Aeneas' turnabout ends his rampage for the moment, and the rest of book 10 is taken up with Mezentius' suicide in despair at losing his son. There is in Aeneas' remorse a *paternal* tone, as if he saw in the young man something of Pallas or the absent Ascanius. Indeed, the father-son relationship is prominent all through book 10, in Mezentius and Lausus, Pallas and the absent Evander, and in the vignette preceding Pallas' death, when the young man prays to the deified Hercules, once a guest of Evander, for strength in his fight against Turnus. Fate will not allow intervention—we have here a reworking of the Zeus and Sarpedon episode of *Iliad* 16—and Hercules is torn:

> Hercules heard him. Deep in his heart he quelled
> A mighty groan, and let the vain tears flow.
> At this the Olympian father addressed his son
> In kindness:
> "Every man's last day is fixed.
> Lifetimes are brief, and not to be regained,
> For all mankind. But by their deeds to make
> Their fame last: that is labor for the brave.

> Below the walls of Troy so many sons
> Of gods went down, among them, yes, my child,
> Sarpedon. Turnus, too, is called by fate.
> He stands at the given limit of his years."
>
> *Aeneid* 10. 464–472

Aeneas, exemplary father that he is, has had more than one opportunity to
find his son mirrored in the faces of dead young men. Wakened from his
nightmarish spree by the sight of a dead youth who might have been his
own flesh, he returns to his former demeanor for a time. We might in
fact see the entire passage of Aeneas' vengeance as bracketed by paternal
responses, beginning with rage at the death of Pallas, one surrogate son,
ending with his own killing of another.

There is, I think, one other aspect of Aeneas' anger, less obvious from
the surface content but ultimately crucial to our understanding of him and
of the second-self motif as it functions in the last third of the poem. Pallas,
though clearly younger than Aeneas, is in the role of Patroclus to his
mentor. Our experience with the pattern of this relationship suggests some
element of *identification* between the two. I am not saying quite that Pallas
is a second self to Aeneas, but there is something of this dimension in their
relationship. And if so, why ought we to be surprised? Anyone who has
had children will recognize the habit of replaying one's own youth through
one's children—getting it *right* this time. Ascanius now being sequestered
for safekeeping, Pallas and perhaps Lausus draw some paternal responses
from Aeneas, and one of these might well be that of identification. Insofar
as this element is operating in the dynamic, we see here both a preview of
the poem's end and a flashback to book 4: Aeneas, dutiful as ever, killing
off parts of himself in the service of the future.

Conclusion

Virgil has covered a large canvas since Aeneas left Carthage: the memorial
games, the underworld, the advent of the Trojans in Latium and subsequent events leading to war. In all of these episodes, Virgil works, as usual,
with Homeric precedents, and we have seen a general shift in focus from
the *Odyssey* to the *Iliad*, especially in books 9 to 11. Meanwhile, various
subplots have been woven into the forward progress of the hero toward his
destined goal: Hercules and Cacus, Nisus and Euryalus, the deaths of Pallas, Lausus, and Camilla. The profusion of events might obscure the coher-
ence of all this, and in particular, we may feel that the second-self motif has
been rather muted. But that dynamic has in fact been steadily developing,
supported by two interrelated elements in the story: the confusion, which I
have called fruitful, about who the other Achilles will be, and the Iliadic

paradigm of Achilles and Patroclus. The former has set up for us the primary duality in the second half of the poem, between Aeneas and Turnus; the latter, by injecting through Pallas a generational shift into the story, has effected the enriching of the primary duality by various overtones. The crosscurrents of association between Hercules, Aeneas, Cacus, and Turnus, between Nisus, Euryalus, Aeneas, and Camilla, between Aeneas, Pallas, and Lausus, between Camilla and Dido, even Camilla and Turnus, build a new context for understanding what is at stake as Aeneas moves toward the ultimate confrontation with his Italian rival. In all of this the sense of Aeneas as still being on trial, an apprentice hero required to prove his credentials, is strong. As the poem draws to its dramatic and rather stark conclusion, that testing will continue.

Buried Selves:
The Aeneid (3)

The mere ability to choose between good and evil is the lowest
limit of freedom, and the only thing that is free about it is the
fact that we can still choose good.

Thomas Merton, *Seeds of Contemplation*

The last book of the *Aeneid* opens with a potent image:

> Turnus now saw how Latin strength had failed,
> How the day's fight was lost and they were broken;
> Saw that they held him to his promise now
> All eyes upon him. But before they spoke
> His passion rose, hot and unquenchable.
> As in the African hinterland a lion,
> Hit in the chest by hunters, badly hurt,
> Gives battle then at last and revels in it,
> Tossing his bunch of mane back from his nape;
> All fighting heart, he snaps the shaft the tracker
> Put into him, and roars with a bloody maw.
> So Turnus in extremity flared up
> And stormed at the old king.

Aeneid 12. 1–9

Much of what follows in the story can be traced here. The image of the
wounded lion, hampered perhaps but undaunted, captures Turnus' situation, his allies weakened by setbacks, the Trojans' fortunes on the rise. In
his defiance of death, his determination to fight even though the cause
looks hopeless, Turnus takes his place beside the many examples of doomed
and — in the perspective of the new Roman settlement — rather old-fashioned
heroism in the poem: Nisus and Euryalus, Pallas, Lausus, Camilla, the

younger Aeneas at Troy. The simile itself alludes to Homer's description of Achilles in *Iliad* 20, as he prepares to face — interestingly enough — Aeneas:

> From the other
> side the son of Peleus rose like a lion against him,
> the baleful beast, when men have been straining to kill him, the country
> all in the hunt, and he at first pays them no attention
> but goes on his way, only when some one of the impetuous young men
> has hit him with a spear he whirls, jaws open, over his teeth foam
> breaks out, and in the depth of his chest the powerful heart groans;
> he lashes his own ribs with his tail and the flanks on both sides
> as he rouses himself to fury for the fight, eyes glaring,
> and hurls himself straight onward on the chance of killing some one
> of the men, or else being killed himself in the first onrush.
> So the proud heart and fighting fury stirred on Achilleus
> to go forward in the face of the great-hearted Aineias.
>
> *Iliad* 20. 163–175

Even as the climactic duel approaches, modeled closely on the death of Hector in *Iliad* 22 and clearly putting *Aeneas* in the role of Achilles, Virgil keeps that legacy open to Turnus as well.

Perhaps most striking of all is the echo here of the opening lines of book 4:

> The queen, for her part, all that evening ached
> With longing that her heart's blood fed, a wound
> Or inward fire eating her away.
> The manhood of the man, his pride of birth,
> Came home to her time and time again; his looks,
> His words remained with her to haunt her mind,
> And desire for him gave her no rest.
>
> *Aeneid* 4. 1–5

The English translation of the passage in book 12 masks a clear parallel here, the Latin *Poenorum* being translated as "African," when it means specifically "Carthaginian." Since as far as we know there were no lions on the coast of North Africa in Virgil's time, the venue for the simile can only signal an invitation to compare Aeneas' two most prominent victims, part of a parallelism that reaches its fullest expression in the stalking of both by the Trojan hero. We remember Dido, wandering madly through Carthage like a doe wounded by an unknowing hunter; to this Virgil will soon add:

> As for Aeneas,
> Slowed though his knees were by the arrow wound
> That hampered him at times, cutting his speed,
> He pressed on hotly, matching stride for stride,

Behind his shaken foe. As when a stag-hound
Corners a stag, blocked by a stream, or by
Alarm at a barrier of crimson feathers
Strung by beaters, then the dog assails him
With darting, barking runs; the stag in fear
Of nets and the high river-bank attempts
To flee and flee again a thousand ways,
But, packed with power, the Umbrian hound hangs on,
Muzzle agape: now, now he has him, now,
As though he had him, snaps eluded jaws
And bites on empty air. Then he gives tongue
In furious barking; the river banks and pools
Echo the din, reverberant to the sky.

Aeneid 12. 746–757

So Dido, last seen in the underworld, lives on through Turnus. And now
we think again of her last curse on Aeneas:

Then, O my Tyrians, besiege with hate
His progeny and all his race to come:
Make this your offering to my dust. No love,
No pact must be between our peoples; No,
But rise up from my bones, avenging spirit!
Harry with fire and sword the Dardan countrymen
Now, or hereafter, at whatever time
The strength will be afforded . . .

Aeneid 4. 612–627

When these words were delivered, they seemed to point to the distant future, to the Punic Wars; now Virgil provides a Hannibal sooner than expected.

Turnus, then, has come to represent a complex set of attitudes and responses in the poem, carrying with him something from each of many
other characters. Though not said to be markedly younger than Aeneas, he
embodies the youthful and at times naive ways of seeing we have encountered so often in other, younger, men, and most strikingly in the earlier
version of Aeneas himself. At the same time, the Nisus and Euryalus episode in particular seems to inject the element of *cultural* difference into the
contrast between the old and new brands of heroism on display in the
poem — there is a decidedly Greek cast to the setting of the vignette and the
attitudes of the young men. This suits Virgil's agenda in that he can cele-
brate the Romans conquering Greece in the triumph of the Trojans, while
hedging to some extent on the more negative aspects of the Greeks from
the Roman perspective by associating the better qualities with sturdy Ital-

ians, always an object of reverence in Augustan Rome. Finally—and this will be confirmed in his death scene—Turnus also appears to preserve something of the gender ambiguity we saw played out in the abortive union of Aeneas and Dido.

All of these associations combine to load the final duel of Aeneas and Turnus with enormous significance for the motif of the second self. When the last sword thrust comes, Aeneas puts to rest with it much more than the character of Turnus. There dies with him an entire world, pastoral, heroic, Greek, early Italian, Homeric; and there dies with him, once more and forever, an Aeneas who might have been. That the death stroke comes directly from Aeneas himself this time is poignant, but consistent with the poem's vision of the interaction of gods and mortals. By playing Turnus' death against the background of *Iliad* 22, Virgil creates an inevitable contrast that marks yet again the strikingly original view of the heroic career to be found in his poem.

The Hero's Duel with a Second Self: Preliminaries

If the lion simile evokes the Achillean soul of Turnus, the scene following puts him back in the shadow of Hector. Latinus and Amata plead with their favorite to forego fighting the Trojans, echoing Priam and Hecuba begging Hector not to oppose Achilles alone (*Iliad* 22. 25–89). Turnus has, in fact, just proposed a duel between himself and Aeneas, his reckless bravado very much to the fore:

> "No one waits
> While Turnus shirks a battle. No pretext
> Allows Aeneas' riffraff to renege
> Or take their challenge back. By god, I'll fight him.
> Father, bring sacred offerings and state
> The terms of combat. Either by this right arm
> I send to hell that Dardan prince who left
> His Asia in the lurch—and let the Latins
> Rest and look on! while I alone disprove
> With my sword-point the charge against us all—
> Or else let him take over a beaten people,
> Let Lavinia be the winner's bride."

> *Aeneid* 12. 11–17

In reply to the old couple, Turnus continues to see himself through the lens of traditional heroism:

My lord, I beg you,
Put this reckoning for my sake aside
For my sake; let me bid my death for honor.
                                                   Aeneid 12. 48–49

Please,
Mother, no tears for me, no parting omen
So unpromising, as I go out
To combat ruled by Mars. No longer
Is Turnus free to put off risk of death.
                                                   Aeneid 12. 72–74

Preparing us for the final duel to come, Virgil seems at pains to paint Turnus in strong colors, to make him embody in particular that pride and fatalistic defiance so often on display in the *Aeneid*'s losers.

A simile alerts us that the duel and its attendant truce are to follow the contours of *Iliad* 3 and 4, the abortive fight between Paris and Menelaus. Lavinia, listening to her mother beg Turnus, blushes, reminding the poet of ivory stained with red dye or lilies mixed with roses. Red dye on ivory is Homer's image to describe Menelaus' wounded leg, struck by the arrow that breaks the truce in *Iliad* 4 — allusion here foreshadows, darkening the truce with failure even as it is being organized. Meanwhile, the overarching theme of sexual jealousy, present from the beginning of the story, surfaces yet again, fueling Turnus' self-destructive fire.

The image of Lavinia in the simile as an object to be decorated is entirely consistent with her utter passivity and lack of definition in the poem. She never speaks, only records reactions to what others do. We return here in some ways to the Iliadic notion of women as chattel, as prizes to be fought over, interchangeable with tripods. But Virgil has transformed the dynamic to fit his own themes: Achilles and Agamemnon use Chryseis and Briseis, nearly interchangeable characters, as vehicles for playing out emotions that have little to do with the captives' identity as women — the issue is honor, signaled by valuable possessions of whatever sort; for Virgil the operation of sexual jealousy in particular as a motive for conflict is always central, embodied in Juno, in Iarbas, in Turnus.

At the same time, we are unlikely to confuse Lavinia with Dido — she will be the foreign bride over whom a war is fought, but there is no chance of her being a soul mate for Aeneas. While Virgil has not abandoned the exploration of gender and power, he will pursue it through Turnus — and, indirectly, Camilla — not Lavinia. Insubstantial, bland, childlike, Lavinia is unlikely to provide Aeneas with anything more than children for the dynasty — in this sense, she belongs, like Ascanius, to the future and Rome's destiny, not to Aeneas. Again, what *he* might need is secondary to what Rome needs.

Juno's Last Stand

The duel is at hand. The armies gather, the gods are enlisted, and the unlikely prospect of a clean decision seems closeby. True to form, Juno appears. Tender creature that she is, she cannot bear to watch the duel, but cannot keep from meddling again, either. Seeking out yet another agent, this time Juturna, river nymph and sister to Turnus, she urges her to help her brother, adding some helpful suggestions: either rescue him from death or sabotage the truce. Choosing the latter course, Juturna appears in disguise to the Italians after Aeneas and Latinus seal the truce agreement. Moving among the foot soldiers, she stirs them up: are they afraid to fight the Trojans; are they not more than a match for the invaders; Turnus will get glory by dying in a lost cause, but they will get slavery. Riled now, the men are ripe for the next ruse, a faked portent from Jupiter's eagle, which pushes one Tolumnius, a prophet, over the edge into action. He spears an Arcadian, and the truce explodes.

The conjunction of a thirst for glory and the breaking of the truce is significant. As Turnus' death looms, the traditional heroic values he represents spread outward, reaching all the combatants. The result is a particularly graphic and ugly battle, one in which Virgil pointedly contrasts a desire for peace with bloodlust:

> One passion took possession of them all:
> To make the sword their arbiter. They ripped
> The altars to get firebrands, missiles flew
> In darkening squalls over the whole sky,
> A rain of steel, while sacrificial bowls
> And hearth fires of the peace were snatched away.
>
> *Aeneid* 12. 282–285

Latinus takes cover, abdicating again, as he did after the first outbreak of violence in book 7, his responsibilities as king, leaving the field to the soldiers and their uncontrolled fury. Gruesome death is all around: a firebrand from the altar itself becomes a weapon to rip open a man's face, and the air, we hear, smells of burning hair and flesh; the man still lives, is kneed in the groin and run through; a shepherd's head is split from behind by an axe. Amidst the horror, Aeneas, bewildered again by divine initiative:

> "Where bound? Are you a mob?
> Why this outbreak of brawling all at once?
> Cool your hot heads. A pact has been agreed to,
> Terms have been laid down. I am the one

To fight them. Let me do so. Never fear:
With this right hand I'll carry out the treaty.
Turnus is mine, our sacrifice obliged it."
                                               Aeneid 12. 313-317

The response to this is an arrow, its sender anonymous, whizzing into
Aeneas' body—diplomacy has no chance against Juno.

Shifting Paradigms for the Hero

Turnus, seeing Aeneas' retreat, goes after him, a trail of bodies in his wake.
The scene shifts, leaving the Italian hero suspended, advancing inexorably,
and we think of *Iliad* 22: Achilles, like the baleful Dogstar, racing across
the plain, then frozen, while Hector stands alone before the walls of Troy
and delivers his great soliloquy, reviewing his past acts, now thrown into
relief by the imminence of death, pondering the choices open to him in his
final moments (*Iliad* 22. 99-130). The reminiscence puts Turnus again in
the role of Achilles, with Aeneas as Hector, a configuration that Virgil
confirms in the scene following the latter's magical healing by his mother.
All thoughts of peace are gone now; Aeneas arms with a grim eagerness.
On his way to the field, he hugs Ascanius,

             . . . embracing him with steel,
    Then through his visor brushed his lips and said:

"Learn fortitude and toil from me, my son,
    Ache of true toil. Good fortune learn from others.
    My sword arm will now be your shield in battle
    And introduce you to the boons of war.
    When, before long, you come to a man's estate,
    Be sure you recall this. Harking back
    For models in your family, let your father,
    Aeneas, and uncle, Hector, stir your heart."
                                               Aeneid 12. 435-440

The echo here is multiple, of Hector's prayer to Zeus for his son, delivered
in his farewell scene with Andromache in *Iliad* 6, of Ajax speaking to his
infant son in Sophocles' *Ajax*, another farewell, this time preceding Ajax's
suicide. Both passages carry a similar resonance, of doomed heroism, of
resignation to fate; both signal the passing of heroic force from one generation to another. And both, one explicitly and one implicitly (so Andromache in book 6: "Dearest,/your own great strength will be your death"
[406-407]) foreshadow suicidal acts, pointing in this beyond the immediate
context to Aeneas' final sword thrust.

The Trojans advance, compared by Virgil to a storm cloud that blots out the sun, and a chill runs through the Italians. Grimly intent, Aeneas threads his way through the melee, looking only for Turnus:

> In the dense murk he tracked Turnus alone,
> Called on Turnus alone to stand and fight him.
>
> *Aeneid* 12. 466–467

The image of *tracking* is specific, the Latin verb, *vestigat*, being the word used for hunters. Aeneas' single-minded pursuit puts him back in the Achillean role; the hunting imagery looks forward to a final stalking, backward to the unhappy Dido.

Aeneas' Rage: Redefining the Hero

This menace frightens Juturna, who decides to remove her brother from harm's way. Disguising herself as his charioteer, she takes over the reins and keeps him away from Aeneas. The result is a retarding of the plot, as the two principals are kept apart. But if the ultimate goal of the story is delayed, the fierce battling that follows does play a part in the ongoing portrait of Aeneas. As he pursues his elusive counterpart, Aeneas is attacked by one Messapus. For some reason, this particular opponent pushes him over the edge:

> At this attack,
> A tide of battle-fury swept the Trojan,
> Overcome by Rutulian bad faith.
> The team and car of his great adversary
> Being out of range, he called on Jove and called
> On altars of the broken peace to witness,
> Many times, then into the mêlée
> He raced, most terrible to see, with Mars
> Behind him, rousing blind and savage slaughter,
> All restraints on wrath cast to the winds.
>
> *Aeneid* 12. 494–499

As he did after Pallas' death, so here, Aeneas loses his characteristic self-control when his *pietas* is undermined. In both instances, the puzzle and the paradox of Aeneas' motivation come into sharp focus.

From the poem's opening lines, we have seen a consistent pattern: Aeneas struggling with a set of divine imperatives that require the obliteration of unrealized or underdeveloped parts of himself. The resulting alienation from his own deepest potential has made Aeneas a particularly opaque character, one whose behavior often lacks emotional authenticity—others rage and lust, Aeneas is usually merely confused, full of good intentions but paralyzed in the face of what life offers him. After Carthage, the theme of the hero's education, or initiation, becomes prominent, in the *katabasis*, in the journey to the site of Rome. Aeneas, it appears, is to be taught how to be a new kind of hero, one fitted for the job at hand. One quality well suited to this role he already has in abundance: loyalty, or, to use the more specific Latin term, *pietas*. So his later moments of uncontrolled rage, at the death of Pallas and at the breaking of the truce, might be—insofar as both incidents undermine bonds guaranteed by his *pietas*—evidence of his assumption of the new heroic agenda.

If so, then Virgil seems to be redefining the boundaries between the old and new heroism here. There has been, up to this point, a contrast implied between the undisciplined passion of a Nisus or a Camilla, fueled by intensely personal motives, and the more controlled responses of Aeneas the public man as he tries to keep his expedition intact and heading for Italy. The Carthage episode appears as an aberration in this perspective, a loss of control that works against the gods' agenda. Now, we might say, it is not so much the issue of self-control that separates new- and old-style heroism, but the *motives* for the passion—extremism in the defense of Roman destiny is no vice, to paraphrase. In effecting this shift, Virgil realigns Aeneas' trajectory as he moves inexorably toward Turnus, and by doing so shifts our perspective on his hero's last act.

Venus calls Aeneas back from his fruitless quest, prompting him to force the issue by attacking the undefended city of Latinus. The resulting siege is refracted through a particularly pregnant simile, of Aeneas as shepherd, tracking bees and then smoking them out of their hive. Combining the recurrent tracking image with the role of shepherd seems to sanction a certain ruthlessness in Aeneas, serving as it does his "shepherding' of Roman destiny. Like his newfound passion, this aggressive quality in Aeneas, which might in another character be evidence of primitive, anachronistic emotions, seems to be redeemed by the ends it serves.

The sight of Trojans at the gates is too much for Amata, who hangs herself, becoming yet another sacrifice to the future glory of Rome. That her death is self-inflicted makes it foreshadow the suicidal implications of Aeneas' final act. Lavinia, as usual, is given no words, but leads the mourners, once again serving as a mute mirror for the actions of others.

The Reemergence of Hector in Turnus

The sound of the citizens' distress reaches Turnus as he is driven around the edges of the battle, and Juturna's ruse is aborted. She tries to lead him further away, but he refuses:

> "Sister — yes, I knew you
> Long since, when you spoiled the pact by guile
> And gave yourself to this war. Now again
> You need not try to hide your divinity.
> But who has wished you sent down from Olympus
> To take this rough work on? That you should see
> The painful end of your unhappy brother?
> What am I to do? What stroke of luck
> Can guarantee my safety now? I saw
> Before my eyes, and calling on my name,
> Murranus drowned — great soul by a great wound —
> And none survives more dear to me. Poor Ufens
> Died as though to avoid seeing my shame;
> The Trojans have his body and his gear.
> But now destruction of our homes — the one thing
> Lacking to my desperate case — can I
> Face that? Should I not give the lie to Drancës?
> Shall I turn tail? Will this land know the sight
> Of Turnus on the run? To die — is that
> So miserable? Heaven has grown cold;
> Shades of the underworld, be friendly to me.
> As a pure spirit guiltless of that shame
> I shall go down among you — never unfit
> To join my forefathers."

Aeneid 12. 632–649

A remarkable speech, and definitive for our understanding of the character. The pride, the willingness to face death before enduring shame, these are not new qualities. And yet there are subtle new shadings. That he has known of Juturna's agency for this long hints at least that he may have been willing to be kept safe while appearing to pursue danger, and this lends the suggestion of human vulnerability — he *could*, it seems, give in to fear. Likewise, his remorse for Murranus and Ufens shows a tenderness and fellow-feeling not evident before. Finally, and most important, his insistence on frustrating his sister's plan and facing death *by his own choice* show him consciously taking responsibility for what happens to him. This is crucial in a character whose behavior has been so vividly influenced by divine intervention. As he turns back to face Aeneas, Turnus takes responsibility for his actions in a way that enhances his personal autonomy and keeps us from seeing him as merely Juno's puppet.

The new qualities, the vulnerability, the thought for others, and especially the sense of civic responsibility, all position Turnus firmly in the line of Hector. Aeneas, meanwhile, with his newfound passion, can reassume the Achillean mantle. All of this prepares us for the final scenes of the poem, as Virgil narrows the focus down to the two combatants, playing out their respective destinies before the crowd of onlookers. Book 12 has been, up to this point, crowded with incident, and perhaps overcrowded, we may say—trying to bring together all the various strands of his narrative, Virgil loses forward momentum at times. But from now on, the pace and the energy are relentless, as we are given one last brilliant reworking of Homer, a transformation of the duel between Hector and Achilles in *Iliad* 22. In its own way, this passage is as fine as anything Virgil ever created, preserving the nobility of Hector's last moments and the raw force of Achilles, but putting these energies to work in the service of an entirely new vision.

The Final Duel: Aeneas and His Second Self

Turnus' anxiety is affirmed by the arrival of Saces, envoy from the Italians, bearing the grim details. The former's reaction sums up neatly the mix of motives inside him:

> Stunned and confused
> By one and another image of disaster,
> Turnus held stock-still with a silent stare.
> In that one heart great shame boiled up, and madness
> Mixed with grief, and love goaded by fury,
> Courage inwardly known. When by and by
> The darkness shadowing him broke and light
> Came to his mind again, wildly he turned
> His burning eyes townward and from his car
> Gazed at the city.
>
> *Aeneid* 12. 665–671

The sight firms his resolve:

> "Ah, sister, see, fate overpowers us.
> No holding back now. We must follow where
> The god calls, or implacable Fortune calls.
> My mind's made up on what remains to do:
> To meet Aeneas hand to hand, to bear
> All that may be of bitterness in death.
> You'll find no more unseemliness in me.
> Let me be mad enough for this mad act,
> I pray, before I die."
>
> *Aeneid* 12. 676–680

In this last reflective moment, Turnus recalls Hector, to be sure, but also Aeneas himself as he looks at another city being consumed by flames, driving himself and his friends to what looks like certain death at Troy:

> "Soldiers,
> Brave as you are to no end, if you crave
> To face the last fight with me, and no doubt of it,
> How matters stand for us each one can see.
> The gods by whom this kingdom stood are gone,
> Gone from the shrines and altars. You defend
> A city lost in flames. Come, let us die,
> We'll make a rush into the thick of it
> The conquered have one safety: hope for none."
> *Aeneid* 2. 352–354

That version of Aeneas, obliterated by the gods' mission, has returned to face the man who replaced him.

The duel begins immediately. Turnus and Aeneas call off their colleagues, a space is cleared on the plain, and the men draw close, soon fighting hand to hand. The scene is enlarged by simile: the two men are like bulls, snorting and bloody, fighting for dominance as "heifers muse on a new forest lord/Whom all the herds will follow" (12. 718–719) — Virgil keeps the motive of sexual jealousy fresh in our minds to the very end. Next, the camera zooms up and away to Olympus, where we see Jupiter holding the scales of destiny, Aeneas' fate on one pan, Turnus' the other. The gesture echoes Zeus in *Iliad* 22, but there we are told the outcome, as Hector's side sinks; here, Virgil leaves the duel literally hanging in the balance and never returns to the image.

The focus shifts back, as Turnus breaks his sword on Aeneas' armor and is forced to flee. Now the footrace begins, with Turnus calling for a new sword from the Italian onlookers, Aeneas threatening anyone who complies. Another simile, quoted above, expands the focus: Aeneas as an Umbrian hound, snapping at the heels of a stag. Then an explicit allusion to *Iliad* 22:

> They raced for no light garland of the games
> But strove to win the life and blood of Turnus.
> *Aeneid* 12. 764–765

> here was no festal beast, no ox-hide
> they strove for, for these are prizes that are given men for their running.
> No, they ran for the life of Hektor, breaker of horses.
> *Iliad* 22. 159–161

The chase is interrupted while both men are rearmed with divine aid, and then turn to face each other again.

The Gods Dispose: The Dira

At this point, again freezing the action at a crucial moment, Virgil turns again to Olympus, where Jupiter and Juno have one more exchange, modeled on Zeus and Athena at *Iliad* 22. 167–185. After some introductory persuasion, Jupiter delivers a blunt order: Juno must now desist from helping Turnus, whose hour has arrived. Meek and submissive, she agrees, but extracts one last concession: the Trojans and the native Italians are to share the kingdom of Latinus, the Latins are to keep their own name. Jupiter assents, and Turnus is finished. All that remains is for Jupiter to warn off Juturna:

> That done,
> The Father set about a second plan —
> To take Juturna from her warring brother.
> Stories are told of twin fiends, called the Dirae,
> Whom, with Hell's Megara, deep Night bore
> In one birth. She entwined their heads with coils
> Of snakes and gave them wings to race the wind.
> Before Jove's throne, a step from the cruel king,
> These twins attend him and give piercing fear
> To ill mankind, when he who rules the gods
> Deals out appalling death and pestilence,
> Or war to terrify our wicked cities.
> Jove now dispatched one of these, swift from heaven,
> Bidding her be an omen to Juturna.
> Down she flew, in a whirlwind borne to earth,
> Just like an arrow driven through a cloud
> From a taut string, an arrow armed with gall
> Of deadly poison, shot by a Parthian —
> A Parthian or Cretan — for a wound
> Immedicable; whizzing unforeseen
> It goes through racing shadows: so the spawn
> Of Night went diving downward to earth.

Aeneid 12. 843–860

In the world of the poem, this creature is virtually interchangeable with Allecto: hair made of snakes, dark in aspect and intent, an instrument of pure evil. But such forces are summoned this time not by Juno to subvert the cosmic order, but by Jupiter himself to ensure it. Here is a rather chilling reassessment of the male regime, heretofore represented by bright agents of order, arrayed against the dark, female forces of disorder. Now it turns out that creatures of darkness sit at the feet of Jupiter, ready to do his bidding. The implications of this image for Virgil's view of the moral tenor of the Olympian regime are beyond our scope here, but we may at least note that Virgil seems to imply that the gulf between the male and female agenda on the divine level is not as wide as earlier parts of the poem might suggest. Or, to put it another way, the use of the Dira by Jupiter shifts the focus from division along gender lines to one that emphasizes — as Turnus stands on the brink of extinction — the great separation between mortals and immortals, whatever their sex may be. We recall that analogous refocusings inform the last scenes of both earlier epics, and then reflect on the differences: both Achilles and Gilgamesh are liberated by realizing their position alongside other mortals; Aeneas and Turnus are neither enlightened nor freed by the acceptance of their mortality.

The Dira is prompt and efficacious, going straight to work. Taking the form of some "night bird," that sits on tombs and desolate rooftops, she flits before the face of Turnus, beating her wings against his shield. Numbness seeps into him; he chokes. Juturna recognizes the creature and what it portends, leaving her brother to die. Indeed, the effect of the Dira on Turnus is clear enough: he is beginning to die even before Aeneas dispatches him. This is reaffirmed by Virgil's gruesome transfiguration of Homeric material. After exchanging taunts with Aeneas, Turnus picks up a stone to throw:

> Then he saw a stone,
> Enormous, ancient, set up there to prevent
> Landowners' quarrels. Even a dozen picked men
> Such as the earth produces in our day
> Could barely lift or shoulder it. He swooped
> And wrenched it free, in one hand, then rose up
> To his heroic height, ran a few steps,
> And tried to hurl the stone against his foe —
>
> *Aeneid* 12. 896–902

This vignette is common in Homeric battle scenes, the usual outcome being that the hero flings the stone easily, being that much stronger than ordinary mortals. Virgil surprises us:

> But as he bent and as he ran
> And as he hefted and propelled the weight
> He did not know himself. His knees gave way,
> His blood ran cold and froze. The stone itself,
> Tumbling through space, fell short and had no impact.
>
> *Aeneid* 12. 903–907

One last image clinches the meaning of this weakness:

> Just as in dreams when the night-swoon of sleep
> Weighs on our eyes, it seems we try in vain

> To keep on running, try with all our might,
> But in the midst of effort faint and fail;
> Our tongue is powerless, familiar strength
> Will not hold up our body, not a sound
> Or word will come: just so with Turnus now:
> However bravely he made shift to fight
> The immortal fiend blocked and frustrated him.
> Flurrying images passed through his mind.
> He gazed at the Rutulians, and beyond them,
> Gazed at the city, hesitant, in dread.
> He trembled now before the poised spear-shaft
> And saw no way to escape; he had no force
> With which to close, or reach his foe, no chariot
> And no sign of the charioteer, his sister.
> At a dead loss he stood.
>
> *Aeneid* 12. 908–918

This moment draws on two Homeric precedents, Athena tricking Hector into thinking she will aid him and then deserting him to Achilles (*Iliad* 22. 228–305), and the dream simile that describes Achilles' frustration at not being able to catch Hector:

> As in a dream a man is not able to follow one who runs
> from him, nor can the runner escape, nor the other pursue him,
> so he could not run him down in his speed, nor the other get clear.
>
> *Iliad* 22. 199–201

In Homer's version, Hector, though tricked into a false sense of security, is nonetheless left with his strength intact, able to oppose Achilles with heroic vigor. Not so Turnus, who is not fooled, but simply *mortified*, in a terrifyingly literal sense. Death, brought by the Dira, has begun to seep into Turnus, leaving him defenseless against Aeneas. And horrifying as the physical manifestations of the possession are, its other dimension is yet more appalling, Turnus losing his grip on reality, on his very self — as Aeneas advances, Turnus is being drained of his existence as a distinct human being, dying in his spirit. Though he has been given some autonomy in his last hours, Turnus finally joins Aeneas and all other mortals as a pawn in a game he cannot understand or control.

The Death of the Second Self

Not much remains for Aeneas to do. One throw of the spear and Turnus is disabled, speared through the thigh. In his reduced state, the Italian begs on his knees for mercy:

The man brought down, brought low, lifted his eyes
And held his right hand out to make his plea:

"Clearly I earned this, and I ask no quarter.
Make the most of your good fortune here.
If you can feel a father's grief — and you, too,
Had such a father in Anchises — then
Let me bespeak your mercy for old age
In Daunus, and return me, or my body,
Stripped, if you will, of life, to my own kin.
You have defeated me. The Ausonians
Have seen me in defeat, spreading my hands.
Lavinia is your bride. But go no further
Out of hatred."

Aeneid 12. 931–938

Though weakened, Turnus retains his sense of personal autonomy. The
supplication is dignified, stressing concern for others who will grieve. His
words invoke two Homeric precedents, Hector's last plea to Achilles in
Iliad 22, and the speech of Priam in *Iliad* 24, come to ransom Hector's
body:

"I entreat you, by your life, by your knees, by your parents,
do not let the dogs feed on me by the ships of the Achaians,
but take yourself the bronze and gold that are there in abundance,
those gifts that my father and the lady my mother will give you,
and give my body to be taken home again, so that the Trojans
and the wives of the Trojans may give me in death my rite of burning."

Iliad 22. 338–343

"Achilleus like the gods, remember your father, one who
is of years like mine, and the door-sill of old age . . . "

Iliad 24. 486–487

There will, of course, be no *Iliad* 24 in this poem, but Virgil brings it into
the present scene, as if to suggest two alternative responses for Aeneas, as
the Achilles of book 22 or the gentler man, softened by thoughts of his
own father, in book 24. Turnus has admitted defeat, thrown himself on the
mercy of his Trojan conqueror. In *Iliad* 22, there was no question of mercy,
but a new way of looking at the world, reflecting reintegration of the
second self, brought a different response later. Which will it be now?

Fierce under arms, Aeneas
Looked to and fro, and towered, and stayed his hand
Upon the sword-hilt. Moment by moment now
What Turnus said began to bring him round

From indecision. Then to his glance appeared
The accurst swordbelt surmounting Turnus' shoulder,
Shining with its familiar studs — the strap
Young Pallas wore when Turnus wounded him
And left him dead upon the field; now Turnus
Bore that enemy token on his shoulder —
Enemy still. For when the sight came home to him,
Aeneas raged at the relic of his anguish
Worn by this man as trophy. Blazing up
And terrible in his anger, he called out:

"You in your plunder, torn from one of mine,
Shall I be robbed of you? This wound will come
From Pallas: Pallas makes this offering
And from your criminal blood exacts his due."

He sank his blade in fury in Turnus' chest.
Then all the body slackened in death's chill,
And with a groan for that indignity
His spirit fled into the gloom below.

Aeneid 12. 938–952

A stark and rather ugly moment, hardly resonant of Homer's final tranquilities, and yet carrying enormous significance. We have seen how Virgil makes Turnus a vehicle for summing up what the future of Rome costs, and in particular for the price to Aeneas. The process crescendos in these lines, as all the ghostly companions of Aeneas and Turnus are summoned once more. The Homeric Hector and Achilles flit in the background, their outlines moving between the two combatants; Aeneas himself calls Pallas to witness; the latter's belt, which ignites Aeneas, driving him past hesitation into action, places Turnus again in the company of Nisus, Camilla, and — remember Venus' work of art — Dido, all undone by a beautiful but dangerous object; the poem's last line — last two in the translation — repeats verbatim the description of Camilla's death; and of course, there is the young Aeneas himself, ready to die if he can do so gloriously, before the faces of his parents in Troy.

From our perspective, another warrior looks on: Gilgamesh. With Achilles, he stands witness to the traditional motif of the second self, which Virgil has invoked with such striking originality. If then, as I have been insisting, Turnus, like Dido, is a second self to Aeneas, then what exactly is Aeneas killing in himself? First, the old heroic impulse, so familiar to us from earlier realizations, to be replaced, one supposes, by something driven by *pietas*. This much seems consistent with the public agenda of the gods within the story itself. But Virgil, as distinct from his divine creations, plays another film for us, one chronicling a spiritual death. Something of Aeneas has already burned with Dido: a man who would, like her, draw strength from both a masculine and a feminine reservoir, would cross over the traditional lines drawn in the poem's ethos between male and female. This death is replayed in the last act of Aeneas, in that Turnus is linked so specifically to Camilla and to Dido, but also perhaps in the circumstances of Turnus himself, disarmed and helpless before Aeneas, "womanish" in his vulnerability. Hector, imagining himself in Turnus' position, gives us the flavor:

> I might go up to him, and he take no pity upon me
> nor respect my position, but kill me naked so, as if I were
> a woman, once I stripped my armour from me . . .
>
> *Iliad* 22. 123–125

It is this vulnerability, so frightening from the traditional male perspective, so potentially fruitful in the world that rushes past so briefly in book 4, that Aeneas — in his markedly *masculine* posture — stabs out of existence.

But this much was evident in Dido's death, and though it is part of Turnus' death as well, something else has been added. Following Virgil's lead, we conclude that matters of *history*, broadly defined, rather than *gender*, are foremost in the working out of the second-self motif after Carthage. What dies with Turnus is the past, in many different forms. On the level of culture, Greek gives way to Roman; in the epic tradition, the youthful heroic impulse toward personal aggrandizement is replaced by something less self-involved, requiring loyalty to a greater, collective good; and, more poignantly, particular young men and women perish, tied to an untenable past, to be replaced by others who are part of a different kind of future. Finally there is Aeneas, who must learn to annihilate his own youth and then live on, cut off from his past but not part of the future, which belongs to his descendants.

We might pause here to consider whether killing his youth can be seen as a sign of Aeneas' *maturity*, a sign that the child must give way to the man. But this particular portrait of the transition seems rather brutal — maturation as spiritual suicide is a disquieting kind of metaphor. In the model of spiritual development we have been working with here, annihilation is the *penultimate*, not the final stage of evolution to adulthood. The ability to *reintegrate* parts of ourselves we have lost track of, *rebirth* coming out of annihilation, is paramount in the motif of the second self that we suppose Virgil to be drawing on here. There will be no integration of what Turnus represents.

Here we must observe an important distinction between the deaths of Dido and Turnus. The former dies by Aeneas' sword, but Aeneas himself is unaware, an unwitting assassin. Thus the crucial detail in Virgil's hunting simile: Dido's wound of love comes from a shepherd who is *nescius* in Latin, "unknowing." Turnus' death, by contrast, is very much something that Aeneas *chooses*. Confronted by his opponent, helpless and supplicating, he wavers, and we are allowed to look inside him, to witness the process of choice. We have seen that opportunities such as this have been rare for Aeneas, whose own preferences about important matters have been regularly swamped by divine initiatives. Now, after what has been a long initiation, comes the moment when he is allowed to define himself, to act out of whatever is left down there inside him. The result is a spiritual suicide, and this time *he* will drive the sword home, *he* will annihilate his own youth. The net effect of this change is to relocate the power that killed Dido, to mark the internalization by Aeneas of what was an external motivation. The gods, we suppose, must be satisfied.

Final Questions

The implications of the act will always be a source of debate, because they call on each reader's working of the calculus of means and ends that Virgil presents to us: is Rome worth it? The poet does not, I believe, choose — it is not a matter of finding the right code to crack. Coming to the *Aeneid* from the Gilgamesh epic and the *Iliad*, and seeing it through the lens of the second-self motif, we read the spiritual topography in a particular way that makes certain features stand out, others recede. From this angle, the last outburst of anger in Aeneas looks like part of a chain that also includes the responses to Pallas' death and to the breaking of the truce, aligning all three as drawing on the same reservoir as Aeneas' *pietas*. Thus we are less likely to see the *furor* — Virgil's Latin word for unrestrained emotion — in these places as linking Aeneas with others ruined by giving in to *furor* — this would undermine the attempt to distance the hero from unsuitably old-fashioned heroism. We are likely instead to mark a distinction between the *source* of his outbursts, *pietas*, which separates him to some extent from the others, who act out of a more the self-regarding set of motives associated with traditional heroic assertion. From this perspective, the dispatching of Turnus looks like an affirmation of the gods' agenda in the poem.

And yet, the second-self motif also urges a particular working of the calculus. The pattern of spiritual evolution marked in the our previous works, from solipsistic self-aggrandizement to a sense of oneself as part of a larger whole, might at first glance seem to be replayed here, at least in part. Aeneas, after all, would seem to have learned to see himself as a servant of the destiny of Rome, to accept the subordination of his own personal needs to the imperatives of empire. But there is a crucial difference: for Gilgamesh and Achilles, the new perspective grows directly out of a confronting of the deepest, most intimate parts of themselves; journeying to the center of one's being — this is one level of the metaphor — brings an

unparalleled intimacy with one's self; at the same time, the journey is analogous with encountering the most *impersonal* force in the cosmos, death,
the ultimate obliteration of the self. Out of this collision of self and selflessness comes a new acceptance of *transcendence*, a displacing of oneself from
the center of the cosmos to a part of it shared with all other mortals. In
short: humility. From this—another paradox—comes a subsequent enriching of the hero's individuality, a deepening of the meaning of personal
autonomy.

Aeneas, in order to accept the transcendent power in *his* cosmos, must
turn away from the journey that Gilgamesh and Achilles take, must forego
the meeting with his own deepest self. There is no paradox in this trade-off,
no blending of personal and impersonal, but rather the annihilation of the
former to serve the latter, with no subsequent enrichment by refocusing.
Thus, the obliteration envisioned in the parade of souls in book 6 seems
not to hold out the prospect of a new level of integrity, but a continued loss
of autonomy. And finally, we observe that whereas both Gilgamesh and
Achilles evolve from seeing the world as competition, as a series of contests
to be won, to a place where what unites all humans is most definitive for
one's identity, Aeneas appears to seal his acceptance of a new perspective
by conquering Turnus. Book 2 shows us that he has always been a good
fighter; by the end of the poem he has become a killer. That he reaches this
status in the very act of annihilating willingly so much of *himself* is troubling—what is left?

Tracing the second-self motif in the *Aeneid* has taken us around a long
and complex circuit. Because Virgil draws on both Homeric epics, the poem
covers more terrain—to preserve the topographical metaphor—than the
Iliad or the Gilgamesh epic. And because Aeneas is the kind of hero he is,
following the trajectory of his personal evolution through the story is a
more involved process than it is for Achilles and Gilgamesh. That is, the
journeys of both earlier heroes are for the most part the backbone of the
plot in their respective poems; Aeneas' journey is more embedded in the
fabric of the *Aeneid*, must be teased out from the background. Another
way of putting this is that, in a sense, *Rome* is the real hero of the poem,
not Aeneas.

This aspect of the poem also makes it harder to read as a mirror of our
own struggles, because personal choice, and the relation of that choice to
personal suffering are overshadowed from the outset by larger forces—we
cannot get close to Aeneas because he cannot get close to himself. Here, in
fact, is the heart of Virgil's reworking of traditional themes in the hero
story. It is the social and political implications of Rome's founding, rather
than the model of personal evolution represented by Aeneas' journey, that
finally obtrude from the narrative. There is also the sense, fostered by
Virgil's prophetic references to the Rome of his own day, that the founding
of Rome can be seen as a portrait of the enduring, fundamental aspects of

the Roman settlement. It is not that Aeneas' struggles do not illustrate the human condition, but that the *arena* of struggle is different. From Achilles, we learn something about, among other things, self-knowledge and the ability to love; from Aeneas, something about how individuals can be co-opted, and thus prevented from self-realization, by supra-personal forces. The prominence of the dimension of *history* in books 5 through 12 is consistent with this perspective. But even the relationship of Aeneas and Dido can be understood on this level: it is the crippling division of male and female prerogatives in the world of the poem (and in Virgil's Rome?) that lies behind the tragedy of Dido. The world of the poem is not ready for the kind of man Aeneas might have become if he had been able to integrate the qualities that the Carthaginian queen reflected back to him. Finally Lavinia, not Dido, is the mirror of Roman destiny.

All of this might suggest that Virgil's refocusing of the hero story obviates the second-self motif as an integral part of his narrative strategy. To put it another way, maybe I am pushing a model of interpretation that is some-how beside the point. But the invocation of elements of the motif at critical moments in Aeneas' journey suggests the opposite, that Virgil draws on this dynamic in the same way he does other precedents in the tradition, particularly the Homeric epics, to establish a set of expectations against which he works in creating his own vision. Finally that vision focuses on the trade-off between personal autonomy and the imperatives of larger forces, in particular the destined founding of Rome. And finally, though it is central in the definition of the struggle within and outside of Aeneas, the thrust of the motif in the story offers no answer to what we might call the Virgilian Question: is the sacrifice worth it?

The poet's refusal to decide for us reaches its most economical expression in the last words of the poem. The English translation I have used renders the verb for Aeneas' sword thrust as "sank," which masks a potent *double-entendre* in the Latin word, *condit*. The basic meaning is "to put something underground," and the range of uses regularly includes burying a human body or laying the foundations for a building; as Aeneas' sword descends it becomes in the metaphor a shovel, digging a grave, founding a city. There is, it seems, something about Rome that calls forth this particular image — like St. Peter under his baldachino, Aeneas lies there still, potent and enig-matic.

Metaphor Revisited

How do you expect to arrive at the end of your own journey if
you take the road to another man's city? How do you expect to
reach your own perfection by leading somebody else's life?

Thomas Merton, *New Seeds of Contemplation*

We began with a metaphor; where has it taken us? Through other metaphors, first of all. The journey has enriched our paradigm from life by
refracting it through particular stories, doing what we ask of art. Now we
may turn around and observe what might be learned from the trip, about
the art itself, about its agency in life. To begin with, we note that these
poems offer a more complicated view of male heroism than we might suppose. The confrontation, denial, journey into darkness, and (potential)
reintegration in the motif of the second self implies an awareness in our
three poets of the narrowing, often destructive aspects of the traditional
heroic career. The "return" of Patroclus affords (however fleetingly) a
wholly different view of the world for Achilles — humility, not the isolating
drive for preeminence often associated with Classical heroism, is the final
goal. Less certain but equally tantalizing are the hints in these poems that
being a fully realized man means integrating traits often associated in ancient Mediterranean cultures (and our own) with women. The Aeneas-that-
might-have-been looks rather more "modern" in this way than we might
expect given the kind of patriarchal culture he and Virgil come from.

I might be reading my modern preoccupations into the texts, of course.
This raises questions about why we read the poems to begin with, takes us
again into that middle ground between the hermetically sealed, historically
bound worlds that scholars try to mine from the texts and the world all
around any reader, messy, frayed at the edges, filtered through the gauzy
veil of subjectivity. Lately theorists have been attacking the very reality of
the first kind of world, pointing insistently to the cultural contingency of

any "meaning." This latter stance is as I have said friendly to my own perspective here, since I insist on the subjective nature of my views – I am indeed reading my own preoccupations into the poems. Whether the result is useful to others depends, I suppose, on whether my ideas have any resonance for them as they look on from within their own subjectivities.

Taking this view positions us to explain why the subtlety and inclusiveness of our poems have been so often missed, why it has been common to take them as one-sided exemplars of the competitive, hierarchical way of seeing. We need no proof, I suppose, of the enduring allure of traditional heroic goals and priorities, judging from their efflorescence through the centuries and all around us at present. Whether culturally conditioned or genetically transmitted or both, this approach to life answers a need felt by many, men and women, to seek the kind of empowerment it seems to offer. Nor is it necessarily a bad thing to answer this call, provided it is balanced by other ways of being. So why ought we be surprised if works of art agreed to be seminal are read in a way that glorifies what we are drawn to for other reasons?

Supposing we *are* guilty of reading the poems in a distorting way that suits our own needs, we only confirm one of the central lessons that these works teach as I have read them: the objective world is very much more a product of our subjective ways of seeing than we would like to admit; Uruk is one kind of place for Gilgamesh before Enkidu's death, another after. And if it were determined by *others* that the integration dramatized in Achilles is clearly good for us, the poems tell us not to be surprised if *we* resist nonetheless. The stories we have read are all about our blindness to what is good for us until we are ready, emotionally, spiritually, to see it.

Somber reflections, these. But finally the stories offer hope, if we will listen to them. Doing so is not always easy, because they tell us that a new life may require going into dark places where the heroic powers we have been straining to acquire avail us nothing. Self-mastery must be preceded by a letting-go of the desire to master the world – Gilgamesh, looking for a way to get power over death, gives in to death's brother, sleep, and awakes newly empowered by the acceptance of his defeat; Achilles, yielding to the gods and letting go of the one dearest to him, comes in the renunciation to repossess both his friend and himself. As the epigraphs to my chapters show, this powerful, paradoxical metaphor is not confined to Greek and Roman culture, and it would be easy enough to add witness from much further afield or much closer to home. The message it sends to us is simple enough to understand, if hard to accept: to be a hero is finally to embrace the person we really are, and to live in the world that this acceptance creates all around us.

Further Reading

Introduction

Jung's ideas about the relationship of literature and psychology are sprinkled all through his *Collected Works* (Jung CW 1–19.1902–1958); see especially "The Origin of the Hero," in *Symbols of Transformation* (CW 5), "The Phenomenology of the Spirit in Fairytales," in *The Archetypes and the Collective Unconscious* (CW 9.1), "On the Relation of Analytical Psychology to Poetry," "Psychology and Literature," "Ulysses," in *The Spirit in Man, Art, and Literature* (CW 15). Of particular interest for the second-self motif are his models for the Shadow and the Anima in the human psyche, for which see *Aion: Researches into the Phenomenology of the Self* (CW 9.2). Campbell 1971 provides a helpful set of selections from Jung and an overview of his work. Discussions of Jung's psychology in general are also available in Jacobi 1951, Jung 1968, and Hannah 1972.

The classic study of the hero story from a basically Jungian perspective is Campbell 1949. On the motif of the second self or double in modern literature, see Tymms 1949, Lesser 1957, Rank 1958, Guerard 1967, Rogers 1970, Keppler 1972, Irwin 1975, Crook 1981.

The reading I offer here has also been inspired by the work of James Hillman and Robert Bly. The best introduction to the former's imaginative revisioning of psychology is Hillman 1990; for Bly's equally vivid, if more poetic working of the same soil, see Bly 1988 and Bly 1990.

Chapter 1

The standard scholarly text for the Gilgamesh epic in English is by Speiser in Pritchard 1969, with extensive commentary on the state of the various texts and on the historical and religious background for the poem. This book is also a good source for studying the place of the Gilgamesh epic in the context of other Near Eastern literature. Jacobsen 1976 is an excellent general study of Near Eastern literature, with a helpful survey of the religious background and extensive bibliography. See also Kramer 1961, Kramer 1969, and Kramer 1979. Maier's notes to the translation in Gardner and Maier 1984 are unfailingly illuminating to the nonspecialist.

On the Gilgamesh epic as myth, stressing the nature-culture polarity, see Kirk 1970.132–152. Tigay 1982 gives a thorough analysis of the evolution of the story through its various versions, and has extensive bibliography on all aspects of the poem. For more on this topic, plus a brief literary analysis, see Jacobsen 1976.195–219. For more of the latter, see also Gardner and Maier 1984.vii–viii.

Keppler 1972.14–26 has an argument for the origins of the second self motif in ancient stories about twins. While I am not convinced that the motif began in this way, Keppler's discussion of the poem is good. On the poem as a story of the double, see also Gardner and Maier 1984.15–16,42.

Halperin 1989 is a thorough and convincing discussion of the erotic context for the friendship between Gilgamesh and Enkidu.

Chapter 2

The scholarship on the *Iliad* is vast. Packard and Meyers 1974 is a comprehensive treatment covering the period from 1930 to 1970; Holoka 1979 surveys 1971–1977. Good recent bibliography can be found in Schein 1984 and Edwards 1987. My discussion of the poem leaves to one side the intricate and controversial subject of oral composition, which has played an enormous part in Homeric scholarship in this century. Parry 1970 provides the seminal texts; Kirk 1966 has an updated version of Milman Parry's theories; Edwards 1987 brings the discussion up to the present for the general reader. Nagler 1974 offers an intriguing and controversial variation on the standard Parryist theory.

For a comprehensive, if at times flat discussion of Homeric epic in general, see Kirk 1966; Edwards 1987.1–164 is an excellent overview of Homeric style; Whitman 1958, though dated on style, is superb on the Homeric epics as poetry; Beye 1976 offers an insightful literary perspective on both Homeric epics and the *Aeneid*; Nagy 1979 places the Homeric concepts of heroism in the context of Indo-European prehistory; Griffin 1980 is an insightful discussion of selected aspects Homeric poetry. For the *Iliad* in particular, Weil 1945 is one of the most forceful treatments of the poem, though the influence of Vichy France on the author's thinking results in a one-sided view that conflicts fundamentally with my own; Owen 1946, a running commentary, is still an invaluable guide to the overall structure of the poem; Bespaloff 1947 is a brilliant set of essays on selected topics in the poem; Redfield 1975 offers some fascinating, if controversial, insights on the poem from an anthropological perspective; Willcock 1976 gives useful commentary geared specifically to Lattimore's translation; Schein 1984 is a sound, balanced introduction to the *Iliad* with good bibliography; Mueller 1984 is also a general introduction, though less successful than Schein, in my view; Edwards 1987 provides a running commentary on selected books of the poem, valuable for its cross-referencing to the earlier discussion of style and for its sensitive appreciation of the *Iliad's* complexities.

On Achilles as a hero, see especially: Bespaloff 1947. 53–58; Whitman 1958.181–220; Redfield 1975.3–29, 99–109; Griffin 1980.81–102; Schein 1984.89–167. For a view of Achilles fundamentally opposed to mine, see MacCary 1982. The relationship between Achilles and Patroclus is discussed in all of the above; see in addition: Beye 1976.85–86; Devereux 1978; Sinos 1980; Edwards 1987.257–259; Halperin 1989. On the implications of Achilles' speeches in book 9 for his evolution as a hero, see: Parry 1956; Reeve 1973; Claus 1975; Edwards 1987.221–237.

On the relationship of the *Epic of Gilgamesh* to the Homeric poems, see: Gresseth 1975; Beye 1984; Wilson 1986.

Chapter 3

Of the general works cited in Chapter 2, the following are particularly helpful on the material covered in this chapter: Owen 1946.164–248; Bespaloff 1947.95–106; Whitman 1958.201–220; Beye 1976.140–157; Schein 1984.128–167; Edwards 1987.267–323.

Segal 1971 provides a thorough discussion of the treatment of corpses in the *Iliad*. See also Redfield 1975.178–179.

For the killing of Hector as a suicide, see Devereux 1978.

Nagler 1974.167–198 is a brilliant analysis of the last book of the *Iliad*, to which my own discussion owes much. See also Van Nortwick 1985.

Chapter 4

The bibliography for Virgil is at least as daunting as for Homer. Surveys of secondary writings on Virgil and his poetry are a regular feature of the journal *Vergilius*. Briggs 1987 is an index of that journal for the years

1938–1987; McKay 1988 has information on recent bibliography. For the period 1964–73, see McKay 1974. Among recent general works in English on the *Aeneid*, the following are noteworthy (all have bibliography): Poeschl 1962; Otis 1963; Putnam 1965; Commager 1966; Quinn 1968; Hunt 1973; Johnson 1976; Lee 1979; Lyne 1987.

On the *Aeneid* as part of the tradition of ancient epic, see Beye 1976 and Newman 1986; for the influence of Hellenistic Greek literature, especially Apollonius' *Argonautica*, on the *Aeneid*, see Otis 1963.73–76; Clausen 1987.

For the political and historical background of the *Aeneid*, see Camps 1969.95–104; Cairns 1989.1–128. On cosmological ideas (with political overtones) in the poem, see Hardie 1983.

The most complete survey of Virgil's debt to Homer is Knauer 1964; see also Heinze 1903.167–232; MacKay 1957; Anderson 1957; Poeschl 1963; Otis 1963.313–382; Wigodsky 1965; Quinn 1968.278–288; West 1974; Johnson 1976.23–48; Van Nortwick 1980; Lyne 1987.217–238.

For a sensitive discussion of possible applications of Jungian metaphors to the *Aeneid*, see Lee 1979.105–118, 143–156; see—in contrast to my own view—especially 105–108, his arguments for Achates as a "shadow" figure. Lee's book as a whole is a fine introduction to the poem which has stimulated my own thinking, and his application of modern psychological metaphors is consistently delicate and respectful of Virgil's own ways of seeing.

Chapter 5

On fathers and sons in the *Aeneid*, see Lee 1979. For book 5 in particular, see Putnam 1965.64–104; Cairns 1989.215–248. Brooks 1953, reprinted in Commager 1966.143–163, is a brilliant discussion of book 6 in general and the golden bough in particular. On the Jungian aspects of Aeneas' trip to the underworld, see Lee 1979.143–156. For the Nisus and Euryalus episode, see Lee 1979.108–112; Pavlock 1985, Makowski 1989. The latter argues for a relatively explicit sexual basis for the relationship between the two friends, which is neither inconsistent with nor strictly necessary for my argument.

Chapter 6

The most thorough reading of the last book of the *Aeneid* in English is Putnam 1965.151–201; Hunt 1973.82–98 is an insightful discussion of the thematic relationship between Dido and Turnus, to which my discussion owes much. Johnson 1976.114–134 is a brilliant treatment of the last scenes of the poem, especially good on the final exchange between Jupiter and Juno. On Turnus, see also Poeschl 1962.91–93 and Otis 1965.372–378.

For a different reading of the meaning of Turnus' death than mine, see Galinsky 1988 and Cairns 1989.58–84.

Bibliographical Essay

Tracing the scholarly genealogy for my work is challenging, because I have been intent on balancing various perspectives, literary, psychological, spiritual, treating each as a system of metaphors describing something prior, granting primacy to none. This means I have often drawn on the work of scholars whose basic agenda differs markedly from my own. To put it metaphorically, I have woven a tapestry using many different kinds of thread, and the final product is not easily compared to any particular component. Thus, while I can and should acknowledge the contributions of others, extended discussion of how my work fits into larger intellectual contexts is often not germane. With that proviso in place, I offer the following as a guide to the provenance of my work.

My major contribution, as I see it, has been:

1. To develop the implications of seeing the companion as a second self.

2. To integrate the resulting dynamic into a comprehensive model for the hero's spiritual evolution (or lack of it) in each poem I study.

3. To draw on these findings to offer a fresh perspective on the ways these poems dramatize issues raised by traditional heroic ideals.

The first item brings me into contact with several perspectives. The closest psychological parallel to the kind of dynamic I see in the stories is Jungian. As I have said in the text, Jung's metaphor of the shadow fits, in some but by no means all respects, the second self as I describe it here. Probably the best source for this model is *Aion: Researches into the Phenomenology of the Self*. (CW 9.2). One fundamental difficulty with pressing the analogies very far is that the second selves I locate in the poems are not dark and sinister. As Jacobi notes (1951.128), Jung's model does not rule out the possibility of the shadow being bright and positive, but in practice Jungians have been much more interested in the shadow as a representation of something dark and threatening. A closer fit appears in certain spiritual metaphors, in particular the notion of the "Twin," as described by Keppler (1972.14–26), or as found in some of the gnostic gospels (see Pagels 1981.21–23).

Extended studies of the second self from a more literary perspective have, as I note in my first chapter, been restricted mostly to modern literature, and have emphasized dark qualities (e.g., Guerard 1967, Rogers 1970, Irwin 1975). That Enkidu and Patroclus may be seen as "doubles" for Gilgamesh and Achilles has been noted by more than one scholar. Maier, in his introduction to Gardner and Maier 1984, touches briefly on Enkidu's complementarity to Gilgamesh (15–16, 42); Whitman 1951 has a characteristically elegant if brief discussion of Patroclus as an "alter ego" (136–137, 200–202); Beye 1976 identifies both Patroclus and Enkidu as types of "alter ego," noting further that the Mesopotamian version is a more fully realized character (85–86); Beye 1984 carries the discussion of Patroclus and Enkidu further, suggesting but not developing in detail the idea that each may be a "shadow" figure; taking a somewhat more anthropological approach, Nagy 1979 analyzes Patroclus as a *therapon*, or ritual substitute for Achilles, drawing on the work of Van Brock 1959 to locate the role in an older Indo-European tradition; Sinos 1980 follows basically the same path to explore the meaning of the Achilles-Patroclus relationship within the larger scheme of the *Iliad*. His reading is probably the closest of these to mine — Patroclus as a surrogate for Achilles and as a representative in some sense of the concern for others that is swamped by Achilles' heroic excess. The emphasis on ritual and cult in Sinos' work puts, however, a somewhat different slant than mine on all of this. His perspective does not, for instance, encourage a recognition of the denial of mortality still present in Achilles in books 18–24, nor does he see the last scenes with Priam as a recapturing of what was lost with Patroclus' death, as the "return" of the second self.

Two other studies address the characterization of Achilles by the projection of parts of his nature onto other figures, Devereux 1978 and MacCary 1982. The former is a basically Freudian treatment of the meaning of Hector's death, portraying it as a kind of suicide to assuage guilt over the death of Patroclus. As I have said in my discussion of Hector's death, this view does not account for the significance of book 24 in the evolution of Achilles. The same may be said of the latter study, which sees in Achilles an infantile, narcissistic personality, unable ever to overcome a fundamental solipsism — Achilles sees everyone else as mirrors for himself. Both studies elevate psychological metaphors above other ways of seeing; neither sees any particular importance in Patroclus after his death.

Halperin 1990, though not addressed specifically to the issue of the second self, has helped me to situate the relationship of the hero with his companion in the larger cultural context of ancient epic. Halperin's analysis of the erotic potential in such a relationship is the most helpful single piece of scholarship to be found on that complex topic.

The use of Homeric models in the *Aeneid* is, of course, a large topic, but not one that has elicited any detailed discussion of the use of a second self or selves in the *Aeneid* as a way of commenting on the character of Aeneas. I have drawn on a few earlier discussions in developing the basic similarities and differences between Homeric and Virgilian heroes: MacKay 1957, an elegant if brief argument for the Achilles of *Iliad* 18-24 as a model for Aeneas; Anderson 1957, a much fuller and more convincing discussion, which sees Virgil initially suggesting Turnus as the successor for Achilles, then showing this role to be only Turnus' delusion, overridden by the genuine kinship of Achilles and the Aeneas of books 10-12; Lee 1979.105-108, which suggests that Achates may have been Virgil's version of the Jungian "shadow," but does not follow out the implications of this in any detail; Van Nortwick 1980, a revision of Anderson which forms the basis for my argument here, that Virgil keeps the figure of Achilles alive in both Turnus and Aeneas right up to the end of the poem.

My argument for Dido as a second self has, as far as I know, no antecedents in the scholarship on the poem, with the exception of one tantalizing hint from Lee 1979.116, that Dido may be an anima figure in the poem.

Little has been written specifically on the second part of my contribution, the second self as part of the hero's spiritual evolution. The more general topic of the hero story as a reflection of psychic or spiritual forces in the life of the hero has, however, been much discussed and I will confine myself here to those works that address in some detail the issues I raise. The most important source is Campbell 1949, still the most comprehensive attempt to read the hero's adventures as representative of a spiritual journey. Enormously learned, passionately presented, this landmark study was the initial inspiration for my work. One caution: though his book has worn remarkably well, Campbell's claim that his analysis is germane to the experience of women is no longer convincing—what he says is clearly all about men. But given the nature of my own texts, this has not been a hindrance. Indeed, the basic model of separation, initiation, and return that Campbell presents is the bedrock on which my discussion rests. The most germane application of this material to the *Iliad* is Nagler 1974.131-166, a detailed look at the way Homer incorporates this universal pattern into his particular agenda. Though Nagler does not take up the issue of the second self, his discussion has influenced my thinking about the latter books of the *Iliad* to a significant degree, as is evidenced by my own previous look at the material, Van Nortwick 1985.

On the hero's spiritual evolution in the Gilgamesh epic, the only detailed treatment I know of is Jacobsen 1976.195–219. The discussion there tries to identify distinct "traditions," literary and historical, to which are ascribed different attitudes toward life. I find this tactic somewhat forced, but Jacobsen's treatment of the theme of mortality in the poem in particular is helpful. At the same time, my reading differs from his in a way that is instructive for understanding the importance of the second self. Because from my perspective acceptance of his own mortality means for Gilgamesh the return of the part of himself that did not die with Enkidu, the end of the story is for me basically positive. Jacobsen's interpretation, lacking the dimension of the second self, portrays Gilgamesh's attitude at the end of the story as one of resignation, tinged with melancholy.

In working from the Mesopotamian epic to its descendants, I have been guided to some extent by three works, Gresseth 1975, Beye 1984, and Wilson 1986. The first two of these look for parallels between the Gilgamesh epic and both the *Iliad* and the *Odyssey*, and so have a less specific agenda than mine; none develops to any great extent the implications of Enkidu's death for Gilgamesh. But each does recognize to one extent or another the similarities in the relationship between Gilgamesh and Enkidu on the one hand, Achilles and Patroclus on the other. Wilson and Beye also trace parallels between Thetis and Ninsun, and between the tone, basically tragic, in both poems. Finally, however, I part company with both in their reading of the Gilgamesh epic, as neither sees any movement toward humility in the hero there as a result of his adventures.

Tracing the spiritual evolution—or lack of it—in Aeneas has not been a popular topic for scholars of the *Aeneid*. Part of the difficulty has been that Aeneas is such an opaque character, so much less vivid than Turnus or Dido—how much can be said of such a cipher? There is also a tendency to subsume any discussion of Aeneas' heroism under the related set of issues surrounding the "Virgilian Question," as I have called it in the book. That is, what happens to Aeneas is less interesting to scholars than the way the Augustan settlement is refracted through the story of the poem. A significant exception here is Beye 1976, a book that has never received the attention it deserves. Beye's discussion (227–234) of the interplay between the fate of Aeneas and the destiny of Rome is the starting point for my own treatment. I go further than he does, because the motif of the second self allows me to define more precisely and in more detail what it is that Aeneas loses in order to be the kind of hero the gods require, but the thrust of my argument is much the same.

My third item, the importance of all this for our understanding of the hero story as representing a certain set of attitudes toward life, again touches on a vast area of scholarship, and I will stay close to the boundaries of my own tapestry. My major departure here has been to argue that the poets of all three works offer a wider, more inclusive view of what constitutes the fully evolved male than has been usually accorded to the heroic tradition. The humility that both Gilgamesh and Achilles achieve is, in my view, presented not as a temporary respite from the "real world" of battle or heroic exertion, but as a perspective that can and should coexist with the competitive, agonal drive in the mature hero. Likewise, Aeneas represents the costs of being coopted by larger forces, of not balancing this with attention to one's own soul. I also argue, albeit somewhat more tentatively, that gender is a more prominent topic in the story of the hero's development as I read it in these three poems than has generally been recognized. The figure of the second self, as I see it, represents with varying degrees of vividness in each work, the feminine potential in the male hero, which he must integrate in order to tap his powers to the fullest.

The more traditional view of heroism, that it entails and is encompassed by the seeking of glory, with all the rewards and all the penalties this brings, is ubiquitous in the scholarly literature, though it often lies unexamined behind the discussion of other, more technical issues. One of the best presentations of this view of the Homeric epics is Griffin 1980, and in particular 81–102. This excellent overview, supported by many specific examples, offers a comprehensive portrait of the traditional heroic perspective. The emphasis here is on the tragic element in the hero's story, that what makes the hero an object of reverence, even awe, must necessarily destroy him. The somber tone such a view creates is captured in Griffin's comment on the meeting of Priam and Achilles (100): "For both Priam and Achilles the war has become an endless process, unrewarding and meaningless, from which they cannot extricate themselves." Here, as in Jacobsen's or Beye's reading of the end of the Gilgamesh story, the focus is on what has been lost, on an emptiness that can only be met by resignation and endurance. What is missing is any sense of what is won from the acceptance of limits, what I see as represented by the reintegration of the second self.

Nagler 1974 again is something of an exception. His discussion of the end of the *Iliad* (167–198) allows for a transformation of Achilles as a result of his suffering, a recognition of the possibility of seeing the world in a new way. While I would not see it as the creation of a new man but rather as the recapturing of what was always there, I am following his lead in pursuing the spiritual aspects of *Iliad* 24.

Finally, the work of Robert Bly (Bly 1988, 1990) has been a model for my attempts to balance more than one perspective in discussing the meaning of these poems. Though I am not sure if he would approve of everything I say about the heroic career as it applies to contemporary masculinity, his deft movement between literature, psychology, and spirituality in pursuit of an integrated view of human life has been inspirational to me.

Bibliography

Anderson, W. S. 1957. "Vergil's Second *Iliad*." *Transactions of the American Philological Association*. 88:17–30.

Bespaloff, Rachel. 1947. *On the Iliad*. New York.

Beye, Charles R. 1976. 2nd edition. *The Iliad, the Odyssey, and the Epic Tradition*. New York.

———. 1984. "The Epic of Gilgamesh, the Bible, and Homer. Some Narrative Parallels." *Mnemai. Classical Studies in Memory of Karl K. Hulley* (ed. Evjen). Chico.

Bly, Robert. 1988. *A Little Book on the Human Shadow*. New York.

———. 1990. *Iron John: A Book About Men*. Reading, Mass.

Briggs, Ward W., Jr. 1987. "Index to *Vergilius*, 1938–1986." *Vergilius* 33:174–205.

Cairns, Frances. 1989. *Virgil's Augustan Epic*. Cambridge.

Campbell, Joseph. 1949. *The Hero with a Thousand Faces*. Princeton.

———. 1971. *The Portable Jung*. New York.

Camps, W. A. *Introduction to Virgil's Aeneid*. Oxford.

Commager, Steele. 1966. *Virgil: A Collection of Critical Essays*. Englewood Cliffs, N. J.

Claus, David. 1975. "*Aidôs* in the Language of Achilles." *Transactions of the American Philological Association* 105:13–28.

Clausen, Wendell. 1987. *Virgil's Aeneid and the Tradition of Hellenistic Poetry*. Berkeley and Los Angeles.

Crook, Eugene. 1981. *Fearful Symmetry: Doubles and Doubling in Literature and Film* (ed.). Tallahassee.

Devereux, George. 1978. "Achilles' 'Suicide' in the *Iliad*." *Helios* 6:3–15.

Edwards, Mark W. 1987. *Homer: Poet of the Iliad*. Baltimore.

Fitzgerald, Robert. 1963. *The Odyssey: Homer* (trans.). Garden City, N.Y.

———. 1980. *The Aeneid: Virgil* (trans.). New York.

Galinsky, Karl. 1988. "The Anger of Aeneas." *American Journal of Philology* 109: 321–348.

Gardner, John, and Maier, John. 1984. *Gilgamesh*. (ed. and trans.) New York.

Gresseth, Gerald K. 1975. "The Gilgamesh Epic and Homer." *Classical Journal* 70: 1–18.

Griffin, Jasper. 1980. *Homer on Life and Death*. Oxford.

Guerard, Albert. 1967. *Stories of the Double*. New York.

Halperin, David. 1989. "The Hero and His Pal." *One Hundred Years of Homosexuality*. London.

Hannah, Barbara. 1972. *Striving Towards Wholeness*. New York.

Hardie, Colin. 1983. *Virgil's Aeneid: Cosmos and Imperium*. Oxford.

Heinze, R. 1903. *Virgils Epische Technik*. Leipzig.

Hillman, James. 1990. *A Blue Fire*. New York.

Holoka, James P. 1979. "Homer Studies 1971–1977." *Classical World* 73:65–150.

Hunt, J. William. 1973. *Forms of Glory: Structure and Sense in Virgil's Aeneid*. Carbondale.

Irwin, John T. 1975. *Doubling and Incest/Repetition and Revenge*. Baltimore.

Jacobi, Jolande. 1951. *The Psychology of C. J. Jung*. New Haven.

Jacobsen, Thorkild. 1976. *The Treasures of Darkness*. New Haven.

Johnson, W. Ralph. 1976. *Darkness Visible: A Study of Vergil's Aeneid*. Berkeley and Los Angeles.

Jung, Carl. 1902–1958. *Collected Works vol. 1–19*. Princeton.

———. 1968. *Modern Man and His Symbols* (ed.). New York.

Keppler, Carl. 1972. *The Literature of the Second Self*. Tucson.

Kirk, Geoffrey. 1966. *The Songs of Homer*. Cambridge.

———. 1970. *Myth: Its Meaning and Functions in Ancient and Other Cultures*. Berkeley and Los Angeles.

Kramer, Samuel N. 1961. *Sumerian Mythology*. New York.

———. 1969. *The Sacred Marriage Rite*. Bloomington.

———. 1979. *From the Poetry of Sumer*. Berkeley and Los Angeles.

Lattimore, Richmond. 1951. *The Iliad of Homer* (trans.). Chicago.

Lee, M. Owen. 1979. *Fathers and Sons in Virgil's Aeneid: Tum Genitor Natum*. Albany.

Lesser, Simon. 1957. *Fiction and the Unconscious*. New York.

Lyne, R. O. A. M. 1987. *Further Voices in Vergil's Aeneid*. Oxford.

MacCary, W. T. 1982. *Childlike Achilles: Ontogeny and Philogeny in the Iliad*. New York.

MacKay, L. A. 1957. "Achilles as Model for Aeneas." *Transactions of the American Philological Association* 88:11–16.

Makowski, John. 1989. "Nisus and Euryalus: A Platonic Relationship." *Classical Journal* 85:1–15.

McKay, Alexander. 1974. "Recent Work on Vergil." *Classical World* 68:1–93.

_____. 1988. "Vergilian Bibliography 1987-1988." *Vergilius* 34:139-178.

Merton, Thomas. 1949. *Seeds of Contemplation*. Westport, Conn.

_____. 1961. *New Seeds of Contemplation*. New York.

Mueller, Martin. 1984. *The Iliad*. London

Nagler, Michael. 1974. *Spontaneity and Tradition: A Study in the Oral Art of Homer*. Berkeley and Los Angeles.

Nagy, Gregory. 1979. *The Best of the Achaeans*. Baltimore.

Neruda, Pablo. 1986. *100 Love Sonnets* (trans. Tapscott). Austin, Texas.

Newman, J.K. 1986. *The Classical Epic Tradition*. Madison.

Otis, Brooks. 1963. *Virgil: A Study in Civilized Poetry*. Oxford.

Owen, E. T. 1946. *The Story of the Iliad*. Toronto.

Packard, David, and Meyers, Tania. 1974. *A Bibliography of Homeric Scholarship 1930-1970*. Malibu.

Pagels, Elaine. 1979. *The Gnostic Gospels*. New York

Parry, Adam. 1956. "The Language of Achilles." *Transactions of the American Philological Association* 87:1-7.

_____. 1971. *The Making of Homeric Verse: The Collected Papers of Milman Parry* (ed.). Oxford.

Pavlock, Barbara. 1985. "Epic and Tragedy in Vergil's Nisus and Euryalus Episode." *Transactions of the American Philological Association* 115:207-224.

Poeschl, Viktor. 1962. *The Art of Vergil: Image and Symbol in the Aeneid*. Trans. Gerda Seligson. Ann Arbor.

Pritchard, James B. 1969. *Ancient Near Eastern Texts Relating to the Old Testament*. Princeton.

Quinn, Kenneth. 1968. *Virgil's Aeneid: A Critical Description*. Ann Arbor.

Putnam, Michael. 1965. *The Poetry of the Aeneid*. Cambridge, Mass.

Rank, Otto. 1958. *Beyond Psychology*. New York.

Redfield, James. 1975. *Nature and Culture in the Iliad*. Chicago.

Reeve, M. D. 1973. "The Language of Achilles." *Classical Quarterly* 23:193-195.

Rogers, Robert. 1970. *The Double in Literature*. Detroit.

Schein, Seth. 1984. *The Mortal Hero*. Berkeley and Los Angeles.

Segal, Charles. 1971. *The Theme of the Mutilation of the Corpse in the Iliad*. Leiden.

Sinos, Dale. 1980. *Achilles, Patroklos, and the Meaning of Philos*. Innsbruch.

Tigay, Jeffrey H. 1982. *The Evolution of the Gilgamesh Epic*. Philadelphia.

Tymms, Ralph. 1949. *Doubles In Literary Psychology*. Cambridge.

Van Brock, Nadia. 1959. "Substitution rituelle." *Revue Hittite et Asianique* 65:117-146.

Van Nortwick, Thomas. 1980. "Aeneas, Turnus, and Achilles." *Transactions of the American Philological Association* 110:303-314.

_____. 1985. "Priam, Achilles, and the Resolution of the *Iliad*." *North Dakota Quarterly* 53:55-65.

Weil, Simone. 1945. *The Iliad: or, the Poem of Force*. Trans. Mary McCarthy. New York.

West, D. 1974. "The Deaths of Hector and Turnus." *Greece & Rome* 21:21-31.

Wigodsky, Michael. 1965. "The Arming of Aeneas." *Classica & Medievalia* 26:192–221.

Willcock, Malcolm M. 1976. *A Companion to the Iliad*. Chicago.

Wilson, J.R. 1986. "The Gilgamesh Epic and the *Iliad*." *Echos du Monde Classique* 30:25–40.

Whitman, Cedric. 1958. *Homer and the Heroic Tradition*. Cambridge, Mass.

Index